Donald M. Scott, an assistant pro-
ssor of history at North Carolina
ate University, graduated with hon-
s in American history and literature
m Harvard, received his Ph.D.
m the University of Wisconsin, and
s taught history at the University of
iicago and the University of
isconsin.

From
OFFICE to
PROFESSION

From OFFICE to PROFESSION

The New England Ministry
1750–1850

DONALD M. SCOTT

University of Pennsylvania Press/1978

Library of Congress Cataloging in Publication Data
Scott, Donald M
   From office to profession.

   Includes bibliographical references and index.
   1. Clergy—New England. 2. New England—Church
history. I. Title.
BR520.S36   253'.0974   77-20304
ISBN 0-8122-7737-6

Composition by Deputy Crown, Inc., Camden, N.J.

To my father
and
to the memory of my mother

Contents

Acknowledgments

Among the teachers, friends, and colleagues whose criticism and encouragement have shaped this study are Merle Curti, Paul Mattingly, Robert Church, William McLoughlin, Barry Karl, Keith Baker, Charles Gray, Anthony La Vopa, and Stanley Suval. Stanley Katz and David Allmendinger went well beyond the call of duty or friendship and read several versions of the study.

Libraries, typists, and publishers really make history books happen. I am particularly grateful to Ruth Davis of the Wisconsin State Historical Society, Evelyn Vradenberg of the Congregational Library, and Tom Owen and Harvey Arnold of Regenstein Library of the University of Chicago. Thanks are also due Kathryn Hardee for turning my scrawl into crisp typescript, to Robert Erwin and his colleagues at the University of Pennsylvania Press, and particularly to Jane Barry for her splendid editing. I am also grateful to the National Endowment for the Humanities for providing a younger humanist's fellowship. Of course, the book in no way represents the views of the NEH.

My indebtedness to a few people demands special mention. Donald Mathews' work as well as his conversation and criticism has been invaluable. Neil Harris has read the manuscript almost as many times as I have, and his confidence in the study has sustained me. More than anyone else, William R. Taylor has shaped my development as a scholar and teacher. Only those who have had the privilege of working with him can know how profound my debt to him is. My wife, Joan Wallach Scott, knows the true dimension of my gratitude to her. Without her aid and encouragement the book would not be what it is—it is doubtful that it would exist at all.

Preface

In eighteenth-century New England, the ministry was the most highly esteemed of the "learned professions." Like the lawyer or physician, the minister "professed" a particular body of knowledge, and the ministry provided a clergyman with his livelihood and defined his standing in the community. But at the same time, the ministry was very different from the other professions. Although it possessed some of the characteristics of an occupation, it was also a form of public office. Public funds sustained the church and minister, and the polity joined with the gathered church in selecting the town minister. Moreover, the minister was a "watchman on the walls of Zion" with explicit, ordained responsibilities for the preservation of social order. As an "ambassador of God" and the "faithful shepherd" of a particular flock, he presided over the faith and knowledge which at once sustained one's personal relationship to God and defined one's position and duties within the community.

It is the argument of this book that by the 1850s the New England ministry had become a "profession" in a modern sense. Just like a lawyer or a doctor, the pastor now offered a specialized service to a particular self-selected clientele, which would not hesitate to dismiss him if it was dissatisfied with the quality of his service. Although clergymen might act in and upon the public in a variety of ways, in no sense did they any longer occupy a public office. Clergymen, moreover, no longer considered themselves part of a broader officialdom, but saw themselves as members of a profession which was defined by a series of separate occupational institutions and associations.

There are a number of important problems which an historical study of a profession might address: how it organized the intellectual, tech-nological, and managerial skills needed for social and economic devel-opment; how it defined intellectual activity and determined what was accepted as knowledge; how it provided avenues of mobility by estab-lishing new occupations that required for admission mastery of a requisite science, rather than privilege or prior status; or how it restricted opportunity by controlling and limiting access to the pro-fession. This study of necessity touches upon matters relevant to these issues—the deliberate recruitment of ministers from social classes that had not previously contributed heavily to the ministry; the organization of professional associations and educational institu-tions devoted exclusively to professional training; conflicts between pastors and parishioners over the control of devotion. But I have been concerned above all with a question of a rather different order. This study analyzes the explicit role of the ministry, not in its char-acter as a profession, but in its character as the body charged with the care and application of formal religion in society. Thus, though the chapters that follow contain what might well be construed as an argument about professionalization, the book is not organized around that concept. Instead, I have examined the emergence of forms of ministerial organization and consciousness which we might now define as professional within the context of changes in the place of religion in personal and public life and in the nature of church and clergy as social institutions. The result is a specific history of how the ministry changed as a social institution, rather than a description of a process that inevitably turned the ministry into a "profession."

I have approached the subject, then, from three perspectives. I examine the ministry structurally and analyze the various institutions which at different times defined the ministry and organized its activi-ties, and I use some of the techniques of collective biography to discern different and changing patterns in clerical careers. But role is as much a matter of consciousness as of institutions. Thus, in order to chart the ongoing responses of the ministry to the conditions, institutions, and pressures that afflicted it, I have analyzed a number of different kinds of clerical expression: sermons at professional rituals like ordinations, resignations, and dedications; journals, diaries, and pro-fessional correspondence of clergymen; advice manuals for ministers; reports and proceedings of ministerial associations; documents attend-ing the establishment of new practices and institutions; and materials surrounding such pastoral crises as the dismissal of a minister by his congregation. By attending to the form and occasion as well as the content of expression, I have tried to uncover the shifts in sensi-bility—in the *idea* of a minister—which are as much a part of the transformation of the ministry as changes in organization and practice. Third, the minister and ministry acted in and were acted upon by the society at large, and I have tried to relate the changes in structure and consciousness to changing conditions in the broader society and culture.

Finally, at the outset of any historical inquiry, some rationale for its temporal and substantive boundaries should be provided. Perhaps there is always a certain arbitrariness in deciding when to begin and end a study. Particularly when the focus is a process of change rather than a sequence of events, exact dates can easily give a misleading sense of precision. Essentially, this is a study of what happened during the first half of the nineteenth century to the public ministry that had existed throughout the eighteenth century in New England. The study draws upon materials from the New England-based and -derived Congregational-Presbyterian ministry. Other denominational traditions shared some aspects of the idea of clerical public guardianship with which I begin, but in its most fully articulated and institutionalized form, the notion was associated with the Congregational minister. His position derived from establishment and from the tradition of a learned and permanently settled ministry. (I have used Presbyterian sources because under the Plan of Union of 1801, ministers of New England origin used Presbyterian churches to carry their vision of social guardianship beyond the geographical boundaries of New England.) The book ends in the 1850s. By that time, after several decades of rapid expansion and institutional improvisation and then a period of severe crisis, a new kind of ministerial structure and consciousness had emerged, which, in some ways, has endured to this day.

The substantive boundaries of this book are complex. What is "the ministry" that I am talking about, and which clergymen does it include? I have tried to address myself to an historically real and identifiable ministry, that is, one which had shared traditions and/or common institutions and which was conscious of itself as a distinct ministry. But because of the temporal and conceptual scope of the study, I have been unable to rely upon a single set of terms. Hence, I have used various designations such as "the New England ministry," the "established clergy," and "the evangelical ministry" to indicate the ministry I am talking about, because categories which are accurate and serviceable at one point in the study become anachronistic and misleading for other periods.

It makes some sense to talk of "the New England ministry" at least through the Great Awakening of the 1740s, since all clergymen except a handful of Anglicans considered themselves part of a common and single clerical establishment and tradition. But with the doctrinal conflicts and denominational divisions of the late eighteenth and early nineteenth centuries, it becomes more accurate to think in terms of several different ministries. Similar problems arise with denominational categories. Throughout the eighteenth century, most ministers in New England, whatever their doctrinal allegiances, served in churches organized according to independent or congregational ecclesiastical principles. But it was not until the 1840s or 1850s that Congregationalists became denominationally conscious and organized themselves as a distinct denomination, and even then this self-consciousness existed within the context of an emerging and broader professional consciousness. Thus, even though the overwhelming majority of ministers discussed in the study served Congregational churches, I have used that designation sparingly.

Doctrinal categories also present problems. When talking of the eighteenth century, I have frequently referred to the "established clergy," for whether New or Old Light, liberal or evangelical, most eighteenth-century New England ministers held the same assumptions about the character of the ministry as a public office and saw even their opponents as members of a common clerical officialdom. (Some Separatists, many of whom became Baptists, were forced to depart from the established structure and developed some rather different conceptions of the office. But since this study is concerned with what happened to the tradition coming from establishment, I have not discussed the Separatists.) By the beginning of the nineteenth century, however, some doctrinal divisions had begun to take on more permanent institutional forms as the evangelicals (usually referred to as the Orthodox or Calvinist clergy) forced the liberals, or Unitarians, to organize themselves as a separate denomination. Thus, for the nineteenth century, upon which the major portions of this study concentrate, I have spoken of the "evangelical ministry." This emphasis partly stems from the fact that the evangelical clergy was by far the largest of the New England ministries during the first half of the century. Mainly, however, I have focused upon Plan of Union evangelicals because they reoriented the tradition of clerical guardianship and took the lead in improvising a series of new institutions that utterly transformed the structure of the ministry.

Not even the geographical scope of the book escapes difficulties. In the eighteenth century, I refer to a regionally based and distinctive ministry, but by the early decades of the nineteenth century, evangelicals of New England nurture and origin were conscious members of a ministry more meaningfully described by a network of new, translocal institutions that was in no way confined to New England. Moreover, in the 1850s, when denominational self-consciousness began to outweigh evangelicalism as an essential badge of ministerial identity, Congregationalism emerged as a national rather than a purely regional denomination. In certain ways, then, the end point of this study comes not only at a particular time but also with the disintegration of the historical meaningfulness of the original categories. By the 1840s and 1850s, the regional designation has little meaning beyond specifying where the ministers I discuss happened to be practicing their profession. By that time the distinctive New England clerical heritage had been utterly dissipated. Moreover, although denominational differences still played an important part in the operations of denominations as separate social and religious groups—to both ministers and communicants it was still important that they were Congregationalists rather than something else—from the perspective of professional structure, consciousness, and experiences, Unitarians, Baptists, Congregationalists, and perhaps even Methodists were becoming increasingly indistinguishable. In this sense, denominations can be seen as ministerial structures analogous to state bar associations, namely, as suborganizations of a broader profession of which more ministers considered themselves members. For the 1850s, in short, it begins to become historically meaningful to think not only of a number of particular ministries but of a clerical profession.

1

The Office of the Minister in Eighteenth-Century New England

The ministry in seventeenth- and eighteenth-century New England was a form of public office. Although ministers did not possess any formal civil authority, the sacred office nonetheless had particular responsibility for the preservation of social order. The character of the Puritan ministry derived from the religious foundations of New England public culture. But if its religious heritage was the ideological source of order in eighteenth-century New England, it was in the individual communities that the clergy's role in preserving social order was most important. Indeed, above all else, the sacred office in eighteenth-century New England was a local office, derived from a special blend of congregationalist ecclesiastical theory and the social order of the New England town.[1]

The English Puritans who made their way to New England came to the New World armed with the conviction that a gathered communion of saints was the only legitimate home for the sacred in the profane world. For them, the universal invisible church had no earthly embodiment: properly speaking, there was no Church but only discrete congregations, over which neither civil nor ecclesiastical institutions had any authority. Almost as soon as they arrived, the Puritans organized their churches into special, covenanted gatherings of confessed saints. The New England version of the ministerial office derived directly from this notion of the covenanted communion.[2] The minister was not part of an official or ecclesiastical caste, for no professional organization, civil authority, or ecclesiastical body could confer the position. He was solely the creation of the individual

church. He was a pastor elected by a church to preach the Word and
to provide the instruction and exhortation that were at the core of
Puritan worship. His spiritual powers and status did not differ from
those of the gathered saints who called him their pastor. Many seventeenth-century New Englanders, in fact, argued that before a man
could become a minister to a church he had to become a member of
the church on equal footing with the other members, equally subject
to the discipline of the church.[3]

The various procedures New Englanders devised for settling a minister in a church reflected this insistence that the office was essentially
a local one under the ultimate control of the individual church. After
a church had issued a call to a preacher, a formal ceremony of ordination sealed the ties between the pastor and his people. Care was taken
to make sure that the ceremony did not abrogate the authority of the
individual church to select its own minister. "Ordination," the Cambridge Platform of 1646 insisted, "is not to go before but to follow
election. The essence and substance of the outward calling of an
ordinary officer of the church, did not consist in his ordination, but in
his voluntary and free election by the Church and in his accepting of
that Election."[4] Ordination, thus, did not confer the office. It was
simply the symbolic expression of the formal assumption of an office
already conferred by the church. Ordination sermons invariably
stressed the fact that the relationship, though archetypal, was nonetheless a particularistic one existing between the pastor and his people.
It was made clear, moreover, that the right hand of fellowship wel-
coming the man to the ministerial fold was not the laying on of hands,
but merely signified his acceptance as a fellow minister of a sister
church.[5] The autonomy of congregations was abrogated somewhat in
the early years of the eighteenth century. The clergy organized neighborhood ministerial associations, which began to license pastoral
candidates after examining them for piety, character, and orthodoxy.
Increasingly, individual churches looking for a minister would ask the
association to suggest likely candidates. In some ways, however, these
devices formalized already existing practices and did not drastically
change the power of the local church to select its own pastor. Though
churches selected properly licensed candidates, they were under no
constraint to select any particular candidate, and they still elected a
minister only after a period of trial and with the vote of at least a
substantial majority of the adult male members of the church.[6]

The parish system that New Englanders grafted onto their congregationalism also helped establish the localistic character of the ministerial office. This system was the basis of the New England form

of religious establishment and required that each church, while retaining its character as a gathered, specially covenanted communion of saints, exist within a territorial parish. Whether confessing Christians or not, the civil population as a whole was taxed to support the Gospel at rates set and collected by the civil jurisdiction and authority.[7] Parish boundaries for the most part were coextensive with town boundaries, and frequently a town was formally organized as a town only after a church had been organized. The town parishes were required to contribute to the salary of the minister and to construct a house of worship, which then belonged to the parish rather than to the church itself.[8]

This development had importance well beyond the practical matter of building churches and paying ministers. The parishes quickly began to assert various rights over the settling of a minister. By the end of the seventeenth century, the practice that Williston Walker considered the most "peculiar feature of New England congregationalism" had been established in law. "Those who weren't members of the church [were permitted] a voice in calling a pastor."[9] The gathered church still called a minister and continued to take the most active role in finding him, but he could not be installed or ordained until a majority of the voting inhabitants of the parish had concurred in his selection. In this sense, a minister belonged as much to the town as to the gathered body of converted saints and was pastor to the town as well as to the church.

The most significant aspect of the localistic character of the ministerial office, however, was the ideal and practice of pastorates of lifetime tenure.[10] The bond established at his ordination was expected to be permanent, lasting until death. The extent of permanence among the established Congregational clergy in New England during the eighteenth century is indeed significant. For example, from the Yale College classes from 1702 through 1794, 550 graduates entered the Congregationalist ministry. Of these men, 392, or 71 percent, ministered for their entire career to only one church, the one to which they had first been ordained. Only 21, or 4 percent, of the 550 served more than three pastorates. A more precise picture emerges if the graduates from the first seventy-five years of the century are separated from those from the last quarter, when an erosion of permanence had begun. For graduates from 1775 through 1794, 57 percent served only one pastorate, although 81 percent still served only one or two pastorates. (Moreover, since the careers of most of these graduates extended well into the nineteenth century, a good portion of the changes in pastorate occurred in the nineteenth century.) For the graduates from Yale up until 1775, however, fully 79 percent served only one pastorate, while only 7 percent served more than two pastorates. Equally revealing is the length of time these men served their pastorates. Of the 392 graduates from 1702 through 1794 who served one church, 74 percent (292) served twenty or more years, while 62 percent (242) served thirty or more years and 38 percent served forty or more years. Moreover, 58 of them served for a half century or more.[11]

The importance attached to a single, lifetime pastorate can be seen in the care with which both sides approached the selection of a pastor. Churches almost never called a man without a period of probationary preaching that usually lasted a minimum of three months, and they often demanded a second and third stint before finally offering the candidate a "call." It was not at all uncommon for churches to try out a succession of candidates before agreeing on the one they wanted to "settle." Different groups in the church and town frequently differed over what pastoral style or doctrinal emphasis they liked and would each favor a particular candidate, and the search would continue until one side prevailed with their man or some neutral candidate could be found.[12] In any case, the scrutiny to which a church subjected a candidate was careful and trying. As one young candidate confided to his fiancée, "the people watch me as narrowly as a mouse is watched by a cat." Indeed, the diaries, letters, and journals of young preachers seeking a settlement are filled with anxieties about how the people were responding to them and to their preaching, and whether, if the signals were unclear, this meant hostility to their candidacy, or, even worse, was a sign of their own spiritual unworthiness for the office.[13]

The candidates themselves were no less scrupulous, knowing full well that if they accepted a call, they were likely to be stuck with the situation for the rest of their lives. They were equally aware of the capacities of contentious parishioners and faction-ridden communities to inflict misery on their pastors by sabotaging the support of the community and withdrawing various supplemental forms of salary support. Thus, it was not uncommon for a young preacher to reject a number of calls before finally settling. If a candidate had prospects for a better position, he would of course reject a church's call. But even without another immediate prospect, a young man seeking a pastorate would reject a call if for any reason the prospects for enduring support were unfavorable. The parish might be poor and have a tradition of excessive parsimony toward its pastor, the people might be seriously divided in their call to him, or the church or town might have a history of contentiousness.[14] Indeed, many a man appears to have chosen a small, but harmonious and respectful, parish over a larger and wealthier, but divided, one.[15] The Reverend Joseph Vaill, for example, decided in 1780 to accept the call tendered by the church in Hadlyme, Connecticut, even though the society was "small and unable to give the minister a large salary." Still, he accepted because the "people gave . . . [him] a harmonious invitation to settle with them and manifested a willingness to support him according to their ability."[16] It proved a felicitous choice: he remained there for fifty-six years. And when in 1798 Lyman Beecher was called as a candidate to the church in East Hampton, Long Island, he wrote tellingly of the things that had made it an attractive post: "There are more Christians, no sectarians; I believe not one. Comparatively few infidels. The people are peaceable. Not a lawyer in the whole country. Industrious, hospitable; in the habit of being influenced by their minister."[17]

Once forged, the ordination bond was not lightly or easily broken. A ministry could only be dissolved for legitimate cause and even then only by following a carefully worked-out procedure. Neither side could unilaterally break the bond: if he wished to remain a congregational clergyman, with full sanction to serve elsewhere, an eighteenth-century minister could not simply resign; nor could a church simply expel a minister. If either party to an ordination became dissatisfied, a council drawn from neighboring churches would be called to examine the situation to see if conditions warranted such a drastic step as dismissal of the minister from his "charge."[18] Throughout the eighteenth century, dismissal was an extraordinary act, justified only by extreme conditions, and neither side resorted to a council unless they felt especially aggrieved. Even then, a council would usually try to repair the bond if at all possible before it would agree to dissolve it. It was not uncommon for a council to refuse to dissolve a pastorate and warn the minister and the church to stop bickering and restore harmony. Conflict sometimes continued for years until a second, third, or even a fourth council finally agreed that the situation was serious enough to break the ordination bond. Sometimes churches or ministers even went to court or to the colonial legislature to challenge a council's decision.[19]

The legitimate grounds for dismissal were clear. A church could usually secure a dismissal only if it could show that the minister's pastoral character had become so flawed that he could no longer be counted a *real* pastor; perhaps he had become intemperate, grossly neglected his duties, or committed some obvious immorality. Even then a council did not always grant dismissal, especially if the pastor was contrite and it appeared that the threat of a dishonorable discharge would restore proper behavior. Thus the Reverend Benjamin Strong, first criticized for drinking in the 1740s, was arraigned before the local consociation for intemperance in 1757 and 1759, confessed his guilt, and was not finally dismissed from his charge until 1767.[20] A minister could ordinarily get out of his ordination bond only if the church deliberately refused to give him adequate support to sustain himself and his family, or if, for some reason—ill-health, loss of piety, or a change of doctrinal position—he no longer thought himself capable of filling the office and intended to leave the ministry altogether. Anything short of these charges was usually insufficient, although occasionally a council would decide that a conflict within a congregation was so deep and bitter that only removal of the pastor would restore harmony, even though the minister neither wished nor deserved dismissal. Disagreement with pastoral chastisement or dislike of a man's pulpit style did not warrant changing pastors. The "charge to the people" in ordination and installation ceremonies invariably reminded the congregation that as sinners whose very salvation might be at stake, they were obliged to endure the hard truths that pastors were called upon to preach. In fact Dexter's six-volume *Biographical Sketches of Graduates of Yale College*, which covers graduates from 1702 through 1815, records a number of instances of dull preachers who nonetheless enjoyed long lifetime pastorates. The easy removal of ministers because parishioners did not think they adequately "edified" them was a thing of the future.[21]

The recruitment practices of the churches respected the ideal of permanency. A church that needed a minister did not violate the sanctity of another church's settled pastorate. In fact, the stricture against raiding was such that in 1782 when Yale College called the Reverend Samuel Wales from the First Church in Milford, Connecticut, to become the professor of divinity, his church refused to dismiss him (even though he was not a very popular preacher) until Yale agreed to pay the church a £200 indemnity. A number of churches might well compete for a young man of talent, piety, and promise, but once he settled he left the pool of available candidates. And even if a church had wanted a settled minister, no council would have been likely to release him from his original charge.[22]

In addition to the formal obstacles to changing pastorates, the character of the ministry as a "sacred office and calling" worked to secure pastoral permanence. The term *calling*, of course, applied to all vocations and professions and referred to the providential action that directed all of life. From the idea of calling, New Englanders derived their notions about both the personal virtues and disciplines and the public obligations that they associated with the various vocations. The idea also reflected the belief that the social order of a community derived from a divine economy in which God had assigned a particular task and a particular place to each person. Thus the ubiquitous teaching that all were obliged to attend faithfully to their calling carried the dual message to work hard and to be content with one's place, because no matter how high or humble one's social standing, all legitimate callings were honorable in God's eyes.[23] The sacred calling, however, while sharing these general characteristics, differed from all other callings because of the nature of the office.

The minister, to use the two central metaphors New Englanders applied to the office, was both an "ambassador" of God who carried God's word to a particular town and congregation, and their "shepherd," responsible for preserving them from sin and directing them into godly paths. Such an office, it was thought, demanded a special ministerial character, one that could be trusted to serve faithfully both God and his people, a character that was born in piety, shaped by learning, and displayed in a special brand of asceticism. The outward badges of this character included the absence of excessive concern about acquiring the material goods and comforts of the world, the absence of spiritual pride, and most of all the absence of personal ambition for power and fame. The clergy itself appears to have been most concerned about ambition. They sought to immunize the sacred office against appropriation as a profession of particular standing and honor by young men of talent and energy who would try to use it to achieve secular ambitions. Ministers of such character would hardly make fit vessels for transmitting a divine message that demanded that man serve God rather than mammon or himself. They would also undermine the very character of the ministry as a divine and public office, transforming it from an agency of public order into an instrument of personal aggrandizement.[24]

The inner sanctions of the sense of the ministry as a sacred calling ultimately secured the ministerial character that protected the office and preserved permanence. In certain ways, of course, the social structure and the procedures for arriving at a vocation limited the initiative a young man exerted on his own behalf. Essentially, a young man was selected out for the ministry, and here the passive voice is used deliberately. Young men of the eighteenth century generally did not play a very active role in determining their adult occupations and stations. The basic decision lay with parents and elders, who tried to equip their sons for a position commensurate with family tradition, standing, resources, and, to an extent, the son's particular traits and talents. But the young man going into the ministry had a particularly acute sense that divine agency was at work in placing him in the sacred office. The initial step toward the ministry—that which set the ministerial candidate apart from young men headed toward secular vocations—was the experience of a "call" to it. Obviously, the intensity of a sense of call varied. Indeed, there is evidence that in the decades preceding the Great Awakening the spiritual standards had slackened and that a portion of the clergy treated the ministry as a secular vocation. After the Great Awakening of the 1740s, there appears to have been a general reassertion of spiritual standards among Old Light as well as New Light clergymen. Most clergymen probably came into the clergy after this point with a discernible sense that God had chosen them for it. The inner hallmark of a call, moreover, was a sense of renunciation of secular ambitions and, among the more evangelical, of self. A young man with ministerial piety measured his fidelity to his call by monitoring his feelings as he worked to purge himself of the selfish and worldly desires that were inimical to the sacred office. Among evangelicals this process amounted to a kind of continuing spiritual test to determine whether one had genuinely surrendered himself to divine service, whether he was willing to actually trust God to sustain him as He saw fit.[25]

The conception of the sacred office as a calling, then, provided a powerful sanction against ambition and hence a powerful buttress to permanence. It labeled as ungodly any feeling of discontent with a position or wish for a better post, and it made such feelings a source of spiritual guilt and doubt. The notion of a call was also applied to the process of settling in a church and thus served to further bind a man to his pastorate. Direct providential action not only brought a young man into the clerical profession, but it also placed him in the church to which he was ordained. The "call" from a church to a young man to settle with them was both the act of a church and, when sealed, an act of God, to be accepted just as one would accept a marriage vow, for better or for worse. For a minister to chafe under the trials and burdens of the station God had directed him to might well be a sign that his own piety was wanting, that perhaps his original call to preach the gospel had not been a genuine one. In fact, the diaries, journals, and letters of ministers reveal that when they did have troubles in the parish they, at least initially, interpreted their problems as a divine chastisement, a sign of God's displeasure over their failure to purge themselves of worldly affections.[26]

These were the constraints John Vaill operated under when he accepted and remained in his Hadlyme pastorate. To him the unanimity of the church's call and its willingness to support him as best it could was an unmistakable sign that the call was indeed "a call of Providence." To violate this call by using his success to secure a richer, more influential pastorate would have been an absolute betrayal of his own divine call, a clear and unmistakable substitution of worldly desires for divine service. The eighteenth-century minister, in other words, simply did not expect to change pastorates. In this sense the eighteenth-century ministry was an office and a calling, rather than a career in the modern sense of the term. A career, according to the *International Encyclopedia of the Social Sciences,* is "a long, if not a lifetime commitment to moving upwards through a series of related occupations and statuses."[27] When an eighteenth-century clergyman did move, his action did not stem from aspirations for something better. He moved from necessity and because his situation was in peril. The 7 percent of the Yale graduates from 1702 to 1775 who had more than two pastorates during their lifetimes were not the clergymen who gained prominence. Rather, they were the ne'er-do-wells of the profession, for when a minister had to move, especially a second or third time, the move was almost always from bad to worse, to a small, poor frontier post, or to a church that had a such a history of parsimony and contentiousness that only someone fairly desperate for a post would accept it. And even when a man did secure such a post, his chances for staying were not very good.[28]

Such were the institutional and psychological sanctions that bound the minister to a particular church and town. But the character of his authority and leadership as well as his overall standing and ties within the community also derived from the general nature of office and leadership in eighteenth-century New England. The ministry was a public office and shared a common character and idiom with magistracy. Pastoral and magisterial authority and the relationships and obligations between magistrate and citizenry and between minister and congregation were similar. Whether through town meeting or church meeting, the people conferred the office, but the office itself bestowed authority which came from God. Once a person was "elevated" to a "chief office," it was the obligation of those who conferred the office (and retained the power of removal) to grant him respect and obedience and cheerfully to acquiesce in his exercise of his office. When someone was installed as a magistrate or a clergyman, in fact, the people were said to be "subject" to him, for their legitimate sovereignty did not extend to the ordinary conduct of the office but only to the violations of its ultimate nature. An electorate was expected to remove a magistrate only when his behavior demonstrated that he did not possess the "character of a good ruler." As one election sermon put it, magistrates were not servants of the people expected to do their will but servants of God, chosen by the people, to do His will; and once chosen, they were due "that cheerful obedience" that by divine writ and immemorial nature subordinates owed their superiors.[29] And as the Cambridge Platform put it when it defined pastoral authority, "when such a people do chuse any to be over them in the Lord, then do they become subject and most willingly submit to the ministry of the Lord, whom they have so chosen."[30]

In eighteenth-century New England, moreover, informal personal and social authority buttressed the authority of office itself. Office was bestowed because a person was thought by the community to possess the qualities—the "character"—that the office required. For civil office there were two distinct ways to determine this merit: demonstration and social standing. In his systematic study of the leaders of seventy eighteenth-century New England towns, Edward Cook has shown that even the major offices of most New England towns were open to a broad portion of the white, adult male population. For the most part, however, office was bestowed only after a person had established a general reputation and bearing in the community and by performing creditably in a series of lesser, essentially service offices had demonstrated that he possessed the character and ability that New Englanders wanted their selectmen and sheriffs to have. Cook has found that in most towns most occupants of the higher offices were first selected for high offices in their late thirties and early forties, and that they then held them until they voluntarily stepped down after reaching the customary age for surrendering leadership to the next generation.[31]

There was, however, a second mode of accession to office and leadership. Some men became leaders because of the families to which they belonged. New Englanders, believers in the existence of a natural social order, held that in any human community there were legitimate distinctions to be made among persons. Moreover, though the degree of social gradation varied enormously in the New England towns, by the last third of the century most towns that were over fifty years old and had over fifteen hundred inhabitants possessed a cluster of families that comprised a recognized social elite. Members of these families were presumed to possess qualities of leadership and were frequently entrusted with high office while in their late twenties and early thirties, without having first to demonstrate their character in lesser service offices. Leaders from this source, moreover, were frequently the most powerful and influential town leaders; and in a few towns the dominance of such leaders appears to have bordered on the oligarchical, though there were not many towns in which leadership was confined solely to such men. Thus, though officeholders were drawn from a fairly large pool of talent, in the towns of moderate size and age that provided the models of the godly community, real leadership lay in the hands of the portion of the community referred to as "the better part" or the "wise and the good," that social elite which was assumed to possess the requisite moral and public qualities because of its wealth, learning, and tradition of leadership.[32]

The minister's authority and overall position in the town derived from his occupancy of office and from social standing, from his possession of the social stature that town leaders possessed whether they had earned or were born to it. The deference and obedience due by nature and divine ordinance to all legitimately conferred authority was especially due to the pastor. In addition to the respect and authority that accrued simply to the fact of office and its special character and importance, a minister also possessed the kind of influence which accrued to superior social standing and which, in turn, enhanced his overall stature and authority. But although this influence was the *kind* that accompanied social rank, it came to the minister with the office and did not accrue to the young man himself. In the first place, the established clergy of eighteenth-century New England was not drawn from a single social class or caste.[33] Just as with civil office holding, the clerical ranks were filled by reaching deeply into the social structure. Some ministers were recruited from the small provincial elite and from such prominent ministerial families as the Elys, the Dwights, the Williamses, or the Huntingtons. But the largest portion was drawn from the sons of local respectables, who would send a younger son into the clergy, and from the hard-working and pious middling families, which would frequently contribute a son who displayed the requisite talents and piety to the clergy. A few young men of extremely humble parentage were also recruited. In such cases (Joseph Bellamy is a prominent example), a young man's striking piety and intellect had brought him the special forms of charity and patronage that enabled him to secure the education needed to become a minister.[34]

A minister was almost never a member by birth or previous residence of the community to which he was called. In social terms, he came as a relative stranger, as one without personal standing in the town. But when a young man did settle into a community, whatever his own social origins, he settled near, if not at, the top of its social gradations. Upon settling, in other words, a minister assumed a local *social* standing commensurate with the importance of his office. This confluence of social and official station was reflected in the sumptuary custom that gave the powdered hair and wig of the gentleman to the clergyman, as well as by the form of address, "the reverend sir," that was applied to a minister. Since he held formal authority of at least a spiritual and moral sort over almost everyone in the community, it would have been unnatural and unthinkable for him to be an obvious social inferior to any of his parishioners. Thus those communities that contained a cluster of families tied into the provincial elite appear to have called men from among their class or men whose early educational and collegiate accomplishments had demonstrated exceptional talent and promise.[35] Moreover, even if a ministerial candidate was of poor and unlettered parentage, by virtue of his education, collegiate associates, and the manner and speech that came with such learning, he had a station comparable to that of the leaders of most towns. In some of the newer, smaller, and less stratified communities, the minister almost immediately assumed a special status, in some ways above that of his parishioners. Such parishes could be faction-ridden and poverty-stricken, but at the same time the combination of respect for the office, deference to learning and manner, and the attentiveness of a "good" pastor could yield a highly stable, felicitous, and influential pastorate.[36]

The ministerial office in eighteenth-century New England, then, was inseparable from the fabric of the New England towns that contained it. But what gave this ministerial presence and office such importance—what, in short, lay behind the ideal and practice of permanence—was the minister's role as the mainstay of communal order. There was, in fact, little in congregationalist ecclesiastical theory that demanded lifetime pastorates: permanence, rather, was a requirement of the social order of the New England town. The most distinctive feature of eighteenth-century New England society and culture was its communalism, a social structure and ideology in which order, harmony, and obedience to all authority were the highest public and social values.[37] This communalism, moreover, can be said to have centered as much in the figure of a settled minister as it did in any other figure or institution, for the clergyman was both the keeper and purveyor of the public culture, the body of fundamental precepts and values that defined the social community, and an enforcer of the personal values and decorum that sustained it.

The clergy occupied the ideological center of New England society and presided over its public rituals. Eighteenth-century New England was still largely a culture built upon the Word; and at least until the American Revolution, and in many ways even well after it, the clergy enjoyed a virtual monopoly over the public forum. The sermon, delivered by a clergyman, was the form of address on all formal "state" and public occasions—such as the annual election day ceremonies and the hundreds of fast and thanksgiving days.[38] On these and other public occasions New Englanders gathered to hear their ministers invoke the basic ideas around which society was based and their communities organized.

New England public rituals were ordinarily local ceremonies, designed to restore and maintain the social order of the particular communities. Though the public culture that was invoked in the various ceremonies was a common New England orthodoxy, the focus usually remained local, addressing either the local institutions that ordered a community or particular conditions that threatened to disorder it. Election sermons dealt with magistracy, with the character demanded of rulers and the need for the cheerful obedience to magistrates that together united a polity in order and harmony. Ordination sermons, describing the bonds between a preacher and his people, dwelt upon the need for religious institutions, and the role of faith and devotion in maintaining a peaceful and felicitous community. Funeral sermons for the eminent held up immediate models of ideal Christian citizenship, while execution sermons dramatized the precepts of order by counterpointing them with vivid examples of their opposites.

The most important—and ubiquitous—public ritual, however, was the fast, for it, more than any other ceremony, expressed the particular public consciousness of New England. Eighteenth-century New England possessed a remarkably coherent and self-conscious public culture that centered on the myth of its special providential founding and upon a deep sense of the exceptional character of its institutions and heritage. In terms that John Winthrop first promulgated in 1630 as the *ArBella* approached the New England shore, God and New England had entered into a sacred and solemn covenant. God had called the Puritans to the wilderness to set up a model Christian commonwealth, and so long as New Englanders remained faithful to this charge, God would sustain and prosper them with special providential oversight. But if New England betrayed its charge, if its people fell into unruliness and its communities into disorder and conflict, and if its churches lost faith, a wrathful God would cast New England aside and punish it for its iniquity. By the eighteenth century, moreover, this myth had been codified into the jeremiad, the rhetorical formula that had become *the* sermon of the fast ceremony.[39]

Above all else, the jeremiad was a deliberate instrument of social order directed toward the local community. It deployed the central myth of the covenant in ways that were designed to restore the personal and communal disciplines upon which the New England localistic model of social order depended. The jeremiad appropriated any event or condition that could possibly be considered special or extraordinary and interpreted it as a sign of God's displeasure with the community. The phenomenon was interpreted as an "affliction," an example of God's wrath at the community's failure to live up to the standards of faith and morality, personal discipline and social harmony that the covenant obliged it to maintain. The fast ceremony was designed to restore the immediate and poignant sense of utter dependence upon God that was thought to be the foundation of all social discipline and felicity. The jeremiad, in fact, contained the two basic values of New England communalism. It embodied both the authoritarianism that underlay social obedience and harmony, and New England civic-mindedness—a sense of mutual obligation and common responsibility for the order and well-being of the whole. Indeed, the sins that the jeremiad catalogued as the source of God's wrath and the effective cause of the community's affliction were invariably forms of behavior—disrespect for elders and betters, persistent feuding, contentiousness, and litigiousness—that seemed to jeopardize the orderliness and harmony of the community. The jeremiad and the fast thus sought to restore both the obedience to authority and the civic consciousness that characterized New England communalism. Indeed, the ceremony itself expressed New England communalism. As a ritual, it referred back to the original act, the collective owning of the covenant that had established the community, and thus drew the public out of individual, self-centered preoccupations into explicit consciousness of its existence as a public, a common body, knit together by bonds of mutuality and obligation.[40] In its penitential aspect, the ceremony sought to restore the ultimate source of obedience—submission to divine will—from which all order flowed and then to translate this submissiveness into individual repentance and reformation and into public and collective watchfulness. It was not at all uncommon for periods of fast to be followed by a reassertion of church discipline, by systematic efforts to punish such misconduct as the failure to conduct family devotions, Sabbath breaking, intemperance, or such breaches of godly carriage as feuding and rumor mongering.[41]

The public role of the clergy was not confined to the performance of these public rituals. Church and pastor played an active role in chastising antisocial behavior, and the town minister was frequently called upon as a wise, learned, and disinterested party to adjudicate personal disputes.[42] Although sin was a personal act touching upon an individual's relationship to God, sin was nonetheless a social matter. All behavior construed as antisocial was ultimately a matter of sin, traceable to a disposition that was hostile to order in all its personal, social, and theological dimensions. Crime thus had both a theological and a civil definition. Social decorum—manners—was never simply a matter of nicety, merely regulating the behavior between kinds of people, but was either supportive or subversive of order and, like a stone cast into a pond, sent its ripples across the whole of the social fabric. When a humble or young man, for example, openly refused to doff his cap and step aside for a public official or a gentleman, it was not simply a personal insult. The act displayed a frame of discontent with one's place and hence was in itself an explicit challenge to social and natural order. Moreover, it eroded the habits of deference that signaled and enforced order by setting a subversive example and by treating authority itself with contempt. Finally, it was a blasphemous assault upon the very foundation of order, both because the discontent with one's place that it betrayed was a discontent with God's workmanship and because a refusal to respect superiors at one level was a defiance of the highest authority, of which all lesser forms were types or shadows. This conception of behavior and wrongdoing was reflected in the significance attached to confession and the use made of crime and punishment in such things as execution sermons. More than simply punish the particular act, New England pastors and churches sought to secure full confessions through mechanisms and rituals that not only restored the wrongdoer to a posture of repentance and submission but also strengthened the fabric of order itself.[43]

The clergy's role in securing the personal behavior associated with harmonious and orderly communities was not limited to defining and punishing wrongdoing. It was part as well of his day-to-day, cradle-to-grave ministrations to his people. The discipline that obtained in the confessing Christian's relationship to God was the prototype and source of the discipline that social order demanded. The social order of the New England town, in other words, resided in disciplines that stemmed equally from religious beliefs and obligations and from the decorum that by nature was thought to inhere in any genuine community. In this sense religious discipline was social discipline, and when the good pastor tended the spiritual needs of his flock he simultaneously tended the social needs of his community. Although New England society was authoritarian, it was not overtly coercive. Obedience to all legitimate authority was perhaps its highest social value, but the obedience needed for a felicitous community was the voluntary acquiescence that was secured through habit, devotion, and deference. Whether the minister fostered the piety of the convert, detailed the limits of the legitimate pursuit of self-interest, instructed children to seek God and obey their parents, comforted the dying and the afflicted, or indoctrinated the populace at large with the basic precepts of social life, he plied the common idiom of obedience and obligation that lay at the heart of a proper conduct of life. It is to this overall public dimension of the pastoral role that the Reverend Azel Backus referred in his 1798 election sermon when he insisted that although rulers were responsible for framing laws, society had to rely upon the clergy "as instruments in the hands of Providence to make wholesome habits."[44]

The minister thus embodied and expressed New England communalism. The minister, indeed, was bound to his community in ways that no officeholder or mere citizen was. No other office in town had the same scope, and no other influence was so comprehensively felt. The minister purveyed the ideas which connected the town to the broader culture and by which New Englanders interpreted life in all its personal and social dimensions. He performed the rituals that gave the community its common consciousness as well as those that distinguished deviance from conformity, and he dispensed the piety and moralism that shaped the devotional life of the New England people and the public discipline of the New England towns. It was this pervasive presence in the life of the community and its inhabitants that gave such significance to permanence and such social importance to the office, for, symbolically if not always actually, the presence of a good minister, permanently installed and bound to a town and church, transformed a mere settlement into a genuine, organic community. In this sense, a town was said to "unite *in*" the man they called, ordained, and settled over themselves. When the Reverend Hezekiah Bissell, the first pastor in Wintonbury, Connecticut, died after a faithful ministry of forty-one years, his epitaph declared that "the remarkable peace and good order that reigned among the people of his charge during his ministry bear witness to the prudence and greatness of his mind."[45]

Localism, then, was the essential characteristic of the clerical office in eighteenth-century New England. Although the tradition of clerical public guardianship derived from the precepts of a common New

England social and religious orthodoxy, the concrete sense of what this guardianship meant and the specific duties it entailed derived from the character of the New England town. Moreover, a minister's authority and influence in his community derived from the office, the general traditions of leadership, and social standing. The minister was at once the occupant of the sacred office which along with magistracy provided the twin pillars of public governance, and a member and leader of the "wise and the good," that social elite which by example, informal influence, and office governed the well-ordered community. Ministers were all ambassadors of God, but they were ambassadors to a specific place, and it was this particular, ordained charge that dominated the eighteenth-century clergyman's sense of himself as a man of God no less than it shaped his sense of himself as a public official.

2

The New England Clergy and the
Transformation of American Politics

Clerical public guardianship in 1790 remained much as it had been since the seventeenth-century beginnings. Gaining independence and organizing a new nation under the Constitution did not appear to most clergymen to have altered either the character of public governance or the clergy's responsibility for it. Public order still seemed to reside in a deferential people and in leaders who were wise, impartial, and faithful. The clergy served as the stewards of this public culture, and into the new century they could be found calling for "rulers of good character" and exhorting the people to obedience and "habits of subordination." But with the rise of systematic electoral competition organized by and around two organized political parties, this traditional public culture all but disappeared. As David Hackett Fischer has put it, "the period 1798–1814, the period of contraction in France, was America's age of Democratic revolution, in which the agency of change was not the action of one party but the interaction of two."[1] This revolution in the structure of political life fundamentally altered the place of the clergy in New England public life.

Political parties in the modern sense—much less a party system— did not exist in eighteenth-century New England before the 1790s. The political groupings which did exist in the sphere of "high" or provincial politics that centered around assembly and executive were informal "factions," "interests," or "connexions." Factions were usually ephemeral, temporary alliances based on narrow interest or a particular short-lived issue. Interests, factions, or cliques, which lasted somewhat longer, were bound together by personal and kinship ties

18

as well as by narrow self-interest. The apparently more enduring groupings like the "court and country connexions" were essentially legislative factions bound by personal ties and by shared attitudes and interests. But they had no formal structure, generated no political machinery, and organized no enduring links with local politics.[2]

Organized politics of even this sort did not really exist on the local or town level, with the possible exception of a few cities like Boston or Portsmouth, New Hampshire. To be sure, when there was a particularly controversial issue like setting up an additional parish, factions might arise, but they would disappear once the issue was settled. It was only in these extraordinary circumstances that office was contested. In ordinary times one "stood" for office rather than solicited it. Moreover, one was selected for candidacy by one's peers, elders, or betters, and voluntary retirement rather than electoral defeat usually ended incumbency.[3] Officeholders in eighteenth-century New England towns thus were not really political figures in any modern sense: they were selected because of their standing in the community to carry out certain necessary communal tasks, not because of views they might hold or policies they might advocate. "The New England towns," as Edward Cook has shown, "filled their chief offices with a special kind of public servant. Major officeholders usually were prosperous townsmen, usually were in their middle age, and generally had been prepared for major responsibilities by serving the town capably in lesser offices. . . . Leaders were elected without organized partisan political machinery, without even a formal nominating procedure, and even when questions of personal interest divided leaders from the voters the assembled electorate rarely failed to return proven leaders to major office."[4]

During the 1790s political structures of a new and more durable sort emerged with the rise of two increasingly distinct and coherent political groups—the Federalist "interest" and the Republican "interest." In the early 1790s Alexander Hamilton put together what many historians have referred to as the Federalist party. In form and function, however, the Hamiltonian structure was similar to the traditional political "connexion." Bound by personal ties and particular interests, it was intended to secure the support Hamilton needed to enact his program. But with the organization and geographical extent of the national polity, Hamilton had to supplement the ties of narrow interest and personal connection with the more durable bonds of ideological and programmatic commitment. Using his powers as secretary of the treasury and confidant of Washington, his acquaintance with leaders throughout the nation, and a semiofficial "court" newspaper,

The Gazette of the United States, Hamilton built links beyond the capital to the broader polity as he tried to foster a firm connection between the government interest and local notables in the various states.[5] In this sense, the Hamiltonian structure contained some of the origins of a durable, national political party. Still, in an electoral and an organizational sense, the structure was far from the modern party.[6] It did not establish any formal political organization, and it did not really address the populace as a democratic electorate. Hamilton and his lieutenants sought only to secure the personal support of local elites, assuming that the notables' local standing would be enough to give the government interest the support it needed to succeed and endure.

Those opposed to Hamilton and his measures quickly put together a rival "connexion," initially referred to as the Republican or Jeffersonian interest, to counter Hamilton's court party. Organized by James Madison, it centered in the House of Representatives, and aside from scattered correspondence its only real presence outside the capital consisted of its newspaper, *The National Gazette.* But after 1796, when the Federalists solidified their domination of the national government, the Republican interest began to organize itself as a national, electoral party. Thomas Jefferson took a more visible stance as its leader, and Republicans began to build a genuine party organization on both the state and national levels. They set up a caucus and committee structure, complete with state and district committees. In addition to persuading previously unaffiliated officeholders to let their name be included on a printed list of "friends of liberty," they used public meetings and party committees to nominate candidates. They improvised a number of electioneering tactics, organizing barbecues and rallies, and distributing broadsides and ballads. And in the last years of the decade they turned some benevolent societies and the Tammany societies into political fronts to help distribute party literature, select candidates and electioneer, and cement party loyalty.[7] The extent and complexity of Republican organization and electoral machinery varied greatly from state to state and from locality to locality, but by 1800 the Jeffersonian interest possessed most of the characteristics of the modern political party.

It was in the first decade of the new century, however, that a full-blown two-party electoral system developed on the state as well as the national level. Jefferson's triumph in 1800 stemmed from many things, but in some measure it was a feat of organization, of the Republican's willingness and ability to engage in systematic electoral politics. Federalist organization had lagged behind for several reasons.

Until 1800 Federalists were the government and did not feel as pressing a need to rally the people to their side. But, in addition, many Federalist leaders had a deep temperamental and ideological abhorrence of electoral politics. They possessed an elitist conception of office and a dread of democratic politics. Officeholders, they believed, were rulers, not servants of popular will; and office was the province of the elite, those who in the nature of things ought to rule because of their station and standing. They also believed that deference and "habits of subordination" rather than the solicitation of popular favor ought to govern the relationship between leaders and the people. Many of these old-school Federalists, in fact, simply refused to participate in the new political forms.[8] By the middle of the first decade of the new century, however, a new generation was taking control of Federalism. These young Federalists were as elitist in their attitudes and their policies as many of their elders. But they were also political realists, fully aware that if elite control and conservative ideals were to survive they would have to do so with the new political methods. As Fischer put it, many of them "despised the people but respected their power. . . . They accepted the idea of party and accommodated themselves to the fact that political power was the gift of the people."[9]

In the years following the Jeffersonian triumph, "these young politicians labored to create a disciplined, popularly oriented, but essentially elitistic political organization which might effectively challenge the power of the Jeffersonians."[10] In New England the young Federalists succeeded in constructing a well-structured, well-disciplined, and effective electoral party. By 1808 all the New England states had fully operating state organizations, complete with open caucus and convention, a state central committee, and county, town, and district committees, which selected candidates, raised funds, distributed party literature, and conducted election campaigns. The Federalists also appropriated Republican electioneering techniques. They organized barbecues and clambakes, maintained careful lists of eligible voters, and made sure that they were canvassed before elections by persons of standing in the community. They too used "runners" to get a printed copy of the Federalist slate in the hands of all voters by election day. (In Salem, Massachusetts, Fischer reports, in 1803 they had 120 runners, 30 for each district.)[11] Finally, they countered the Republican political clubs by setting up their own political front—the Washington Benevolent Society. By 1810, in fact, there were probably more than a hundred of these societies in New England.[12]

Although Federalist organization never succeeded nationally, it proved effective in the New England states, where Federalists remained a powerful and usually dominant political force almost until 1820. It was not, however, an easy or unchallenged success. As Noble Cunningham has written, "The national triumph of the Jeffersonians in 1800 stimulated such a rapid growth of Republican machinery in areas where Federalist resistance was most vigorous that New England, the stronghold of Federalism, soon became the region where Republican organizational efforts were most concentrated."[13] Thus, from about 1804, when both parties were fully organized, through to at least 1815, New England was the scene of intense party combat. Elections were close, participation extensive, and the combat fierce as the unrelenting and vituperative clash of party wracked New England from the top to the bottom of its social and political structure.[14]

The established New England clergy had an ambiguous relationship to the new politics. On the one hand, churchmen had a deep and unrelenting antipathy to the very idea of party and especially to the "vile practice of electioneering." They let few opportunities pass without condemning the new politics, and the election and fast sermons, the sermons occasioned first by Washington's retirement and then by his death, and funeral sermons for local leaders of these years invariably contained a ringing denunciation of the politics of party.[15] The clergy, reflecting the organic communalism of the New England town, possessed what can best be termed a service or civil rather than a political conception of public office. (In fact, the modern phrase, "political office" with its conjunction of political process and governmental position is anachronistic when applied to eighteenth-century New England.) To the clergy, order was the function of office. The public stability and harmony born of good rulers and deferential people was their highest political value. Ultimately, a politics of deference rested upon reputation and trust, upon the shared belief that a leader possessed the traits of character that would make him a good ruler. A leader had to possess wisdom and virtue, but most of all his character had to be grounded in principles that led him to conduct his office as a form of higher duty, a divine and public trust that he took on out of a "sense of duty, rather than a thirst for distinction."[16] The "good character" of a magistrate established the "sinews of public confidence" necessary to secure both the authority that magistrates needed to rule effectively and the deference essential for public harmony. Character and standing, as readily discerned qualities, vouchsafed by earlier service and personal and familial reputation, gave legitimacy to a magistrate's acts, for only a leader with the right character could be trusted to use his talent and power for the public good rather than for private gain or special interest.[17]

To the clergy, the politics of party and electioneering appeared to violate these axioms. Churchmen were deeply suspicious of most forms of concerted political behavior and perceived faction and party —in the eighteenth century the two terms were synonomous—as illegitimate institutions. By definition, they were partial and partisan, instruments of special interest and of personal ambition rather than of public service.[18] Officeholders and leaders who allied themselves with a faction or party could not be trusted to use their power of office impartially or for the public good. Indeed, the clergy's public sermons of these years increasingly stressed what they referred to as "independence" as perhaps the most important trait of good magisterial character. By independence they meant the inner strength to stand steadfast against both the pressures of party and the clamors of popular fashion and sentiment. In addition, they insisted in a rather new way upon the need for rulers to possess personal godliness: it was considered the essential ground not only of independence but of a proper conception of office as well. As one clergyman put it, only men who "connected the retributions of eternity with the use or abuse of a post of honor" could be trusted to possess and follow the traditional principles of public governance.[19]

The "vile practice of electioneering," according to these clergymen, not only kept the populace in a state of utter turbulence, but also inverted the hierarchical principle, ordained by God and nature, that underlay all forms of social organization. Giving political judgment and illegitimate power to the populace at large made as much sense from the traditional point of view as turning family government over to children. In addition, it undermined the deference that kept the lower orders in check. The constant flattery of the people, it was feared, gave them false notions of their capacity and authority and encouraged the inferior and untutored to think themselves the judge of those to whom they should defer.[20]

The politics of party thus seemed to undermine the essential, ordained character of public office itself by making the officeholder the servant of the people rather than a servant of God, chosen by the people to rule over them in accordance with what the office, in its nature as an office, dictated. In addition, it replaced the civil conception of office holding with a political conception that seemed to transform a public trust into an instrument of personal ambition and partisan purpose. Moreover, rather than the locus of order, harmony, and stability, the politics of party turned office into a counter in a continuing struggle for power. The clergy had characteristically condemned the presence of conflict in a community as a sign of deep public malaise, but the politics of party appeared to institutionalize conflict. This in turn snapped the sinews of confidence and trust that sustained an orderly, peaceable polity. Electoral combat subjected officeholders to constant attacks on their policies, their principles, and their character. Thus did it "poison the fountains of public life."[21] As men driven by partisanship and personal ambition set out to destroy the "good character" of those in office, the public tranquility associated with a politics of character and deference gave way to a politics of suspicion and conspiracy, a condition that eventually would lead to anarchy or tyranny.[22]

But in spite of its unrelenting condemnation of the new politics, the clergy found itself drawn more and more deeply into it. By 1800, the overwhelming majority of the established clergy, especially in Connecticut and Massachusetts, was a Federalist clergy.[23] Nor was this simply a matter of electoral affilation and ideological sympathy. By 1800, Federalist rhetoric and clerical public spokesmanship sounded many of the same themes: both condemned the French Revolution, lamented the breakdown of public discipline, warned against the dangers of democracy, and condemned the rise of party. And many churchmen immersed themselves deeply in the partisan warfare of the first decade of the new century. To a young Republican from the South who was attending Yale College, it appeared in 1803 that "the clergy so far from being the meek and lowly followers of Christ . . . are the most violent partisans, the most busy electioneers, the source of violent animosities and discussions and the very essence of political wrangling and disturbance! . . . They tell their charge that they must vote for such and such men to represent them, or their religion and their peace will be in danger."[24]

A number of things drew the established clergy into the Federalist orbit. There was considerable ideological affinity between the clergy and Federalist leaders, most of whom shared the clergy's deep antipathy to democratic and electoral politics. Federalists considered themselves "Friends of Order," and the clergy saw itself as the guardian of order. Moreover, they shared the same vision of order: both equated it with elite rule and a politics of deference, with a public discipline built upon habits of subordination, self-control, and religious nurture, and with strict enforcement of public morality.[25]

In addition, there was the fact that the Republicans were an opposition force appealing directly to the electorate against incumbent officeholders. Little in the clergy's ideology or experience permitted them to accept such attacks as legitimate public behavior. To them, rousing the public against rulers was legitimate only when officeholders had violated their office by using their authority to satisfy their own lust for power and thereby jeopardized the liberties of the people. Under such circumstances, it was the duty of patriots to rally the people against tyranny just as the clergy itself had helped mobilize the colonists against the tyranny of crown and parliament.[26] In this sense the only legitimate popular politics was what might be called an ultimate, or crisis, politics in which the stakes were tyranny and liberty. The corollary of this conception of legitimate patriotic opposition was the idea that any public attack on good and faithful rulers was wholly illegitimate, a demagogic attempt to exploit the people's jealousy of their liberties in order to grasp power for one's own nefarious ends. The fact that the clergy itself, by class and by office, was part of the overall governing establishment and the fact that to the clergy the leaders under attack were men of competence and character who had long served the public made it difficult indeed for the clergy to perceive Federalist officeholders as men bent on tyranny.

In addition to the fact of opposition, there was its style and form. To the Republicans it was not simply differences of opinion about banks, taxes, manufacturers, and foreign policy that separated them from the Federalist interest. They too perceived politics in ultimate terms and looked beneath the surface of behavior and rhetoric to the fundamental problem of power and liberty. To them, Hamilton and his lieutenants were bent upon a scheme to turn the new government into a monarchical or aristocratic power that would deprive the people of the liberties for which they had just fought. Accordingly, they went before the public as "friends of liberty" and couched their criticism in terms of the age-old struggle between liberty and tyranny, filling their letters and pamphlets with invective against the character and motives of their opponents.[27] Thus, by 1796, Republican agitation increasingly appeared to the clergy much as the Federalist politicians had been portraying it: as the work of demagogues and disorderers who were driven by ambition for fame and power. Moreover, the caucuses, political clubs, and open electioneering of the Republicans struck them as the unmistakable machinery of conspiracy rather than legitimate forms of political organization.

Somewhat paradoxically, the clergy's implication in the new politics also grew out of its traditional nonpolitical role as the keeper of the common public culture. It increasingly appeared to the clergy that order itself was at stake, that it was threatened in ways extending well beyond the matter of party and electioneering. With the outbreak of the French Revolution and Republican enthusiasm for it, even after it seemed to be heading into excess and anarchy, and with the emergence of organized, proselytizing Deism in apparent league with Republican power, the Republican party had taken on an altogether more ominous dimension.[28] In any event, by 1796 it appeared to many clergymen not only that Republicanism threatened to "level" society, but also that it represented a Deistical and libertine conspiracy against the fundamental base of the New England social order—its Christian belief and institutions. As the Reverend Isaac Lewis put it in a 1796 election sermon: "to maintain that godliness is of no importance in a civil point of view—that it is a matter of no consequence to the political happiness of a people what religious system, or whether any at all prevails among them—to support these and similar sentiments not only tends to encouragement of immorality, but to the propagation of political heresy."[29] A brief sentence from Azel Backus' 1798 election sermon, *Absolom's Conspiracy*, suggests the chain of association that linked freethinking to disorder and anarchy. "We find," he asserted, "all zealous disorganizers, somewhere on that climax of error that begins in what is called modern liberality in religious sentiment and ends in atheism."[30] To most clergymen, libertarian ideology, allied with Deism and armed with the machinery of party, added up to conspiracy and, ultimately, subversion. With this perception of the problem, the clergy could not and did not remain silent: their role as the guardians of order demanded that they cry out against the public danger.

By the late 1790s, then, clerical public discourse had become largely indistinguishable from Federalist partisan rhetoric, and the clergy found itself cast as Federalist ideologues. The adoption of this role, however, did not signal any deliberate departure from the clergy's traditional sense of public guardianship. In their own eyes, churchmen were neither guilty of partisanship nor did they violate conventional notions about the respective domains of civil and religious office when they attacked the new politics and warned of the political consequences of infidelity. As "watchmen on the walls of Zion," they were doing what they had always done: pointing out the dangers to order, decrying the apostacy from basic principles, and invoking the time-honored axioms about the nature of office and the role of revealed religion in securing order and liberty. In some ways, it was an accurate self-portrait. It was not so much the clergy or its public ideas, but the place of this ideology in public life, that had changed. The vocabulary that had once provided the common grammar of New England public life had become a partisan political code. Even the clergy's general condemnation of party no longer seemed very nonpartisan. Most churchmen would have agreed with Connecticut Federalist Jonathan Brace when in 1799 he said, "I do not think that those gentlemen who are in the habit of supporting all the measures of government ought to be denominated a *party*; those only who oppose such measures deserve that appellation."[31] Thus their denunciation of party and electioneering in general sounded much like a condemnation of Republican efforts in particular. In certain ways, moreover, elitist politics and the traditional social order were the issues separating Republicans and Federalists, and the clergy's defense of deference and their evocation of an organic, hierarchical society were thereby increasingly perceived as partisan acts.

After 1800 clerical implication in political warfare deepened. Jefferson's triumph and the Republican's intense organizational efforts in New England heightened the clergy's sense of the danger the "standing order" faced. Equally importantly, however, the clergy's public behavior and establishment itself became central issues around which much of the political warfare revolved.[32] It appeared to the Republicans that clerical influence played a crucial role in helping the Federalists maintain their political dominance. To them, the established clergy had become a "political priesthood" that used its privileged position and its steady access to the public to further partisan ends. Accordingly they denounced clerical interference in government as a violation of civil and religious liberty and made disestablishment and the end of Congregationalist privilege a central part of their electoral platform. This served to entangle sectarian and denominational controversy with political cleavages as the Republicans tried to rally dissenters like the Baptists and Methodists, as well as the Episcopalians, to their side.[33] Most significantly, however, it wedded self-interest to ideological affinity and forced the established clergy to depend upon Federalist political control for the preservation of its special status, a status that the clergy still associated with the preservation of a Christian Commonwealth.

The clerical alliance with Federalist power, however, proved an increasingly troubled one. With the development of a full-blown party structure, Federalism increasingly came under the control of "party-managers," men who had developed the taste and energy for political organization and manipulation and whose allegiance to the party and its success transcended their ties to tradition, custom, or ideology. Whether they actually held office or remained behind the scenes, these political brokers had adopted politics as their real vocation. As James Banner has written of them: "Except for the remunerative occupations needed to support their families, politics was their chief activity and interest. For the energetic young politicians, life was a ceaseless round of travels and meetings, planning and fund-raising, corresponding and speechmaking. Most young Federalists not only served in elective or appointive office at one time or another but concurrently managed parts of the party organization."[34]

Such men had developed attitudes toward government and politics that differed radically from the ideas about office holding that the clergy still embraced. This is not to say that the ideological discourse which had dominated Federalist rhetoric in the 1790s was absent from their politics. On the contrary, the young Federalists were sometimes even more virulent in attacking their opponents as demagogues lusting after power and threatening to plunge the republic into anarchy and irreligion. But for them this rhetoric no longer really bespoke an engrained outlook that controlled their perceptions and shaped their attitudes about political behavior and institutions. It had, in a way, become "mere" rhetoric. They invoked slogans about order, discipline, public virtue, and the dangers of democratic excess, less out of deep conviction than out of their desire to rouse an electorate. In any conflict between traditional precept or procedure and party necessity, they opted for party necessity. Though they could match the clergy in decrying the corruption of the community and vilifying Republicans as enemies of religion and morality, they were ever ready to sacrifice custom, candidate, or ideology if electoral success demanded it.[35]

As public office and its pursuit became more exclusively the province of these party managers, clergymen found themselves outsiders, more part of the Federalist constituency than members of a governing elite. In fact, many clergymen, like many of the older public servants and some of the old school Federalists, left over from the days before the politics of party, were never able to adjust to the new ways and simply withdrew from public activity. Even those individual clergymen who did try to participate in Federalist political councils found themselves increasingly at odds with the pragmatic party managers.[36] Churchmen continued to take the ideology of order with the utmost seriousness. For them the rhetoric of order, harmony, discipline, and fidelity was far more than a set of electoral slogans. These were the real issues, and far more than simple political power was at stake. Federalist politicians also wanted to preserve the standing order, but they increasingly associated it only with political power. But to the clergy the standing order was far more—it was the complicated fabric of custom, cultural tradition, institution, and social discipline that appeared to depend upon established religion.[37]

The Federalist managers increasingly found the clergy's ideological seriousness to be a political burden, and they began to treat the clergy simply as another bloc within the Federalist constituency, a kind of special interest whose claims had to be weighed against those of other interests and even sacrificed if the success of the Federalist party demanded it. Connecticut politics provides a good example of the situation the clergy increasingly faced throughout New England.

In the spring elections of 1811, Connecticut Federalists split over whether to support the acting governor, John Treadwell, for election to the governorship. The year before, some party managers had balked at the promotion of Treadwell to the governorship, even though it was customary for the lieutenant governor to succeed to the office and even though Treadwell had been lieutenant governor for eleven years. Consequently, in 1811 the Federalist managers nominated Roger Griswold, who defeated Treadwell with the aid of the Republicans. Treadwell's rigid adherence to religious principle and his unwavering defense of Congregational privilege had made him a political liability. As acting governor he had tried to enforce Sabbatarian legislation, and his bearing so resembled the Republican portrait of the Puritan bigot that the party managers feared he would lead the Federalists to political disaster. The son and grandson of governors and a Connecticut leader of long standing, Griswold was considered a much more popular candidate. He was not a formal professor of religion, and hence his backers thought he would be immune from the increasingly telling Republican charge that the established clergy controlled Connecticut politics. They hoped Griswold would regain the support of the Episcopalians, whose natural political home was Federalism but who were increasingly attracted to Republican disestablishmentarianism. To the clergy, of course, dumping Treadwell simply confirmed their worst fears about what the new politics was doing to public order.[38]

By the second decade of the new century, the established clergy found itself in a precarious position. It appeared to be almost entirely dependent upon Federalist political supremacy for the protection of its privileged position, but the public priorities of Federalist ministers and politicians were becoming increasingly incompatible. Though clergymen and party publicists still traded in the same ideological coin, they each attached very different value to it, for beneath the common rhetoric lay an irreparable gap between a new culture of politics that accepted the party system and a vision of public order in which electoral competition for public office was the antithesis of order. Furthermore, the deeper ideological affinities between Federalism and the clergy were dissolving as ministers and politicians came to perceive government and order in wholly different ways. By about

1810, what Fischer refers to as "the revolution of American Conservatism," brought about by the Federalist adoption of democratic electoral methods, was well underway. Although the young Federalists remained committed to elite rule, the instruments they had adopted for securing it had eroded much of the ideological and institutional substance that had originally informed New England conservatism.

The embracing of electoral politics by both parties had of course ended the politics of deference and fundamentally altered the relationship between the electorate and officeholders. Though the same kinds of people still gained office, they came into office, not out of respect for their standing and wisdom, but because the party had selected them as candidates and then mobilized its constituency behind them. Even more importantly from the clergy's point of view, the new politics eroded the very nature of magistracy. Churchmen still perceived civil office largely in terms of its function in preserving order. To them, the chief criterion in selecting magistrates remained whether they would enforce public discipline, not the "measures" they might advocate. In their view magistrates were "the fathers of the people, the guardians of their virtue as well as of their rights and privileges,"[39] and it remained an unassailable axiom to them that "a firm and faithful execution of law is necessary to preserve and promote good morals in a community."[40] By 1812, however, it appeared that magistracy in this sense had all but disappeared. Office had become an instrument for carrying out popular will as expressed in the electoral process and a counter in the ongoing struggle for political power. No longer magistracy, civil office had become thoroughly politicized. Moreover, as William Nelson has shown, by 1810 civil action against traditional breaches of moral conduct—against public profanity, fornication and adultery, and violation of the Sabbath—had all but disappeared in New England.[41] It was widely believed—as the Griswold affair demonstrated—that such enforcement was unpopular. Thus, neither the community at large, nor, certainly, the Republicans, nor even the Federalist political managers any longer believed that it was a function of civil office to enforce traditional public moral discipline. They had become, in the words of one churchman, "the dupes of the wild absurdity" which condemned "all compulsory measures to enforce self-discipline as an encroachment upon personal liberty."[42]

The clergy thus confronted both an immediate political crisis and what churchmen saw as the more far-reaching threat to the standing order. With establishment under systematic attack by the Republicans and with a powerful force within the Federalist Party willing to sacrifice public morality and even establishment itself to electoral success, the standing order faced the political battle for its life. The clergy, however, was not in a very strong political position. The structure they had turned to for protection was steadily abandoning the standing order. Even more seriously, however, the clergy's active involvement in the new politics was itself a source of the broader public crisis, because it had compromised both the clergy's public role and its message. Blending clerical and Federalist rhetoric had contaminated the fundamental principles of order with partisanship, and the clerical alliance with Federalist power had eroded the clergy's legitimacy as spokesmen for the common public culture. The clergy's response to this conundrum was ambiguous and at times perhaps even contradictory. On the one hand, churchmen kept up a rear-guard battle against disestablishment and continued to bring pressure to bear on the conduct of public office and the character of the men selected for it.[43] But at the same time, they deliberately set about to try to disengage clerical public guardianship from the processes of politics. This rather complex process of extricating the religious foundations of public order from the new politics can be seen best in the clergy's turn to a new agency—the moral society—as an essential instrument for the preservation of public order.

Moral societies first emerged in the early 1790s (the first one appears to have been the society that the Reverend Nathaniel Emmons set up in Franklin, Massachusetts, in 1790) in response to what churchmen feared was a wholesale breakdown of morality and public virtue.[44] The societies were local institutions designed to stem moral declension—an attempt, as it were, to give the jeremiad some teeth and bring about a "reformation of morals" by resuscitating "the wise and the good" and reviving its sense of public watchfulness and restoring its moral hegemony. These societies spread rapidly throughout New England, and by the end of the first decade of the new century they were a familiar feature on the New England social landscape. They exerted their influence in several ways. First, they gathered what they referred to as the "better part of the community" into "a special" and "extra-ordinary" institution beyond the churches, social class, and familiar institutions through which it had customarily exerted its moral influence. Second, they served as agencies for the personal reformation of those whose position and reputation were thought to give them influence over the manners and morals of the community. They encouraged their members to set rigorous examples of good behavior by binding them in formal, public pledges of personal reformation. Finally, moral societies provided "an auxiliary band to strengthen the hand of the magistrate." They operated as "a disciplined moral militia"[45] which uncovered and reported vice. They ordinarily had a standing committee to report at each monthly meeting on all "evils of a moral nature" that they could find, pinpointing the causes and suggesting specific measures that the society should take against the evils. Remedies ranged from resolutions by the members themselves to desist from hard liquor on all occasions to the dissemination of moral tracts and pressure on the town watch and informing officers to report vice to the authorities.[46]

These societies had emerged in response to the general erosion of public discipline. They had grown up outside the new political culture and indeed were built around the traditional antipolitical conception of public order and office. During the early 1810s, however, churchmen and lay traditionalists began to look to the moral societies as a remedy for the overall public crisis. They set up new societies and organized some county societies, and in 1812 Connecticut churchmen launched a state-wide moral society, The Connecticut Society for the Reformation of Morals and the Suppression of Vice. These societies of the 1810s reflected the ambiguities of the clergy's public position. On one level they represented a direct response to the fear that Federalist politics would sacrifice principle for power. In Connecticut, for example, the sense of an immediate political threat partly accounts for the timing of the founding of the Connecticut Moral Society. When Governor Griswold died in office, John Cotton Smith, whom the pragmatic party managers had accepted as lieutenant governor to placate the traditionalists, moved into the governorship. Churchmen and lay traditionalists like Tapping Reeve and John Treadwell were convinced that an effort was afoot to dump Smith in the spring elections of 1813. If this "coalition with democracy" succeeded, they feared, Connecticut would lose its "habits and institutions piecemeal, as fast as democracy and innovation and ambition shall dare to urge on that work."[47] Many of the founders of the society hoped to forestall this process. Lyman Beecher, perhaps the chief architect of the society, wrote to the Reverend Asahel Hooker that Smith was sure to go unless "at an early date the noise of a rising opposition shall be so great as to deter them." The moral society, he went on, would serve to so "unite the friends of good morals and good government" as to "create a public opinion which nothing can resist."[48]

Some historians (as well as many contemporaries), looking at the partisan identities of most of the founders of the societies, the immediate political circumstances, and Beecher's letters, have interpreted the moral societies of these years in wholly political terms, as either Federalist fronts or as instruments of political priestcraft.[49] To dismiss the moral societies as simply, or even chiefly, political institutions, however, is a mistake. It overlooks the broader dimensions of the clergy's problem and the character and behavior of the societies. Most of all, however, it disregards the fundamentally antipolitical nature of the clergy's conception of public order and office. The founders spoke openly of the need to mobilize public opinion and to protect the standing order from "innovation and democracy." Some founders certainly hoped that the societies would have some impact on the character of people brought into office. But what is important is how this public influence operated. Essentially, the moral society was an attempt to go over the head of the politicians to the community, because even Federalist officeholders could not be relied upon to behave as magistrates ought to behave. In this sense, the moral society was intended to counter "innovation and democracy," not by jumping into the fray with a political counterforce, but by stepping outside and above it.

The moral societies of the 1810s rested upon a crucial distinction between *public* opinion, on the one hand, and political or partisan opinion on the other. The societies addressed the community, moreover, not as an electoral public but as a moral constituency, for the public opinion they promulgated was not political opinion in any direct electoral sense. Indeed, the societies, including the Connecticut Moral Society, did not engage in electioneering, but continued to operate as the local moral societies had, addressing themselves to breaches of public decorum, to the execution of moral legislation, and to self-reformation. The opinion they sought to resuscitate as a force in public life was moral opinion; the body of beliefs which in the proper order the societies were meant to restore existed antecedent to and independent of electoral opinion and practice. In fact, the effectiveness and appeal of the moral society as a public agency were thought to lie precisely in its independence and nonpartisanship. As Lyman Beecher put it in his address inaugurating the Connecticut Moral Society, the society would "provide an influence distinct from that of government, superior in potency to individual efforts, and competent to enlist and preserve public opinion on the side of law and order."[50]

As an agency of collective public action, the moral society's effectiveness was thought to be dependent upon its independence from government. The new politics had eroded the traditional moral elite whose public leadership was considered essential to social order. First, it had forced good men out of public life as the caluminous personal attacks drove men of standing and virtue into private life. In addition, "the wise and the good" itself was losing both its character as a self-conscious public elite and its moral hegemony over the community. The politics of party, it appeared, had introduced systematic division and bitter conflict into its midst, dividing "the better part of the community" into parties and sects and hence destroying its traditional, unified force. The great evil of the age, as one moral society sermon put it, was that "individuals, be their motives never so pure and their weight of character never so great" were "isolated," with no sense of moral solidarity with other such individuals and with no common mechanism for injecting their moral leaven into society.[51] The moral society was expressly designed to provide a mechanism to restore the moral force of good men without implicating them in politics. As the *Columbia Magazine* wrote extolling the "formation and constitution of the Columbia Moral Society": "It was gratifying beyond expression to behold men of various religious and political feelings and sentiments unite cordially for the suppression of vice and the laying aside of every feeling but the benevolent desire to promote the happiness of the community."[52] The moral society, then, was a new kind of public agency, outside politics and, in a sense, beyond government. In some ways it tacitly accepted the new politics and represented the clergy's recognition of its powerlessness over it. Its fundamental purpose was to immunize the foundations of public order from the effects of politics rather than to change or control the new politics. Essentially, the moral society of the 1810s defined and institutionalized new boundaries between the principles of moral order and the processes of politics. It isolated moral opinion and deployed it in an agency of public pressure which gained its force from its pressure tactics, its reformation of its own members, its moral propaganda, and from the collective moral influence it gathered and unified. By 1815, moreover, the moral societies had dropped their initial attempts to pressure magistrates into enforcing the laws against breaches of self-government and turned more exclusively to attempts to directly reform the Christian community.[53] This reflected the clergy's growing sense of fissure between sacred office and civil office and embodied the conviction that the two were no longer the twin pillars of public order. Essentially, the clergy had abandoned public office to the electoral culture in what amounted to an admission that magistracy, in the traditional sense, had itself disappeared.

Thus was the moral society a new kind of institution, a transitional one whose very emergence signaled the erosion of the traditional social order and the development of a different public order, in which the political culture and the moral culture and their respective agencies and activities were kept separate. Public office now belonged wholly to the domain of power and conflict, while the promotion of moral order and social discipline resided in a special fabric of voluntaristic institutions.[54]

This does not mean that the clergy had relinquished its sense of public guardianship—far from it. Instead, with the moral society—the first of many such institutions—the clergy had begun to organize a domain of what can be termed moral citizenship, a domain beyond government, protected and isolated from electoral politics, and under the clear dominion of men of religion. In some ways, the clergy's strategic retreat into this domain was a forced one. But the clergy did not wholly despair, for it too had evolved new views—a conception of public order as far removed from eighteenth-century communalism as the political party was distant from the politics of deference.

3

The Rise of an Evangelical
Conception of Social Order

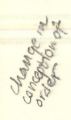

Eighteenth-century clergymen had worked to embed their parishioners firmly in the institutional and social fabric of their communities, considering anyone outside the community a threat to order. They labored to endow communicants with "the habits of deference and subordination" that would lead them to accept their place in family and community, and they tried to instill in those in positions of authority the responsibility to ferret out anything that weakened external discipline or inner submissiveness. During the first two decades of the nineteenth century, this conception of social order all but disappeared. By 1820, the New England clergy associated order more with self-control than with the exertion and acceptance of institutional authority. They no longer looked to an organic, hierarchical community as either an agency or a locus of social order. Instead, the vast majority of New England clergymen considered the revival to be the essential instrument of social order and associated it, not with a well-ordered town, but with the creation of a pious national community gathered into a vast network of new institutions attached to the individual churches.

This shift was partly a consequence of the clergy's growing immersion in the burst of revivalism (usually referred to as the Second Great Awakening) which from the mid-1790s on quickened the New England churches with ever intensifying waves of spiritual awakening. By about 1815, most established clergymen outside the liberal enclaves of Boston and Salem were staunch "revival men" who measured a preacher's fidelity to his call to the ministry by his com-

mitment to revivals.[1] Indeed the churchmen just coming into leadership of the clergy had spent their careers in revivals. Many had
undergone fairly dramatic conversion experiences, and many had
themselves been spiritually quickened in revivals. They had conducted revivals in their own churches, sometimes as frequently as
every half-dozen years, and had assisted colleagues with their revivals. Conversions and revivals became the center of their ministry,
the object to which even their day-to-day ministering was directed,
and they did whatever they could to push their communicants to
recognize their need to repent and seek salvation. They devised new
institutions and used older ones, such as home visits and ministerial
associations, to promote revivals. They instituted new Friday and
Monday services and set up various study and inquiry societies to
help them work their congregations into the state of readiness that
might lead God to bless them with the special dispensation of grace
that marked a revival. They used home visits to assess the precise
state of their communicants and find the spark of anxiety that could
be fanned into a concern for salvation. They transformed ministerial
associations and ecclesiastical meetings from reunions of friends and
colleagues into revival workshops where they could compare notes,
share techniques and particularly effective sermons, and map out joint
campaigns.[2]

This immersion in an ever expanding, ever more carefully organized and comprehensive revivalism fostered a self consciously instru-
mental conception of revivals. The early nineteenth-century evangelicals did not abandon the axiom that revivals were divine events,
brought about by a special or extraordinary dispensation of saving
grace rather than by direct human agency. Nonetheless, in the day-to-
day conduct of their pastorates they increasingly approached revivals
more as something for preachers and churches to do than as a special
gift that God might bestow in his good time. Evangelicals had developed a morphology of conversion that separated it into a sequence
of distinct stages: inquiry, awakening, special seriousness, anxiety,
conviction, regeneration, and sanctification. Moreover, they had
worked out what might be termed an applied science of revivalism.
Armed with their morphology of conversion, the revival men of the
early nineteenth century had become adept at diagnosing a communicant's particular spiritual state and applying the doctrinal dosages
needed to enable one to "come out a Christian." They also had a
pretty clear sense of what they referred to as the spiritual "economy"
of revivals, of how often and under what conditions they might be
expected, how long they ordinarily lasted, and what kinds of things

were "hindrances" to them. Thus, though churchmen could not provoke a revival at will—a few years usually had to pass before another full-blown revival could be expected—they were pretty adept at making sure that most of their communicants were eventually converted members of the church.[3]

This instrumentalism had a social dimension that differed from that of the First Great Awakening. Eighteenth-century evangelicals had certainly been aware of the social significance of revivals. In his narrative of the first Northampton revival in 1734, Jonathan Edwards had made much of how the revival had restored both harmony and moral discipline to the community.[4] (By 1745, of course, this sense of the social consequences of revivals had been replaced by the bitter controversy and disorders that had accompanied the Awakening.) Communicants, moreover, had experienced a sense of importance, participation, and communion, which led some evangelicals to see in the Awakening the shadow of the new order Christ would establish with his second coming.[5] Most established eighteenth-century evangelicals, however, viewed revivals essentially as extraordinary spiritual outpourings whose central meaning lay in the heavenly kingdom. The revival men of the early nineteenth century obviously did not relinquish the salvational emphasis—the escape from damnation and the quest for salvation, after all, fuel all evangelical revivals. After a decade or so of highly peaceable revivals, they no longer looked upon the social dimensions of revivals simply as desirable side effects, but had come to envision the revival as a deliberately deployed instrument of social order.[6] To be sure, when eighteenth-century church men had addressed social disorder in their jeremiads they had spoken of the need for renewed piety and fidelity. But they had stressed such external remedies as the restoration of family government and the exertion of church and civil discipline most heavily. By the second decade of the new century, however, churchmen increasingly argued that the revival itself provided the only reliably effective remedy for disorder. To this generation of clergymen, in other words, revivals became not only their major pastoral tool, but an essential instrument of public guardianship as well.

The deliberate application of the revival to the problems of order was not solely a function of evangelical momentum. It also reflected an altered sense of the nature and power of the forces of disorder. As churchmen surveyed the behavior of their people, they detected not only an alarming moral declension but what appeared to them to amount to a fundamental transformation of manners and morals. As Barbara Soloman has suggested, New Englanders, pointing to their

social arrangements and their Puritan heritage, had long been conscious of themselves as "a distinct, recognizable people, sharing the
identity of an ethnic group."[7] By the early years of the century, however, clergymen as well as other spokesmen began to argue that New
Englanders had become "a new people" imbued with a character and
genius that was very different from the habits of deference and subordination that had long distinguished them. In the language of Timothy Dwight's *Travels in New England* (which was echoed in the
sermons and writings of innumerable other clergymen), their "peculiar genius, situation, and climate" had created an "extra-ordinary
people," distinguished by enormous "energy," "activity of mind,"
and "ingenuity." Increasingly discernible as the Yankee, this New
Englander was driven by a "spirit of enterprise" and possessed an
unquenchable "spirit of independence and self-importance."[8]

Most importantly, however, the new New England character posed
difficult problems of social control. Enterprise and energy, self-importance, independence, and ingenuity, one clergyman insisted, were
certainly "desirable when duly regulated, but dreadful when perverted."[9] In fact, the images that play across clerical social rhetoric
in these years suggest something of the clergy's sense of the potential
for social disorder that the new character contained. They warned of
"lusts" for wealth and drink and of "thirsts" and "cravings" for
fame and power; and as they groped for language to capture the force
of such drives, they frequently adopted metaphors of torrents, storms,
and volcanoes, whose waves of "malignant energy" they pictured as
shattering barricades, snapping ligaments, and rupturing bonds. One
clergyman spoke of the "desperate daring of unrestrained sin" as he
warned that if New England should "break the bands of Christ and
cast his cords from us and begin the work of self-destruction, it will
be urged on with a malignant enterprise which has no parallel in
the annals of time."[10]

But it was not simply the force that a perverted spirit of enterprise
and independence could muster that was the problem. The very language used to talk of the new character reflects the emergence of
new and disturbing social values and patterns of behavior. In fact, the
society of the early decades of the nineteenth century was rapidly
becoming a different society. As Gordon Wood has put it, "by 1820,
Americans had moved into another century, not only in time but in
thought, in the way they perceived themselves and the world. They
had experienced a social and cultural transformation as great as any
in American history."[11] Enterprise, self-importance, and a spirit of
independence were part of this new society. At once descriptive and

normative, the terms both portrayed and legitimized behavior and attitudes very different from the values and disciplines churchmen had associated with order.

It was as if some time during the first decade or so of the century, the cultural spring of colonial New England had snapped and the combined and continuing force of geographic dispersion, defiance of parental authority and social custom, and the improvisation of new procedures and institutions had finally overwhelmed the traditional configuration of organic and hierarchical social precepts. In kind, though not in scope, the behavior which this vocabulary meant to describe was not new: almost from the beginning, New England had strained to contain such pressures. In some ways, in fact, the expansion during the last half of the eighteenth century of the concept of liberty to include the power of individual talent, effort, and character to find its just place in society represented a cultural accommodation to these pressures and the social changes impelling them. Nonetheless, at least until near the end of the century, even though New England society had remained fluid enough to permit some mobility, it had not been so entirely given over to relocation and social striving as to level all distinctions and erode all sense of place and rootedness. Thus it had remained an axiom of the culture that a discernible and enduring social order existed and set the boundaries for individual initiative and enterprise. Legitimate prosperity and social elevation did not violate this order; people might rise or fall in rank, but rank itself remained, and people might do many things to sustain or improve their individual lot, but they still had obligations toward the community as a whole.[12]

The vocabulary of self-importance, independence, and enterprise, however, embodied values and attitudes that were incompatible with this social vision and the disciplines that had sustained it. In fact, many older clergymen, men who had entered the clergy in the 1760s and 1770s, simply condemned the new spirit out of hand, seeing in it and the behavior it seemed to inspire nothing more than the all-too-familiar defiance of authority. To them, enterprise, independence, and self-importance were simply the unruly opposites of modesty, subordination, humility, and the adherence to custom.[13] The terms, however, echoed a very different social sensibility, one in which the sense of society as a discernible order that existed antecedent to the individual had all but evaporated. These values reflected lives that were in fact increasingly free of traditional restraints. Containing little room for the proscriptive authority of fixed institutions and customs, they suggest a sense of life in which the individual rather than family, custom, or a fixed social order was the essential arbiter of his life.

This new social character, then, possessing a sense of self at odds with traditional social decorum, posed a serious problem of social order. In some ways, the local moral societies around the turn of the century had been an initial response to behavior and attitudes that seemed increasingly impervious to the traditional restraints. Among other things, the societies had been set up to supply auxiliary coercive force by grafting new techniques of organization and propaganda onto traditional agencies of social control. By the second decade of the century, however, churchmen had come to believe that external constraints could not really control the forces arrayed against them and began to center their attention more upon internal restraints. Clergymen, of course, had always considered order a function both of internalized habits and external controls. They now believed, however, that social order depended far more upon the capacity of individuals in society to control themselves than upon their willingness to submit to the various authorities above them. And it was to conversions above all else and to revivals as the essential instrument for securing them that they now looked to provide these controls.[14]

revival as control

The complete process of conversion in early nineteenth-century New England ordinarily took place over a period of time ranging from several months to two or three years. It usually occurred when an individual was between fifteen and thirty years of age. A carefully modulated, though frequently intense process, it took place within the context of thorough doctrinal preparation which centered on three basic ideas: the sovereignty of God, the depravity of man, and the atonement of Christ. God, the moral governor of the universe, demanded obedience to his will and law, but fallen mankind, driven by self-love and animal lusts, was wholly defiant and needed Christ's intercession to gain God's mercy and eternal salvation. Salvation was thus doubly a gift of God: it came through Christ's taking on mankind's sin as his own and suffering in its stead the punishment it deserved; but it came also as a free gift of grace, which a person did not deserve and could not earn. Conversion itself was a distinct experience in the communicant's life. It involved a new comprehension and love of God, and it took the form of an explicit and deeply emotional act of submission to God, an utter "surrender of the will," to be disposed of as God wished.[15]

The process began when a person was "awakened" to the fact that he or she was indeed a sinner who deserved God's wrath, and moved through deep "anxiety" about the eternal fate of one's soul to "conviction," the dread sense that one had in fact been tried and found guilty of sin and condemned to eternal perdition. It was at this point that conversion—the saving change—occurred, if by God's grace it was going to happen at all. The convicted sinner, realizing his utter helplessness, threw himself entirely on God's mercy and, with an infusion of divine grace, entered into a totally new and deeply felt comprehension (the "saving knowledge") and acceptance of Christ's atonement and the nature and glory of God's sovereignty over the universe. As this understanding deepened, the convert entered into a wholly different state of being—a "regenerate" state—one in which the "disposition of the heart and will" was grounded, not in defiance, but in acceptance of His sovereignty, and in the desire to do His will and obey His moral law. Conversion thus united devotion and duty as the sanction behind Christian morality. Sinner and saved alike were obligated to obey God. But the regenerate Christians' continuing sense of reconciliation and spiritual peace—the inner assurance that they had in fact been saved—depended in considerable measure upon a continuing sense that they were actively meeting this commitment to God's will.[16]

The turn to conversionism and revivals to some extent represented the clergy's attempt to preserve the tradition of religious social hegemony by adjusting to the new conditions, much as the Federalist leaders had tried to maintain elite rule by accommodating to the demands of democratic politics.[17] But just as the Federalist adoption of the machinery of party had dissolved much of the substance of the conservatism they had set out to preserve, so too the new evangelicalism transformed much of the character of religion as the leaven of social order. The discipline to which churchmen increasingly tied social order was no longer construed in terms of authority and social subordination. In the eighteenth century, the submission and obedience that characterized the relationship between God and man had provided not only the source but also the "type," the ultimate model, of all the basic social disciplines. Increasingly, however, churchmen used the term to refer almost exclusively to the individual's personal relationship to God rather than to one's position and obligations in society. The surrender of the will to God was the ground, not of disciplines which were themselves forms of subordination, but of the inner controls needed to restrain the new, more autonomous character of the New England people. In this sense, evangelicals had evolved a sense of social discipline centered far more upon self-repression than upon internalized habits of deference to authorities.[18]

Their reliance upon self-control does not mean that churchmen sub-

[margin note: changes in clerical conceptions of control?]

scribed to what has sometimes been referred to as an anti-institutional conception of social order.[19] Conversion also brought the communicant into a more binding and continuous relationship with the church as an institution. During these years the evangelical churches had begun to play a greater organizational role in their communicants' lives. There was a remarkable proliferation in the number and kind of devotional meetings and services. In addition to the Sabbath services and the traditional Thursday lecture, most churches added at least one other general service, and during periods of awakening services were held almost daily. Special weekly prayer meetings, organized by sex and age, and inquiry and bible study societies were also set up. Moreover, most communicants belonged to one or more of the many voluntary associations—charitable, education, moral reform, or mutual improvement societies—which were being attached to the local communion. Indeed, churchmen in these years were almost frenetic in their institution building as they worked to encase the Christian community in a dense fabric of groups, societies, and associations that would extend institutional coverage to every age and kind of person. Richard D. Brown's recent study suggests something of the dimensions of this binge of institution building. For Massachusetts during the forty years from 1770 to 1810, Brown uncovered fewer than 40 such societies, but for the next twenty years, from 1810 to 1830, he detected more than 350 such societies in that state alone.[20]

This institutional fabric was very different in character from the organic, hierarchical community of the eighteenth century. For the most part, the new organizations did not operate in authoritarian modes: they were not overtly coercive, nor did they induct their members into relationships of authority and deference. They were strictly voluntary associations. Many were composed of people of the same age and sex, and they all bound their members together by common purpose, sentiment, or belief. Insofar as they can be said to have provided a means of social control, they worked less as direct agencies of discipline than as awareness or mutual-support societies in which members helped each other develop and maintain their own capacities for self-control. Members would gather periodically for various devotional and educational exercises intended to heighten their consciousness of doctrine or of a particular need or problem. The temperance, moral, and young people's mutual improvement societies, moreover, bound their members in open pledges of self-reformation, mutual assistance, and public evangelical activism.

In addition, these organizations were designed to draw people into a network of "friends" and institutions which would lead them—if

[margin note: conversion brings Xn into church—more order]

they were unconverted—to personal reformation and conversion. In the eighteenth century, the local community itself had operated as a superintending agency, but by the early decades of the nineteenth century, most of the older forms of communal watchfulness had broken down. Civil institutions no longer concerned themselves with merely "private" morality, and a common church no longer encompassed the community. Most importantly, perhaps, increasingly large numbers of people were on the move away from home and ancestral communities to places where their ties were fragile at best and where they could easily remain outside the formal and informal surveillance by which the eighteenth-century community had monitored the behavior of its inhabitants. Revealingly, churchmen (as well as other anxious elders) used the term "lost" to describe those who had slipped outside the new evangelical institutions. The innumerable moral tableaux in newspapers, tracts and sermons, and advice manuals abound with people of every social type—young and old, men and women, rich and poor —who quite literally sink from sight. Invariably of moral upbringing and Christian nurture, and apparently possessing steady habits, they nonetheless become victims of depravity. Through their own human weaknesses and the influence of "unwholesome entertainments," taverns, and "evil companions," they become "submerged" in vice and "engulphed" by iniquity. Just before they die, dissipated, diseased, and distraught, they are found just long enough to stand as a warning to all who venture forth without the shield of evangelical piety.[21]

The new evangical organizations were designed to foil the treacheries of the world. They withdrew the seeker and the believer from dangerous secular attachments and secured them against the contaminations of the world. New Englanders, of course, had always possessed an acute sense of the fundamental opposition between the sacred and the profane and had viewed life as a continuing struggle against the temptations of the world. The new evangelicalism of early nineteenth-century New England, however, embodied a subtly different sense of the world as temptation and of religious devotion and institutions as the antidote. Nineteenth-century evangelicals perceived the opposition in almost physical terms, as one between two separate and hostile domains. For colonial churchmen, this distinction would have been somewhat anachronistic. In their social vision, the sacred and the profane were entwined in all things: a godly community was one in which all activities and institutions were organized according to divine ordinance. In theory, at least, no institution was purely secular: all social forms were ordained by God, and most had religious and moral dimensions. The individual household was formally integrated into the church, and a properly ordered family was expected to provide regular religious nurture and devotion. Although the civil polity was separate from the church, the duties of rulers and ruled derived from divine writ, and civil authority had punished the behavior which religion condemned as hostile to order. Even economic activity was thought to be circumscribed by religious sanctions. Although work was the means for worldly sustenance and personal prosperity, the notion of calling subordinated the pursuit of gain to a broader sense of divine and communal obligation.[22] The nineteenth-century evangelicals, however, considered the whole fabric of life outside the specific institutions surrounding the church, not simply the temptations the world contained, to be entirely hostile to the sacred. To them, moreover, the conquest of worldliness consisted, not in organizing the world along godly lines, but in providing the individual with a set of inner and institutional barriers against it.[23]

The fabric of evangelical institutions, associations, and commitments with which churchmen surrounded their communicants thus provided a kind of quarantine against the outer world. In fact, evangelicals invariably talked of these institutions in terms of the "safety" they provided. They brought people together for "wholesome" recreation, provided the "safe" fellowship of the mutual improvement society rather than that of the tavern, and furnished people with godly companions. Indeed, it was a central axiom of the burgeoning literature of advice to young men that the only safety for young men setting out on their life course was to "attach" themselves to an "ecclesiastical society" as soon as they came into a town. The institutions they would find there amounted to a set of buoys to keep people morally afloat amid the currents of life and provided a kind of spiritual prophylaxis to keep them from contamination whenever they did penetrate the world outside evangelical precincts.

In addition to providing a different kind of social discipline, the new evangelicalism also altered both the relationships among communicants and the way the church stationed them in the society at large. The local church had increasingly become a community of sentiment and love in which secular distinctions between the members were of little importance. To some extent, of course, the eighteenth-century church had operated as a devotional community, but in its arrangements it had reflected and, indeed, reinforced the social order of the community. The church, for the most part, had encompassed the social community, and its officers, like those of the town itself, had been men of standing in the community. (Frequently the same people who served as selectmen or militia leaders served as deacons and elders in the church.) In the seventeenth century and well into the eighteenth, men and women had been kept separate, the deaconate had been stationed at the front of the church, and youth and servants had sat at the rear. When family groupings and pews become more common in the eighteenth century, they had been allocated according to social status, and special benches for the poor of the parish were placed at the rear of the church.[24] By the nineteenth century, this correspondence between church and the social order had weakened in a number of ways. First, the church no longer encompassed the social community. Churches, even more than before, had become purely voluntary associations, joined and attended only by those who chose to participate. In addition, communities had a number of different churches: most had more than one Congregational Church as well as churches of other denominations, particularly Baptist and Methodist. Moreover, rather than contain members from across the social spectrum, the particular churches tended to be socially homogeneous.[25] In the larger towns, the original, or "first," church might retain many of the more prominent people, but as additional churches were set up, they drew their members from younger families, newcomers to the town, and new converts, all of whom probably had a weaker consciousness of the social distinctions in the town as a whole. Second, although some of the older forms of pew allotment persisted into the nineteenth century, the designations probably began to reflect duration of church membership more than they did explicit recognition of social standing. And many of the dozens of new churches set up in these years discarded the older forms of pew allotment. Thus, by the 1820s, with the possible exception of the oldest first churches, most New England churches had at best an oblique relationship to the social distinctions of the towns in which they were situated. They had become relatively homogeneous and essentially self-contained associations of those who wanted to congregate together for religious nurture and devotion.[26]

The nature of the relationship that evangelicals forged among communicants was even more important than these external changes in altering the social character of the churches. Evangelicalism centered in a kind of spiritual and essentially egalitarian communion that largely transcended formal and secular distinctions. Evangelical and revival preaching was explicitly designed, not only to explicate doctrine, but also to *move* the congregation to heightened personal piety and greater collective emotion. The less formal sessions—the inquiry meetings, prayer meetings, and special lectures—were more communally expressive than the traditional sermon and involved communicants in a direct sense of active and common participation in a devotional community. But the character of evangelical piety was as important in its communitarian and leveling effects as either the frequency or style of devotion itself. Evangelicalism essentially established a community of love. Much of its devotional activity—for example, prayer meetings and hymn singing—involved joyous expressions of love to God and Christ. In addition, evangelicalism fostered "disinterested benevolence," the deeply and openly expressed feelings of concern for the sin and salvation of those one cared about the most, feelings born of one's understanding of the meaning of Christ's atonement for one's own life. Indeed, this concern was the explicit focus of many of the new services and devotional exercises. Prayer meetings, for example, revolved around explicit prayers for the souls of those within families and the congregation who were not yet saved. Thus communicants increasingly related to each other less in terms of their positions in the secular community than as fellow evangelicals who had the equal spiritual standing born of their common experience of conversion and who were bound together by new and expressive forms of communion and fellowship.[27]

Although the communalism of this evangelicalism was neither so total nor so intense nor so radically democratic as the Methodist communion with its "love feasts," it was nonetheless the same kind of social experience. It not only established bonds of mutuality and feeling which differed in kind from the relationships of secular life, but it also provided communicants with a sense of belonging and fostered and then institutionalized a firm sense of personal and group identity. With conversion, the penitent gained a new sense of selfhood as a Christian, as one who was no longer enslaved to the depravity of human nature, no longer bound by the anxieties of the secular order, no longer in defiant rebellion against God. Instead, communicants developed a sense of Christian identity, grounded in their reconciliation with God and his sovereignty, and built from the feeling that they had entered into a new and better, more secure and enduring order of being. In addition, evangelicalism provided communicants with separate and continuing fellowship with those who were either seeking or already enjoyed the comforts of grace. And it brought them into a structure in which the boundaries between the church and the world and between the communicant and the infidel or unregenerate were kept clear and distinct, a network of institutions and acquaintances which reinforced the communicants' sense that they were different from and better off than those outside evangelical precincts. This is not to say that the older social distinctions had entirely disappeared, but that with the erosion of the social order of the eighteenth-century

New England town, the church had become an essential institution for ordering communicants' lives. Not only did evangelicalism provide forms of self-discipline and a sense of belonging and self-esteem, but it also hedged the anarchy and anonymity of a life of geographical mobility. When communicants moved to a new town, they found in the evangelical church a ready-made community in which they were quickly accepted as genuine Christians and quickly forged trustworthy acquaintances. There is evidence, moreover, that nineteenth-century evangelicals, just like seventeenth-century Puritans and eighteenth-century Quakers, sought business partners and associates, apprentices, and marriage mates from among the ranks of fellow evangelicals.[28]

The emergence of evangelicalism as a culturally and organizationally distinct sphere is reflected most clearly perhaps in the public rhetoric of churchmen. In the eighteenth century, whatever the particular concern or occasion of a fast, thanksgiving, election, funeral, or execution sermon, the frame of reference had been the communal order as a whole. Whether Sabbath breaking, unruly children, social conflict, or even murder, the particular evil was invariably portrayed as a violation of one or more of the relationships of authority and subordination that kept the overall structure of order intact. By 1820 this kind of social sensibility—the sense of a community as a discernible order in which each person was bound in a series of relations of authority and obedience—was all but absent from evangelical public rhetoric.[29] To be sure, churchmen retained a clear sense of the secular world and of their communicants' immersion in it. But the sense of the secular world as an order had largely evaporated; they saw all situations and structures—social class, the condition of youth, the world of economic activity—as dangers, snares to trap the unwary and lead them to sin and eternal damnation. Moreover, their public address—their moral tracts, didactic biographies, and advice literature—was designed not to reinforce the disciplines of a social order, but to induct their audiences into religious commitments and institutional attachments that would break the power of secular attachments to trap them in temptation and sin. For example, the Reverend Joel Hawes's 1827 *Lectures Addressed to the Young Men of New Haven and Hartford* was designed as a species of evangelical success literature, telling young men the "safe" way to get ahead in the world. Hawes accepted —at least rhetorically—the social ambitions of his audience and then deliberately and artfully tried to lead them out of their exclusively personal and worldly concerns and into an active thirst for salvation. After picturing the secular world that they faced as a confusing,

community sense is lost

anxiety-ridden, and morally treacherous labyrinth, he held out evangelicalism to them as a kind of counter-world, a sphere of refuge, security, and wholesome recreation and warm communion and fellowship.[30] Lyman Beecher's 1825 *Six Sermons on the Nature, Evils, and Remedy of Intemperance* approached those a little older, those already burdened with the cares of family and the anxieties of commerce and business, in a similar fashion. Like Hawes he evinced deep sympathy for their situation in life. In fact, he traced the origins of intemperance to the need for recreation, refuge, and relaxation to counter the hard work and anxieties of adulthood: it began with a seemingly innocent drink and then became a raging "thirst" that inevitably led to utter physical, economic, and moral "ruin." Beecher used intemperance to construct a vivid and terrifying portrait of the perils economic life posed for the soul, a portrait explicitly designed to lead his audience to seek refuge, security, and relief from worldly anxiety, not in drink and the tavern, but in evangelicalism and its forms of fellowship. In fact, his sermons were initially preached in the course of a particularly successful revival.[31]

The most revealing example of the clergy's growing sense of a deep separation between evangelicalism and the structure and distinctions of the secular world can be seen in *The Christian Spectator*, an evangelical magazine launched in 1819. Initially at least, the magazine was explicitly directed to that portion of the community which had traditionally been referred to as "the better part" and "the wise and the good." But the approach to this social elite was very different from what it had been in the eighteenth century. The magazine's rhetorical strategy was identical to Hawes's approach to the young man about to set out on life and Beecher's to the struggling young family man. *The Christian Spectator* was essentially a form of proselytizing literature, aimed at the social class which, New England evangelicals feared, was apostatizing to Unitarianism and the Episcopalians. Like Hawes's *Lectures* and Beecher's *Sermons*, it evinced appreciation of its audience's situation. Announced rather disingenuously, since it was wholly a clerical effort, as "a magazine conducted by a group of gentlemen," it applauded good taste, elevated sentiment, and decorous behavior.[32] This extolling of gentility, however, was essentially a device, an attempt to gain an entry which they could then use to draw readers into the evangelical orbit. For all the *Christian Spectator*'s embrace of gentility, it portrayed the world of the upper classes, with its taste for profane literature and intellectual speculation and its embrace of luxury and fashion, theater going and

critical of gentility

frivolous partying, as a world as perilous to the soul as evil companions were to the unwary youth and drink was to the humble tradesman.

Most revealingly, however, *The Christian Spectator* contains almost no sense that *as a class* this social elite possessed any particular and unique public responsibilities. This is seen most clearly in the opening article of the first issue, a memoir of Miss Julia Strong, a recently deceased daughter of the governor of Massachusetts, Caleb Strong. In every way—family position, education, religion (she was converted by Timothy Dwight, the President of Yale)—she was a Christian gentlewoman, a young lady whose demeanor, whether at occasions of "gaity" or in the "habitations of want," was always marked by true godliness and true gentility.[33] Yet, the piece displayed those elements of Miss Strong's bearing which were most obviously religious in ways that had very little to do with her social class. She was portrayed as the complete evangelist, one whose concern for those around her came not from the obligations an elite possessed toward those less fortunate, but from her character as a converted Christian. Her desire for the salvation of those unconverted never flagged and, indeed, was no different in kind from the concern an evangelical youth was expected to have for his unconverted companions or a pious wife for an unregenerate husband. Moreover, her gentility and her ability to mingle with her social circle and establish friendships among them were all portrayed as making her a more effective evangelist. They had rendered her "peculiarly qualified" to "reprove with firmness and attention," to point out to her friends their wayward attachments to luxury and frivolity. Even as she mingled in scenes of "innocent cheerfulness" and "refined effusions of taste and sentiment" (without, of course, "descending from her dignity and Christian character"), she "secretly lifted up her prayers for those" about her.[34]

Finally, the new evangelicalism created a new kind of Christian citizenship. In colonial New England, Christian duty had mirrored the social structure. Churchmen had associated order with the exertions of a pious elite at the core of society: if the saints occupied the stations of formal and informal authority, churchmen had believed, their influence would be such as to imbue the rest of the people with habits of deference and to invest social institutions with sufficient force to restrain the unregenerate. Moreover, the particular duties toward the public weal that religion ordained had reflected a person's place and function within the community. As a public force, however, the new evangelicalism centered in a form of public obligation that believers bore toward society, not because they belonged to a polity or because of their particular place in the community, but simply because they were evangelical Christians. Though communicants had been organized into a special domain apart from and protected against the temptations of the secular world, they nonetheless retained responsibility for maintaining moral and social order. As regenerate Christians serving divine will, they had a mission to seek the reformation and conversion of the unregenerate around them.[35] This obligation, moreover, knew no social distinctions, but derived from the fact of conversion and the power of their own evangelical love. No matter what their position or standing, whether male or female, eminent or obscure, young or old, all evangelicals had the same obligation toward society—to fight the sin and seek the salvation of those still outside personal evangelical dominion.[36]

By 1820, then, Second Great Awakening evangelicalism did not simply contain different ideas about society and its ills. It had generated what can best be understood as a whole new social grammar— a new and distinctive way of perceiving how the social order was composed, operated, and maintained.[37] This grammar, moreover, directed the public guardianship of the clergy. Churchmen had arrogated responsibility for social order to themselves and now associated it with forms of self-control that could only come from personal piety, rather than from external coercion or the operation of a well-ordered, organic community. The avowed public goal was to "evangelize the nation." These were the years that saw the construction of the evangelical empire, a vast network of regional and benevolent associations—the tract, bible, education, home missionary, temperance, and Sabbath school societies—designed to convert, reform, and church the American people. As Lyman Beecher, the foremost architect of the new evangelicalism, rhapsodized in 1815, evangelical Christianity, quickened with regenerate zeal and deployed through its ministers, churches, revivals, tracts and associations, would not only restore New England to godliness. It would also extend the "special influence" that had been New England's blessing and virtue to the South and West and thereby "produce a sameness of views, of feelings, and interests and lay the foundations of the empire on a rock."[38]

4

The Ministry Transformed

The rise of an evangelical conception of social order had a profound impact on the structure and character of the ministry. Evangelizing the nation demanded a vast expansion of the clergy, and beginning in the second decade of the century, New England churchmen made a concerted and increasingly systematic effort to recruit young men into the clergy. They set up education societies to find deserving young men and provide them with the means to obtain the education they needed to become ministers; they founded new colleges like Amherst, Bowdoin, Williams, and Hamilton to educate the new recruits; and they devised the theological seminary to provide a new and systematic form of professional training. In addition, of course, they had launched the various benevolent associations for carrying out their campaign to bring the American people under direct evangelical dominion. These new institutions were not designed to change the ministry. Churchmen improvised them to meet specific needs and solve such practical problems as finding and training enough young men for the ministry, putting Bibles and tracts in the hands and homes of Americans, and providing new or feeble churches with missionary pastors. Together, however, they transformed the institutional environment of the ministry by adding a new and rather different organizational tier to it. The new institutions were neither community-based and -controlled, nor ordained ecclesiastical structures. Under the control of clerically dominated boards of directors, and eventually under the daily direction of full-time clerical functionaries, they added up to a separate, translocal structure of ministerial and evangelical institutions. And this new ministerial structure in turn fostered a form of ministerial identity and professional commitment that fundamentally transformed the localism that had circumscribed the clerical office in eighteenth-century New England.

During the eighteenth century, young men were selected out for the ministry locally, by members of their home communities. Moreover, recruitment did not violate, but worked through, the hierarchical relationships and organic values of the local community. Becoming a clergyman depended upon the decision of an elder—father, pastor, or perhaps patron—that a young man was a "suitable" candidate for the sacred office, that he possessed good character, piety, and intellectual tastes and talent.[1] The discernment of these qualities in particular young men took a variety of forms, all of which depended upon direct, first-hand knowledge of a young man and his personal and familial history. Particularly pious fathers often in effect tithed a son in whom they had detected piety and talent to the ministry and went to great lengths to provide him with the education he needed to become a minister. Frequently, if a boy had a frail or sickly constitution that seemed to unsuit him for a physically demanding vocation, he would be directed from an early age toward the ministry by teaching him to read and exempting him from many of the tasks boys ordinarily performed on the family farm. Similarly, fathers sometimes designated for the ministry younger sons who could not be easily or satisfactorily placed in the family economy and estate.[2]

The New England clergy had, of course, been open to some "poor" young men whose families did not have the wherewithal to fit them for the ministry. The recruitment of such young men also worked through the detailed knowledge that their elders and superiors had of them and their life situations. In fact, poor boys could not become ministers unless some local patron or sponsor gave them the charity necessary to obtain the schooling they could not provide for themselves. Occasionally laymen of piety and means would fasten upon a youth of exceptional piety and promise and give him patronage, and sometimes an uncle would aid a poor but talented nephew. Usually, however, the most important sponsor for a poor boy was his town pastor. When a pastor discerned a youth of exceptional piety and talent, he would in effect adopt him, preparing him for college and then using his influence to secure locally available charity or one of the several scholarships that Yale and Harvard had set aside for such young men.[3]

Eighteenth-century ministerial recruitment, then, at once reflected and reinforced both the notion that the ministry was a sacred office requiring special qualities, and the sense that the minister *as a minister* occupied a particular place among the elite of the community. Whether a recruit was of humble or high origin, he was dependent upon persons recognized as superior to him for his admission into such a high office and station, and was well aware that he had been selected because he was thought to have particular piety and talent. For the son from "the wise and the good," the ministry was a vocation appropriate to his station, if not, indeed, a service he owed the community because of his character and station. For those of middling rank, the ministry provided a way for a father who did not have the economic base to secure all his sons in the family station to place a surplus son in a vocation commensurate with his standing. For the poor recruit, moreover, the very act of charity, both because it was an "extra-ordinary" act (probably no more than 10 or 12 percent of the eighteenth-century clergy was recruited from the poor) and because it lifted him into a position that was otherwise beyond his reach, reinforced in him the traditional conception of the minister's office and station.[4]

Both the scale of ministerial recruitment and the procedures used to bring young men into the clergy changed during the early decades of the nineteenth century. Eighteenth-century recruitment had been essentially informal, proceeding at what must have seemed a natural pace. There had been little concern with numbers, with whether there were too many or too few clergymen. The major concern had been with obtaining clergymen of the proper character, piety, and learning. The rate of entry into the clergy had remained relatively steady, with a gradual increase that appears to have reflected the growth of the population. Beginning at the end of the century and continuing well into the 1840s, however, a dramatic expansion of the clerical ranks took place as the rate of entry almost tripled. For the state of New Hampshire, for example, entry of young men into the clergy for the years from 1790 to 1815 increased from about 40 per decade to 60 per decade. Within fifteen years, by 1830, however, young men were flooding into the New Hampshire clergy at the rate of almost 160 per decade.[5]

A number of things had conspired to bring about this sudden and dramatic invasion of the clerical ranks. As David Allmendinger has made clear, a confluence of demographic and economic conditions were forcing large numbers of young men to seek new occupations beyond family farm and home community.[6] In addition, the revivals of the Second Great Awakening furnished hundreds of these young men with piety and an inner "call" to the ministry. Equally importantly, however, the clergy itself had embarked upon a policy of deliberate clerical expansion, and had created the institutions for recruiting and training a vast corps of new preachers. In 1826, for example, the American Education Society promised to support "every young man of proper character in the United States who may apply for aid and who may not otherwise be provided for," and projected a goal of 4000 beneficiaries.[7] In 1829 it was supporting over 400 young men, and by 1835 it was dispensing $50,000 to more than 1000 recipients. The pool of college students similarly expanded. During the decade from 1780 to 1790, New England colleges produced around 1000 graduates. But by the 1820s, more than 3000 young men were graduated each decade from New England colleges, with approximately two-thirds of them coming from the newer, "provincial" colleges rather than from Harvard or Yale. Until the 1840s, moreover, well over half of the graduates of these colleges set out to become ministers. Clerical expansion thus was a result both of a vast new pool of potential ministers and of the institutions to channel them into the ministry.

[margin handwritten note: began to provide $]

This expansion significantly altered the social composition of the ministry. About 10 percent of the eighteenth-century clergy came from the poor. The clergy itself provided a good number of clergymen. Most ministers were followed into the sacred office by at least one of their sons, and approximately 15 percent of the Yale graduates who entered the clergy in the eighteenth century were sons of clergymen, while another 15 percent had grandfathers or uncles who had been clergymen.[8] The remaining 60 percent of the clergy had come from families which could both spare a son and pay for his education.[9] Nineteenth-century clergymen did not neglect these sources by any means. An 1814 appeal for funds for a Connecticut education society urged those it was soliciting to do everything they could to direct their own sons to the sacred office.[10] And Lyman Beecher, though not the most typical minister or father, succeeded in drumming all seven of his sons into the clergy. Nonetheless, it was clear from the outset that if the clergy was going to expand enough to meet the evangelical goal of one settled pastor for every one thousand souls, it would have to draw far more extensively than it ever had from "the sons of the middle class downward to the cottage of the poor."[11]

[margin handwritten note: more clergy from lower classes]

Although precise figures are practically impossible to garner, it is clear that most of those entering the clergy in the first half of the nineteenth century were "poor" young men whose fathers could not furnish them with a liberal education and who thus depended for it upon self-help, some form of charity, or a combination of the two. By 1830, between 150 and 200 men whose education had been financed at least in part by the education societies, particularly the American Education Society, were entering the clergy each year. Moreover, David F. Allmendinger's recent study of early nineteenth-century New England colleges and their students, while not concerned explicitly with the ministry, nonetheless makes possible a firm understanding of the ministerial population, for the clergy was drawn from these students and these colleges were among the institutions that channeled young men into the ministry.[12] In many ways these provincial colleges bear a stronger resemblance to the community colleges of the twentieth century than they do to eighteenth-century Yale and Harvard. It cost half to two-thirds as much to attend them as it did to go to Yale or Harvard. Most of their students were the first of their families to receive higher education and came from neighboring agricultural communities of the sort that had provided few students to eighteenth-century Harvard and Yale. In addition, probably close to half of the students, if not more, needed financial help. By the 1830s nearly 15 percent of all the students in New England colleges were formally designated "indigents," recipients of funds which they received from the education societies by documenting their poverty. Another sizable portion had to rely upon at least some charity from the college itself. According to Allmendinger, "about 500 of the first 1300" students at Amherst and about one-third of the Bowdoin students in 1828 and 1829 received help from this source.[13] In addition, almost a third of the students in these colleges were those Allmendinger labels "laggards" or "mature students," who entered college after the age of twenty-one and graduated after the age of twenty-five.[14] These students, some of whom received financial help, were almost all poor and essentially on their own. Many, if not most, had delayed entry while they earned money (and perhaps scraped together a scanty precollegiate education), and they were frequently forced to interrupt their education and earn money by periodic bouts of school keeping. (Colleges accommodated this need by arranging their winter vacation times to correspond with the winter term of the district schools.)[15]

This massive influx of young men of such origins into the clergy was bound to have some corrosive effect on the traditional coalescence between official and social standing. These young men had very little sense of themselves as members of a social or cultural elite. They were not in college or headed toward the ministry because it was something members of their families and persons of their social rank had always done or were expected to do. Even more importantly, however, the process itself eroded the traditional social sensibility that had informed eighteenth-century ministerial consciousness. Rather than reinforce the hierarchical relationships and values of the local community, the procedures and institutions that now recruited a young man and made him a minister operated outside, if not against, them.

By the mid-twenties it could no longer really be said that ministers were recruited locally by their immediate elders and social superiors. Most of the new ministers of these years were probably converted in the increasingly frequent and intense revivals of the 1810s and 1820s. Their conversions usually occurred during the middle teens through the middle twenties, the period of life when they were confronting an increasingly anxious process of occupational choice.[16] Many of these "poor" youths, it appears, had not previously considered the ministry among the options open to them. They emerged from conversion, however, with the inner piety that made them candidates for the office and for the charity needed to go to college. Moreover, both the new procedures for recruitment and the new colleges made it possible for young men of clerical inclination to present themselves as candidates for the ministry. With the relative inexpensiveness of the provincial colleges, the availability of charity, and the opportunity to earn money keeping school, almost any young man who was determined enough could secure a college education. Indeed, the laggards making up a third of the student population of the provincial colleges were in fact independent young men. They had reached their majority and were outside parental or local control, and in most instances they had been fending for themselves for several years. The greatest break with local control over clerical recruitment came, however, with the emergence of new mechanisms for distributing the aid that eventually brought thousands of poor young men into the ministry. Under these mechanisms, selection no longer centered in a young man's home town. Nor was it done by superiors who knew him well and based their determination that he was "suitable" for the office and station of a minister on this personal familiarity.

During the first decade of the nineteenth century, neighboring ministers all over New England joined to set up local societies to raise money to fit "indigent young men for the gospel ministry." With their constitutions, timetables for canvassing the local churches for funds, and annual reports, these societies represented a more systematic and collective attempt to do what individual patrons and churches had done sporadically and informally during the eighteenth century. They sought out pious young men of the area, pieced together the small contributions of many donors and several churches, and maintained careful scrutiny and control over their beneficiaries. They thus preserved many of the traditional procedures and assumptions about the bestowal of charity and patronage. Not only did they choose young men known to them and subject them to the traditional controls, but they also expected some of their beneficiaries to come back to serve the vacant, impoverished parishes in the neighborhood.[17]

Out of these scattered efforts, broader and more comprehensive societies were established. In 1814, for example, the Connecticut Education Society was established to raise a corps of ministers to fill Connecticut's "waste places" and to provide aid for the dozens of poor young men of piety who were clamoring for the means to attend Yale College. As one fund-raising appeal put it, "For a number of years past, from 16 to 20 applications have been made and refused. There are at this time several young men in Yale College, who, hearing that this society had been organized, have come and flung themselves upon us. We could not send them away, and yet, unless we are patronized by the public, they must go away despairing of their object."[18] (It was hoped that the society could eventually help up to 100 poor young men of piety go to Yale.) Just a year later churchmen established the American Education Society in Boston. Although it began modestly and drew most of its early beneficiaries from eastern Massachusetts, within a decade the American Education Society had become the central agency dispensing funds to poor and pious young men. By 1819 the AES was aiding 191 beneficiaries, and by 1830 it was aiding close to 500 young men each year.[19]

It was certainly not the intention of the founders and directors of the education societies to trammel the traditional social values that had governed the recruitment of ministers from the ranks of the poor. The Connecticut Education Society, even while projecting an enterprise that stretched well beyond the confines of any particular locality, gave first preference to descendants of life members and permitted large donors to designate the recipients of the funds they gave.[20] Yet, under the pressure of numbers—the seemingly unending need for new ministers and the seemingly limitless supply of poor young men clamoring for aid—the AES developed into a totally new kind of institution. Part-time volunteer clergymen whose main jobs were in the classroom or parish could no longer cope with the flood of applications, raise the funds to support hundreds of beneficiaries, or scrutinize the needs and expenses of young men scattered through dozens of academies, colleges, and seminaries. What was needed was an administrative structure whose personnel could devote themselves totally to the business of the society and, equally importantly, effectively superintend its far-flung operations. Accordingly, in 1826, the AES moved its headquarters from Andover Seminary to Boston, Massachusetts, and reorganized its operations. The board of directors hired the Reverend Elias Cornelius as a full-time general secretary to administer the society. And to help him, they provided a full-time assistant secretary, a number of part-time and full-time clerks, and several full-time "agents" to course the country setting up auxiliary societies and raising funds. As Allmendinger has put it, with the 1826 reorganization of the AES, "a bureaucratic organization without precedent in American higher education" was born.[20]

The important thing about this reorganization of the AES was that it meant that ministerial recruitment now essentially bypassed the local community. As early as 1819, the AES had been forced to stop assigning the funds a local church or society had contributed to it to the particular young men these societies might have wanted to support. In effect, the local affiliates had become little more than fundraising devices for the parent society: no longer needed to discover or select candidates, they served as conduits for local philanthropy to flow into the centrally directed efforts. Candidates no longer were filtered through local personages and organizations. Instead, young men, knowing of the existence of a formal institution that had pledged to help all young men who were qualified, simply applied directly to the AES in Boston. In addition, in the name of efficiency the AES had been forced to adopt procedures for selecting beneficiaries that were based far more upon bureaucratic necessity than upon local custom or traditional social values. A series of examining boards, usually meeting quarterly at the various colleges or seminaries, were responsible for screening applicants. Though these boards were made up of local clergymen and pious laymen, they passed on applicants who were essentially anonymous to them. The sheer number of applicants they had to screen made the traditional ways of assessing talent, character, and piety wholly unworkable. When men had selected one or two young men from their own communities, they could easily draw upon their familiarity with a young man's life and family history to assess his suitability for patronage and the ministry. Now, however, more abstract and more quickly accessible standards came into play. As Allmendinger described the process: "If a young man could prove he had pursued studies for a few months, he had talent; if he could demonstrate that he had been a professor of religion for six months, he was pious; if he pledged himself to a thorough course

but this had never happened across the board...

of theological education and if his references revealed no misbehavior, he had dedication and good character."[21]

There was a comparable change in the institutions that turned the clerical recruit into a minister. New England churchmen, of course, had long been committed to a learned ministry, and it was rare for a man without a collegiate education to become a minister in one of the established churches.[22] The education a minister received at eighteenth-century Harvard and Yale, however, was only secondarily a form of occupational training. Though both colleges had been set up initially to provide New England with a learned ministry, they had become broader cultural institutions. As Karl Kaestle recently put it, eighteenth-century colleges were directed "more to general social leadership than to occupational roles."[23] In its first twenty-five years, for example, 67 percent of Yale's graduates entered the clergy, but from 1725 to 1750 the portion had dropped to 42 percent, and during the second half of the century only 454, or 28 percent, of its 1622 graduates became clergymen.[24] Harvard and Yale were thus among the most important agencies for forming and preserving a self-conscious, colony-wide social and cultural elite. Indeed, in their make-up the reality and significance of social rank was clear and unmistakable. Until the late 1760s, class rank was assigned at matriculation according to the social standing of father and family.[25] Even when this practice ended, the distinctions remained. Present in almost every class were sons of colonial officialdom, members of the clerical families that had dominated New England culture for generations, and descendants of the Puritan fathers. A young man of middling or humble origin might well be the classmate of the son of the local squire to whom everyone in his community paid deference. Harvard and Yale, then, gathered the scions of local notables and respectables together and gave them the common styles of discourse and bearing that distinguished the gentleman, as well as the higher learning that the "better sort" needed to meet their obligation to provide leadership for the community.

For the young man of the eighteenth century who made his way into the clergy, then, college had not only provided a preministerial intellectual training but had also given him the education and manners of the station to which he would automatically belong as a minister, whether or not he belonged to it because of his own family. The concept of learning applied to the ministry, moreover, had embodied the notion that the minister, as a minister, occupied a position among the cultural elite. It referred, in fact, more to the "liberal education" and general "mental culture" of the college than to the more explicitly professional or theological education which ministers picked up in a far less systematic way. A minister, it was believed, needed such general, liberal learning not only to effectively transmit the divine message, but also to "command the attention" of the wise and the good and to "exert that moral and literary influence that it belongs to the ministry to exert."[26]

The colleges that produced the overwhelming majority of the New England ministers of the first half of the nineteenth century were in no real sense institutions for the consolidation of a social and cultural elite. Partly, the change reflected the difference in their student populations. Not more than a handful of the students present at any given time at eighteenth-century Harvard and Yale were "poor," and many of those who were poor were impoverished descendants (frequently orphans) of families of respectable history and standing. But if the poor were scarcely visible in the eighteenth-century college, the well-born were rarely present in the provincial colleges of the nineteenth century. (The wealthiest youth from an Amherst, Williams, or Bowdoin student's home town was much more likely to go to Harvard or Yale than to the poorer local college.) In these colleges the poor made up the dominant population, and they, rather than the scions of the traditional cultural elite, shaped the character and tone of the institutions. School calendars, eating and housing facilities, and patterns of supervision and control were all adjusted to accommodate their needs.[27]

These provincial colleges were a different kind of collegiate institution, even though they retained the traditional liberal curriculum and were set up to educate the clergy to exert the traditional kind of moral and literary influence. Their students approached these colleges with attitudes very different from those of their eighteenth-century counterparts. They did not look to these colleges primarily as agencies of the genteel culture that was the badge of social class. Nor did they enlist in them because of the social station to which they belonged. They went to them for a kind of preparation that would be useful, if not essential, to their subsequent vocational lives. Those who entered them without a clear-cut decision to become ministers came because they had to find their life pursuits away from family farm and home town. They were young men in search of a vocation and went to college to try to expand their life chances, to open up a field of opportunities that might offer them an escape from the constricting and dreary possibilities that otherwise confronted them. In this *no, not a vocational school.*

sense, they looked to college, not for a specific vocational education, but as a general educational platform that would open up a career in teaching, business, law, or the clergy.

The majority of the students in these colleges, moreover, were headed from the outset for the clergy, and they were even more vocationally purposive. Their firm commitment to the clergy justified their collegiate education, and what appears to have characterized them more than anything else was their maturity and sober-mindedness. Many of them, in addition, were older, mature young men rather than college boys. For these poor young men, gaining a college education was a continuing financial and psychological struggle that left little room for the traditional collegiate sensibility and life style. Their vocational and evangelical sobriety, moreover, was reflected in their behavior: they would go off periodically to keep school, set up and teach in Sabbath schools, and conduct devotions and revivals in their colleges. These provincial colleges, then, were more vocationally utilitarian and culturally spartan than eighteenth-century Harvard and Yale had been. Although they could not be termed vocational institutions, they were approached by their students, and in fact functioned, as agencies of occupational preparedness rather than elite acculturation.[28]

(much more positive view, here)

The ministerial population emerging from the provincial colleges thus was a population that had been stripped of much of the social sensibility that had informed the eighteenth-century clergyman's sense of himself as a minister. Moreover, the theological seminary, which by 1830 had become the major institution providing New England ministers with their specific professional training, reinforced this process. Eighteenth-century theological education had followed several patterns. A few young men had stayed on at Harvard and Yale to read divinity while they served as tutors in the colleges. The vast majority, however, received their training by reading theology and living with a practicing minister for several months or a year. A few ministers, like John Smalley, Joseph Bellamy, or Nathaniel Emmons, became particularly well known as trainers of clergymen and spent a good deal of their time fitting young men with a theological education. It is estimated, for example, that Emmons trained over ninety ministers, while more than sixty young men read theology with Hopkins.[29] In the last several decades of the century, Charles Backus and John Smalley improvised what came to be called the "schools of the prophets," in which they dispensed a set regimen of reading and lectures to about a half-dozen young men at a time.[30] Several things, however, characterized all these forms. The course of theological education was brief, extending from about six months to a year, and was fairly informal and unsystematic. Moreover, theological preparation did not draw young men into a separate, exclusively ministerial environment or institution. Rather, they remained in a college or in the home and community of a man who still had to carry out all the ordinary tasks of a town minister.

The theological seminary, instituted in New England with the founding of Andover Theological Seminary in 1808, was a significant departure from the earlier forms.[31] It represented both a formalization and standardization of ministerial training and a dramatically increased emphasis upon purely "professional" training. It erected and institutionalized as the norm a formal three-year curriculum, divided into a series of subjects, each of which was taught by a professor who had come to specialize in a particular branch of what came to be referred to as "the theological sciences." In addition, the seminary involved a dramatic transformation in scale. In the "schools of the prophets" or eighteenth-century Harvard and Yale, only a handful of ministerial candidates were present at any one time. In contrast, by 1820 Andover gathered well over 100 students and teachers each year.[32] Equally importantly, however, the theological seminary was a separate, exclusively ministerial institution, which in effect removed the clerical candidate from earlier forms of immersion in broader, secular institutions and communities. It gathered young men into an institution designed solely for professional training and under the direction of the soundest and most learned leaders of the clergy, thereby removing the rising generation from the provincial and secular influences that study with a single, settled pastor had entailed. In a removed and tranquil setting, with only ministers in training, visiting clergymen, and the seminary professors present, recruits to the ministry were subjected to the theological training that was increasingly looked upon as the most essential step in the creation of a minister.

The theological seminary, then, both embodied and created a new, more exclusively "professional" form of ministerial consciousness. It was the capstone to a process of clerical socialization that was almost the opposite of that of the eighteenth-century minister. Eighteenth-century forms of recruitment and collegiate and theological education had all reinforced a sense of clerical consciousness in which official and social station had coalesced. The colleges through which most of the clergymen now came contained little that fostered the traditional organic and hierarchical social sensibility. And the other institutions, like the AES and the theological seminary, that helped turn a young *didn't have a sense of belonging to a ptclr class*

man into a minister were exclusively ministerial institutions that operated outside the customs and values of the broader secular community. Thus, the young men flooding into the ministry in the 1810s, 1820s, and 1830s emerged from their training with very little of the traditional sense that as ministers they belonged, as both a cultural and clerical necessity, to a particular social class. Their sense of their role and its social importance remained unchanged, but their identity as ministers was now informed far more strongly by their sense of belonging to a professional community than by a sense of their place in the status system of the local community.

Finally, the emergence of this new ministerial consciousness and identity can be detected in the delineation of new canons of pastoral deportment. Indeed, a deliberate attempt to mark out a special set of ministerial manners can be seen in a variety of sources—in articles in the newly formed evangelical journals such as *The Panoplist, The Christian Spectator, The Spirit of the Pilgrims,* and *The Boston Recorder*; in ordination and installation sermons; and most especially in a manual of clerical manners written in 1827 by the Reverend Dr. Samuel Miller, the president of Princeton Theological Seminary.[32] In

traits of a minister

these sources, traits previously associated with gentility—such qualities as decorum, refinement, temperance, and prudence—were recast more as signs of piety, of a soul at ease with divine government, than as the hallmarks of class. In addition, clerical manners were delineated in such a way as to distinguish the minister from those whose education he shared and to whose social class he had previously belonged. What these documents represent, in short, is the enunciation of a code of conduct that was construed as exclusively ministerial and which applied to no other group. The minister was urged to deny himself many of the "gratifications" and "indulgences"—quite innocent in themselves—of social associates and to conscientiously "cultivate and manifest an indifference to worldly enjoyments,"[33] and, in general, to bear himself in such a way as to immediately identify himself as a man of God and godliness.

To a certain extent this represented a continuation of the eighteenth-century ideal of pastoral asceticism, in which the "good" pastor was one who was beyond "worldliness." But what distinguished the discussion of the early nineteenth century was the way in which the minister's pious deportment was connected to a general notion of manners. At heart the idea of manners was a concept of social relationships based on the premise that there were distinct types of people, each of which required a particular style of approach. Miller in fact devoted the greatest portion of his manual to prescribing how the minister ought to address various groups distinguished by age, sex, education, wealth, belief, and affiliation. What is clear from his discussion is that the minister properly belonged to none of these groups.[34] This construction of ministerial manners and deportment thus not only reinforced unworldly asceticism, but also rendered the minister aloof from his community. It reinforced a sense of special clerical position, but did so by extricating the minister from an explicit social position. In this sense, the import of the notion of special ministerial manners was almost the opposite of what had been associated with the ordination bond in the eighteenth century. Those bonds were seen to inextricably enmesh the minister in a particular community, while the ministerial manners of the early nineteenth century sought to remove the minister from entanglement in the community in which he served. In the end, the concept of ministerial manners placed the clergyman outside the social distinctions of the secular community and put boundaries of ministerial caste between him and other groups.

The new ministerial structure and consciousness not only removed the clergyman from the status vocabulary and distinctions of the local community, but also transformed the localistic character of the pastoral office. The ever broader reach of evangelical and benevolent associations spiralling out from the local communion had greatly expanded the scope of the ordinary clergyman's responsibilities. Most ministers still settled into local pulpits, but a clergyman had become a good deal more than simply a local preacher. Lyman Beecher's 1814 sermon installing the Reverend John Keyes in the Woolcot, Connecticut, pulpit provides a revealing description of the ordinary clergyman's concern. This widely distributed sermon, which Beecher repeated all over the state, can be read as the blueprint of the new ministerial life. Beecher urged Keyes to spare no effort in his attempts to awaken his congregation, as he catalogued all the new devices a pastor could use to gain "an all pervasive influence among his people": systematic home visits that would take him into each home in his parish at least twice each year, prayer meetings, special young people's bible and inquiry groups, and a series of weekday lectures and sermons. The sermon, however, devoted even more time to the activities and obligations of the parish minister beyond his own parish. Beecher flatly insisted that "no minister liveth for his own charge exclusively."[35] Joining others to fill empty pulpits, constant attendance at ecclesiastical meetings, and service for the various benevolent societies were as much a part of official clerical obligation as were a preacher's local ministrations. As Beecher put it at one point, exhorting Keyes not to confine his "eye, heart, and hand to the narrow limits of an association": "The State, the nation, the world demand your prayers and charities and enterprise."[36] He went so far as to suggest that attentiveness to these larger enterprises was a crucial mark of a man's fidelity to his divine call, and warned Keyes that "a neglect of ecclesiastical meetings and of enterprise in the business of the church will limit your influence to do good, diminish your zeal to do good, and subtract essentially from your stimulus to pastoral fidelity among your own people."[37]

The new, translocal evangelical institutions also began to impinge upon the pastor's day-to-day work in his home parish. The tract, bible, education, mission, reform, temperance, and Sabbath school societies had all sprung up locally as attempts to achieve greater evangelical force through collective neighborhood action. But as the local societies and associations amalgamated first into state and then into national societies, they, like the AES, became incipient bureaucracies which began to exert greater and greater influence over the individual pastor's conduct of his ministry. The direction of these efforts increasingly came from outside the parish, from decisions made by boards of the various benevolent societies which would call upon each of the local churches to devote a Sunday service to preaching about, say, the cause of home missions or of the tract society. During the twenties, moreover, most of the major societies had "agents"— frequently seminary students—who would go from town to town preaching about their particular cause, distributing tracts, and organizing local auxiliaries. Eventually, the claims of the national societies for local time became so intense and demanding that regional ministerial associations had to set up annual calendars, specifying which Sundays of which month would be commonly devoted to each of the benevolent enterprises.

Even the content of a minister's preaching and writing occasionally fell under the influence of these new agencies. Religious journals, for example, with sermons, sermon sketches and suggested pulpit themes were published for use by the preacher in the field. Traditionally, most writing by clergymen had been inspired by local circumstances and addressed to local audiences. Indeed, in the eighteenth century only a small portion of the clergy ever published anything, and even then all but a handful of the productions of the writing parson were inspired by local events, such as funerals and ordinations.[38] By 1820, however, clergymen wrote increasingly under the commission of a devotional quarterly or the tract society, and they wrote less for a specific, local audience than for an abstract, anonymous, and generalized evangelical community.[39]

It was, however, the clergyman's local ties and commitments that were most severely strained by the emergence of a translocal ministry with the national community as its constituency. The rise of nationally organized evangelicalism transformed the occupational structure of the ministry and inspired very different patterns in clerical careers. With the exception of three or four college presidents and professors, eighteenth-century clergymen had occupied local pastorates, and though the occupants of some posts certainly had higher social standing and greater clerical influence than many of their clerical brethren, there had been no essential spiritual distinction among pastorates. If a man labored in the church of New Fairfield, Connecticut, he labored in the part of God's vineyard to which he had been called, and he was no less crucial an ambassador of God than the man who had been called to the First Church in Boston. Some ministers had had leadership bestowed upon them simply because of who they were: thus the Dwights, Williamses, the Huntingtons, the Edwardses, and the Elys filled the pulpits of the major Boston Churches and the first churches in towns like Salem, New Haven, Litchfield, Northampton, and Springfield. In this sense, leadership and pulpit coalesced: a young man in these pulpits almost immediately took on the mantle of clerical leadership. Other churchmen, however, earned leadership by their achievements as ministers and exerted it, whether it consisted of writing doctrinal tracts or reconciling clerical factions, from whatever pulpit they happened to occupy. For these men, the fact of leadership was in no way tied to their particular pulpit, and when a man who had become influential from an ordinary pulpit died or retired, his successor did not automatically become a leader but might well spend his life as little more than a moderately successful local preacher. Thus, though there were these distinctions in standing and influence, what might be thought of as an occupational hierarchy was essentially static, with little room for movement within it. The major pulpits to which leadership adhered automatically were not open to just any young men, but fell, through a sure but informal process, to those who were deemed "appropriate" for such posts. In addition, of course, the ideal and practice of pastoral permanence precluded the construction of a clerical career by moving from lesser to more important pulpits.

The new evangelical and ministerial institutions spawned both a greater number and a greater variety of nonpastoral posts, all of which were esteemed for the importance of their service to the greater evangelical cause. By 1830, dozens of new professorships, secretary-ships and agencies in the national benevolent societies, and editor-ships had been established, not to mention the foreign and domestic missionaries. Indeed, 34 percent of the 164 matriculants in Andover Seminary from 1810 to 1820 spent more than half of their careers in nonpastoral positions, and almost a third more spent at least a portion of their careers in a nonpastoral post.[10] The new college and seminary professorships were given particular prestige. That these posts were immediately filled with pulpit ministers who were com-monly recognized as among the most talented leaders and preachers of the profession indicates the importance attached to them. The First Church in New Haven, indeed, lost Moses Stuart to Andover Seminary in 1810, only four years after it had settled him, and then lost his successor, Nathaniel Taylor, when Yale set up its divinity school in 1822. Moreover, men like Samuel Miller, Heman Humphrey, Lyman Beecher and even Charles Grandison Finney, who had en-joyed influence and renown as giants of the cloth outside college and seminary, often crowned their careers by assuming the presidency of one. As good an indication as any of the prestige and honor attached to such posts can be seen in the lament of a young man, who, sensing the unattainability of such a post, decided to put aside the ministry entirely:

> I have thought that no situation would be so agreeable to my mind and taste as a professorship, or the presidency of a college, provided my talents and learning were adequate to the duties of such a station. But to attain either of these (allowing it possible) it would be important for me to have commenced my education earlier, and to have gained a higher reputation for scholarship while in college. . . . No branch of learning was ever pursued by men with so much pleasure and interest as the Philosophy of the mind, and among the different branches of collegiate study, I am obliged to consider this my forte. But the professorship in this department in college is usually united with the Presidency, and requiring talents of the very first order, as well as dignity and reputation, it is the most difficult of the professorships to be obtained by a young man.[41]

In addition, missions and agencies began to siphon off many of the most talented, zealous, and promising young ministers. Beginning with Samuel J. Mills, Adoniram Judson, Samuel Nott and other Andoverians of the class of 1810, missionary service became perhaps the most highly honored form of divine service to which a young man could dedicate himself. In 1829, moreover, a group of the Yale Divinity School's best students formed the "Yale Band" to go to Illinois to set up an outpost for the evangelical crusade to bring the Great Valley of the West under New England and Christian dominion. Such missionary efforts were given enormous play in the burgeoning evangelical periodical press, which celebrated the zeal and self-denying dedication of the home and foreign missionary as the perfect embodiment of piety and ministerial spirituality.[42]

This rise of clerical posts and goals beyond the individual parish subtly downgraded ordinary pastoral labor. It created and then celebrated a series of nonpastoral positions. But it also introduced ways of ranking pastorates that would have been alien to the eighteenth century. For eighteenth-century ministers, a "good" post was a stable and secure one which was conducive to lifetime tenure. Increasingly, however, churchmen weighted a pastorate according to its usefulness to the greater evangelical cause. They tended to measure the overall usefulness of a parish by its suitability for writing or organizational activism, the two major forms of general evangelical influence. How centrally placed a pulpit was and the access it afforded to the cities, like Boston and New York, that headquartered the national benevolent societies, became important considerations. For example, when Lyman Beecher, the archetypal new-style evangelical leader, first began to amass professional influence, he moved from his original secure, but rather isolated, pulpit in East Hampton, Long Island, to the First Church in Litchfield, Connecticut. His predecessor, Samuel Buell, who filled the East Hampton pulpit for more than fifty years, had been looked to as one of the great preachers of his day, one of the stars who had emerged during the First Great Awakening of the 1740s and whose sermons were printed as general devotional literature.[43] The East Hampton pulpit, in other words, was perfectly suited for the kind of eminence and influence Buell enjoyed, and there was no real reason or compulsion for him to leave it. By 1808, however, after a pastorate of ten years, Lyman Beecher had begun to exert a style of leadership for which the East Hampton pulpit was ill suited.

Beecher had not simply attained repute of the kind Buell had enjoyed. Although he was known as a powerful preacher, he had made his greatest impact as an organizer. Notice from beyond his own parish had first come to him because of his skill in improvising new ways to exert clerical social guardianship and prodding other ministers into action. In the two central events that brought him to the brink of leadership, his initial impact had been made at ministerial or professional gatherings where he had proposed more effective ways to reach evangelical goals.[44] More than anything else, this style of leadership dictated Beecher's move to a more strategically located parish. Though it might—and did—appear that in going to Litchfield, Beecher was simply going to a wealthier, more prestigious pulpit, the move was equally a transfer to a post from which his kind of leadership could best be deployed. In fact, while Beecher was entertaining the call to Litchfield, the leaders of the New York City clergy, arguing that his talents could best serve evangelicalism if he were located in the city, tried to get Beecher to the newly formed Brick Street Church. And although the Litchfield congregation wanted Beecher as a preacher, the leaders of the Connecticut clergy, especially Timothy Dwight and his protégés, were eager to bring Beecher to a centrally located pulpit from which he could more easily direct evangelical forces. And, indeed, it was from Litchfield that Beecher emerged in the 1820s as the field marshal of New England evangelicalism.[45]

The size, wealth, and relative sophistication and cosmopolitanism of the congregation also took on importance. A clergyman who played an active role in the larger evangelical and professional community needed a parish which would pay him enough to amass the library a "writing parson" needed or to support the travel that was a necessary part of influence and leadership. In addition, it was helpful if a man had a congregation that took pride in having a man of more than local eminence as their pastor. Indeed, it was not at all uncommon for ministers in the smaller and more rural parishes to get into trouble with their parishioners just as they began to emerge as leaders on the larger scene. Here, too, Beecher's move to Litchfield is indicative. In late 1809, Beecher formally requested East Hampton to raise his salary. His financial problems were in fact serious: he was $500 in debt, and it was clear that his annual salary of $400 was no longer adequate to cover inflation, a growing family, and his increasingly far-flung travels and commitments. But his congregation did not see it that way. Just the year before (as indeed on other occasions) they had supplemented his salary, and they now balked at Beecher's request. Beecher responded to their recalcitrance by threatening to leave if his needs were not met, and the controversy quickly descended into irreconcilable bitterness.

Though salary provided the focus of the dispute, as was often the case in disputes between pastors and their people, the real source of the controversy lay in deeper antagonisms. At the heart of the quarrel was the character of the ministry Beecher had developed. Many of his parishioners resented his activities outside his parish, and they expressed their pique by charging that Beecher had become excessively "proud," that his influence and professional travels provided him with self-gratification at the expense of his own parish. In 1807 and 1808 Beecher had had a powerful revival, and since he had traveled outside his parish on ministerial business as this revival waned, many of his parishioners traced the collapse of their revival directly to Beecher's "neglect." When Beecher came to his people once again for more money these resentments surfaced, and the congregation adamantly refused to meet his request. Some of his parishioners probably did want Beecher to leave, but most wanted him to stay and were simply trying to chastise him for his neglect with the only real weapon they had. In effect, they were asserting that his salary was adequate for the kind of local minister they desired. In the subsequent negotiations, in fact, the church expressed its willingness to meet Beecher's fiscal needs in ways that would guarantee his staying. They offered to give him $500 to clear his debts if he would formally agree to repay the sum if for any reason, as they put it, he "deserted" the parish. But compromise did not work, and after failing to reconcile the parties, the Long Island Presbytery agreed to dissolve the bonds between Beecher and his people and release him to take the "call" to Litchfield. The Presbytery agreed to this not because of any failing of either party but because of a "simple difference of opinion" as to the "sum necessary to render adequate support for the Gospel."[46] Ultimately the two parties could not agree because they had very different kinds of ministries in mind: the congregation was fully willing to support a good local pastor, but Beecher was no longer the traditional local pastor. He needed a position that could and would, in effect, subsidize his services to and leadership of the whole ministerial and evangelical enterprise.

In effect, then, what amounted to a prestige ladder had been introduced into the ministry, and this structure unintentionally but subtly undercut the sanctity of ordination bonds and eroded the tradition of pastoral permanence. Clerical leaders themselves were increasingly willing to break ordination bonds as they sought to recruit the most talented, zealous, and dedicated churchmen into the posts that they now considered more important to the larger cause than a simple pastorate. Thus the claims of evangelicalism as a whole were marshalled to justify taking Elias Cornelius from his Salem, Massachusetts, pulpit to the general secretaryship of the AES, and Moses Stuart to Andover Theological Seminary from the First Church in New Haven, and to justify transferring men who had made a mark in a small parish to more "important" metropolitan ones. In 1826 Lyman Beecher, for example, left Litchfield, Connecticut, to take on the pulpit of the newly formed Hanover Street Church in Boston, Massachusetts. He had become the leader of New England evangelicalism, and he, as well as other leaders, thought it was more important for the evangelical cause that he locate in Boston, where he could more directly lead the fight against Unitarianism, than that he remain in Litchfield.[47]

This kind of promotion set up patterns of achievement and esteem which ran directly counter to the eighteenth-century ideal of pastoral permanence. The eighteenth-century clergyman had confined his expectations and clerical goals largely to his home parish, hoping to achieve stability, local esteem and influence, and, perhaps, some notice by clergymen outside his neighborhood. But eminence was not pursued but came to one, and it certainly had not taken men out of their parishes. The young men entering the clergy in the teens and twenties, however, began to envision a career in the modern, technical sense—an occupational course composed of a sequence of steps upward to positions of greater prestige and influence.[48] They now looked beyond the local communion to the larger structure for the measure of personal and clerical achievement. Their letters and diaries, in fact, betray a wholly new kind of self-consciousness about the relative merits and career potential of particular posts. They ranked pastorates or nonpastoral opportunities according to the *kind* of career they wanted and the chances for advance and influence the posts offered. One young man, for example, pointing to Professor Moses Stuart of Andover as a model, confided to his diary that " I hope to become a good writer and thus I can do good on a greater scale; for the press is becoming the great engine for moving the world."[49] And John Todd, an AES beneficiary and 1825 Andover graduate, was utterly unabashed in the care with which he assessed the potential for influence and esteem of every situation, whether it was a boarding arrangement or an invitation to preach before his clerical leaders. When Todd had finished the regular course at Andover Seminary, he accepted a postgraduate fellowship rather than take a parish which he considered to be beneath his talent and promise. The fellowship, Todd confided to his diary, would provide "great opportunities for mental and moral improvement and a good stand from which to take a good settlement, whenever I do settle."[50] In his third year at Andover, the three most important evangelical churches had asked Todd to deliver a fourth of July address "on behalf of the cause of Africa." The invitation was an enormous honor and opportunity, but it had placed Todd in rather a quandary. He knew he was under consideration for a missionary post (the churches were trying to raise

[handwritten margin note: a little romantic...]

[handwritten margin note: a different interp of being "literary"]

money to support an additional missionary, and Andover was the seat of the foreign missionary movement). But even though his elders considered such a post one of the choicest plums that the ministry could offer a young man, one clerical leaders reserved for the most pious and promising, Todd, in the retrospective words of his son, "did not wish to bury himself in heathenism." Yet clearly he could not reject the invitation, which he finally accepted with this assessment of the risks: "If I succeed it will be a great advantage to me. The subject is trite, distant, and stale. If I fail, it will ruin me as to all my prospects."[51]

In addition, the new structure eroded the expectation and, to an extent, even the desire for permanence, especially among those who found themselves in small, remote parishes. "I know," wrote a young man, disappointed at the "circumstances" that had placed him in an obscure church, "that it is better to spend the first years of a man's life in a small town, where he can have more time for study than in a large place."[52] From there, he hoped, he could more easily write himself into a more influential position. A further anecdote from Lyman Beecher's career is perhaps even more illustrative of what had happened to the ideal of permanence by 1830. When Beecher left East Hampton for Litchfield in 1810, the move was of a kind that was still rare, and Beecher was plagued with spiritual doubts about it, even though the justification of greater usefulness certainly fitted the situation. His East Hampton parishioners accused him of ambition, and Beecher himself was troubled about his motives, wondering whether an ungodly enjoyment of fame and esteem had crept in with his growing eminence. At times he fell into a deep "gloom," a preoccupation with "the dark side of appearances," and his wife, Roxanna, would have to reassure him that he had not "done wrong" in the "steps" he had "taken in the affair."[53] (By the time he moved to Boston, moves to stations of greater usefulness had become so common and Beecher's leadership so dominant that he felt no such doubts.) But John Todd, who was perhaps as typical of the rising generation as Beecher was of his, viewed Beecher's move very differently. Todd looked to Beecher as a model and a hero and referred in awe-struck tones to how Beecher had "burst forth upon the world" from the total "obscurity" of East Hampton.[54]

By the 1820s, then, the new ministerial structures and the evangelical crusade that defined and unified them had come to dominate the individual clergyman's sense of himself as an ambassador of God no less than the local town and individual communion had framed the eighteenth-century clergyman's sense of the sacred office. The procedures for recruiting and training him fostered a far stronger sense of himself as a member of a translocal, professional community than as a member of the governing elite of a specific community. The religious press, the annual celebrations of the various benevolent societies, the exhortations at clerical gatherings, as well as the lectures he had heard at seminary extolling the grand evangelical design— all these deluged him with an expansive, general conception of clerical duty. As he took on a parish, he was thus far less likely than his eighteenth-century counterpart had been to think of himself as one who had been called to minister to one congregation for his whole career. He no longer saw himself as permanently bound and belonging to a place because of the character of his office. Instead, he entered it as an agent of organized evangelicalism, the dutiful occupant of a particular post which he might have to surrender if service to the greater evangelical cause demanded it.[55]

Just as the longevity and permanence of pastoral tenure had provided the demographic underpinnings for the localistic, communal character of the ministerial office in eighteenth-century New England, so too the erosion of this localism is revealed in the career patterns of those entering the clergy after 1795. It will be recalled that 71 percent of the Yale graduates entering the ministry from 1702 to 1795 served one pulpit for their entire career, and that until 1775, 79 percent had served only one pulpit while only 7 percent had served three or more churches during their career. By 1815, the pattern was reversed. In technical language, the modal pattern was no longer a single, lifetime pastorate, but a career involving four or more different positions. Of the 162 Yale graduates from 1795 to 1815 who entered the clergy, only 39, or 24 percent, held one pastorate, while more than half had three or more pastorates and 29 percent had four or more positions. An erosion of permanence can be detected in the two decades after the American Revolution, but the really dramatic shift takes place in the next decade. For the years from 1775 to 1795, 57 percent still held just one pulpit, while another 24 percent held only two pulpits. In the next decade (Lyman Beecher's cohort), the reversal occurs: 24 percent had one pulpit while 28 percent had four or more.[56] The figures for the first decade of Andover Seminary matriculants are even more revealing. Of the 164 matriculants from 1810 to 1820, only 14 percent had a career comprising a single pastorate (more than half of these, moreover, lasted less than twenty years.) A third had careers principally outside the ordinary parish, while another 36 percent held between three and ten pastorates, and of these, more than half spent some time in at least one

very important.

nonpastoral position. [57] Put in somewhat different terms: of the Yale-graduated pastors through 1775, 60 percent had a single pastorate lasting more than twenty years, while less than 10 percent of the Andover matriculants from 1810 to 1820 remained in a single pastorate for as many as twenty years.

From one perspective, there was considerable continuity between the eighteenth-century and the early nineteenth-century New England clergy. Churchmen retained a firm sense of public guardianship, even though they looked to the collective ministry, rather than to the combined exertions of clergy and magistracy, to maintain social order and associated order with a special evangelical domain rather than with a well-ordered town. Moreover, the focal point of evangelicalism remained the individual communion, even though pastoral permanence had been undermined and was rapidly fading away. In their design to evangelize the nation, churchmen had set out not only to convert, but to church, the American people, and their strenuous efforts to expand the clergy and support home missionaries were designed to provide every thousand souls with a settled, full-time, and fully trained preacher. But the structural transformation beneath this continuing tradition of clerical public guardianship should not be underestimated. The clergy had become a different kind of social institution: organized within society along new lines, it stationed the minister toward both his particular constituents and the broader community in new ways—ways that altered the character of clergy and religion as public forces and as social institutions. The full consequences of the change, however, emerged most clearly in the abolitionism that developed out of the new evangelicalism and the challenges it posed to clergy, communicant, and society.

5

Abolition Now! The Emergence
of the Evangelical Abolitionist

In the early 1830s a new and demanding style of public commitment emerged from within evangelicalism as a small number of evangelicals began to insist that slavery was a sin and that the true Christian was bound to work for immediate emancipation.[1] The new evangelicalism was the immediate source of one significant strand of immediatism, for evangelicalism was a direct outgrowth of the ideology and institutions of evangelical public guardianship that had emerged in the 1820s. In some ways, indeed, abolitionists carried the logic and structure of evangelical public guardianship to a logical end point. The vocabulary of sin that they applied to slavery, their conception of clerical duty, and their organizational models and strategies were all extensions of evangelical ideas and agencies devised in the twenties.[2] Moreover, immediatism was largely a generational phenomenon, taking hold most broadly and firmly among those who had reached adulthood and whose formative spiritual experiences had taken place during the 1820s and early 1830s under the aegis of the new evangelicalism. In addition, those evangelicals who did adopt abolitionism in the early 1830s were almost all ministers or candidates for the ministry who came to their immediatism out of an earlier commitment to the Gospel ministry and took their cues as to the nature of their sacred calling from the evangelical campaign to redeem the nation.[3] In this sense, abolitionism became the focal point, not only of their Christian commitment, but of their sense of ministerial calling as well.

In certain ways, the origins of this abolitionist commitment lay in the particular character of the spiritual episodes that had driven the immediatist cadre toward the ministry in the first place. From the 1760s to about 1820, conversion among communicants of New England's established churches had been a gradual process.[4] Even when it took place within a revival (which by 1800 was increasingly the case), the overall spiritual hegira had begun months, if not a year or two, earlier and was not fully completed until well after the converting episode itself had taken place. Of the various stages a person went through on the way to becoming a regenerate and sanctified Christian, only conviction and conversion had centered within the revival itself. Although the general tone of awakening in a community frequently moved penitents to anxiety about their souls, the first step of heightened personal interest in the doctrines of salvation had ordinarily begun privately and well before the revival. In fact, these revivals usually happened only after a sufficient number of communicants had been prepared to receive evangelical Truth. In this sense, conversion—a real event in time—planted the seed of grace in carefully prepared soil. But this seed then had to be nurtured through a "growth in grace" which was marked by "clear and consistent piety" and witnessed in solid Christian deportment. Conversion was certified by formal admittance to full, communing membership in the church only after the immediate emotionality of the converting episode had subsided and consistent piety and moral behavior practiced for several months.[5] By the mid-twenties, however, many evangelical youths were having conversions of a rather different character. Though they certainly had been subjected to a firm regimen of evangelical indoctrination and nurture and may well have had bouts of spiritual concern and anxiety before, they *experienced* conversion not as a gradual process, but as an abrupt, cataclysmic, and deeply transforming event. Conversion and regeneration for them was less the careful construction of a mature Christian personality than a concrete experience of "rebirth," in which they felt themselves to have in fact died to sin and been born again into righteousness, to have broken abruptly, immediately, and utterly with their sinful past.[6]

The intensity and totality of this sense of transformation partly reflected the combined force of the spiritual and secular anxieties that particularly encumbered coming of age for this generation. The twenties converts were perhaps the first generation to be fully reared within the new evangelicalism of the early nineteenth century, which both doctrinally and institutionally had come to center upon conversion and which had ever more firmly encased the life and sensibility of its communicants within an evangelical idiom. At least one parent, if not both, and most, if not all, of the significant elders in their lives were professing and active Christians who considered furnishing children with a solid Christian character the highest parental duty. The responsibility did not stop with the inculcation of the appropriate moral and spiritual precepts: conversion was the ultimate parental goal.[7] By 1800, in fact, conversion had essentially become an experience of youth, that period in the life cycle that we separate into adolescence and young adulthood. Indoctrination and preparation for the event began at an early age, but as children approached youth, their elders used all the means at their disposal to push the young toward conversion. Youth was the time of life when conversion was expected to happen if it was going to occur at all, and elders thus worked to ensure that it would occur before adulthood was reached.[8] But the intensity with which elders bore down on youths of this generation also stemmed from the fact that various economic, demographic, and cultural pressures were forcing youths to make their lives away from family farm and home community. Coming of age increasingly involved departing from parental vision and control, and the prospect of their children leaving parental control without having become Christian filled elders with terror. Thus the youth of a congregation were gathered into special study, inquiry, and mutual improvement societies and deluged with lectures and advice manuals, all of which were designed to press the basic ideas of sin, repentance, and salvation upon them. Everyday events, the personal traumas and anxieties of youthful life, and local tragedies were all held up to them as matters freighted with the warning that they should look to their souls before it was too late, that only the bosom of the Lord could keep them safe from temptation, the ravages of sin, and the terrors of death.

Evangelical anxiety was not the only travail this generation faced as it came of age. In the seventeenth and eighteenth centuries, arriving at adulthood had frequently meant settling into the occupation, station, and place to which one was "bred" and occupying it for the rest of one's life. In addition, a young man's father or some surrogate, because of his control of the resources needed to prepare for and enter adulthood, made the basic decisions concerning a young man's adult vocation and community. Independence had come with the assumption of the marital status and occupational position that ensured stability and freed one from economic dependence upon elders.[9] The generation coming of age after 1815 was, on an unprecedented scale, a dislocated generation, forced to strike out on its own, making its way as it went with few family resources to begin with or fall back upon, with few clear-cut institutions to channel it, and with few unambiguous cues to follow. For them, coming of age and young adulthood had become an unavoidable process of continuing self-construction, which at times amounted to a kind of vagabondage, moving from place to place and pursuit to pursuit, trying, in the words of one particularly battered young man, to "get a hold" on life. Circumstance forced them to leave the parental household well before they were ready to marry and become the head of a household and to forge a life beyond family farm and home community. The initiative in the process, moreover, increasingly fell to young men themselves. How to begin, where to go, what to do, and how to proceed once they had struck out on their own were all matters over which their parents could exert little control. They were essentially free to construct their own lives.[10]

But if it was a condition of unprecedented freedom with a myriad of apparent choices and opportunities, it was at the same time a formless and fluid world that carried a heavy tax of anxiety and uncertainty and seemed to demand will, persistence, and extraordinary degrees of self-control if it was to be mastered or survived. Indeed, the language young men fell back upon to describe their lives reveals something of the character of the world they faced. They refer to life as a scramble, a treacherous maze, a whirlwind; and they speak of the hopes dashed and expectations disappointed and of the obstacles, treachery, and opposition they continually confront. Preoccupation with mental and physical health, notations of melancholy, dyspepsia, and depression, and fears of madness parade across the pages of their letters, diaries, and journals, and all bear painful witness to the psychic burdens they carried. One young man, for example, confiding to his correspondent that children seemed to turn away in fear whenever he passed, wondered whether in fact he "had crossed the Rubicon of madness."[11] A letter John Todd (born in 1800) wrote to his fiancée at the age of twenty-six, just after he had negotiated the shoals of youth, provides a revealing example of this generation's experience of coming of age:

> My father fell under a heavy blow of providence . . . and I was born an orphan, shelterless, penniless. I was about six years old when I knelt over my father's grave and vowed, even then, to rise above my circumstances. I soon determined to have a liberal education. My friends opposed, obstacles were thrown in my way, everything opposed. I rose above all; I went to college half-fitted; I was sick much of the time owing to too

severe application and anxiety. I pressed on, rose above all, and now stand where I can see my way clear.[12]

Evangelical youths of the 1820s and 1830s thus found themselves caught in a psychological whipsaw as they approached adulthood. As they consulted their own impulses and wishes and relied upon their own judgment to work out life goals and improvise strategies to meet them, they came to feel, as John Todd did, that they stood alone, with only their own will and exertion to enable them to survive and succeed. They found themselves immersed in petty details and small but burdensome daily decisions—whether to live with a relative or in a boarding house, whom to seek out for employment or patronage, whether to change situations and seek out different "advantages" and other dilemmas. And unlike many of their seventeenth- and eighteenth-century counterparts, they could no longer take their worldly portion as a given, ordered by God's providence, defined by parental resources, and maintained by their own virtue and hard work. With few institutions to protect and guide them, they, like John Todd, who vowed to "rise above all" (and whose address at his Yale commencement was entitled "the Influence of a High Standard of attainment"), gave free rein to self-assertion and pride and projected dreams of fame, wealth, and success as they constructed myths of self-help and the sure reward of virtue and hard work to sustain them.[13] Thus was theirs a condition of acute self-preoccupation, which fostered, if it did not demand, a sense of self-esteem and autonomy. (It was a situation to which Ralph Waldo Emerson's doctrine of self-reliance spoke with considerable resonance.) But at the same time, their religion subjected this sense of self to sustained attack. As their elders tried to drive them toward conversion and the surrender of self it demanded, they deliberately undermined this confidence in what amounted to a sustained assault on the very self-esteem and autonomy toward which the young were groping. Again and again, pastors told them that their concerns with self and dreams of fame and fortunes were the symptoms of their depravity.

Evangelical youths might well live within this tension for some time, attending services and listening to their ministers preach the doctrines of divine sovereignty, sin, and the atonement, without any immediate sense that they themselves were directly implicated in them. Many, in fact, groping toward autonomy, went through periods of at least tacit rejection of the idea that nothing they did or were could help them earn salvation; and some even found release in apostasy as they sought out religions with devotional styles that built upon autonomy and self-esteem rather than demanded renuncia-tion of them.[14] But for most of those who remained within the fold, sooner or later the evangelical message would strike home and cata-pult them into a transforming conversion experience. The immediate circumstances of vulnerability to the message varied—the crises of departure and vocational decision, familial conflict, the death of a peer, a particularly acute sense of disappointment, loneliness, or isola-tion. But whatever the particular weakness in their resistance to evangelical exhortation, the spiritual process that broke through it was much the same. The doctrines of sin and salvation took on deep personal meaning as penitents came to feel that their pastor's descrip-tion of sin and the torment of a life outside God's embrace was a direct portrayal of them. They came to see their lives in a wholly new light as a sense of their utter depravity hit them with cataclysmic force. They became convinced that they were slaves to their own implacable desires for self-gratification and that their whole lives had been given over to a welter of forbidden desires. As this conviction of their total depravity washed over them, guilt and self-loathing over-whelmed them, and they succumbed to such an intense sense of their deserved condemnation that they almost craved death and damnation. Release, in the form of an overwhelming sense of deliverance, came with their realization that under Christ's atonement God could and would grant salvation and that they could have it if they would truly repent and throw themselves on God's mercy. Powerful feelings of joy and love for a God who would grant them eternal life in spite of their sin replaced their anxiety and self-loathing as they came to feel that they had entered a wholly different mode of being.[15]

The intensity of this sense of transformation and deliverance undoubtedly reflected the power of the anxieties behind conversion. But the sense of rebirth itself was equally a function of changes in the central ritual—the revival—through which conversion took place. A revival of the earlier decades was less a specific event than, in their terms, a "season" through which a church periodically passed. The term essentially described a condition of deepened spiritual concern among communicants and a period in the life of the church when it had a greater concentration of converts than usual. Revivals had built up gradually, lasted from six to eighteen months, and then had gradu-ally waned. Whenever a minister detected enough spiritual concern (concern which he had tried to cultivate, of course) to indicate the possible onset of a season of revival, he would preach a sermon announcing the presence of "special grace" and warn those outside the fold to turn to God before the extraordinary opportunity passed.

Throughout the period of revival, special prayer meetings would take place. In addition, those concerned about their souls would gather in anxious or inquiry meetings, penitents would intensify their private, or "closet," devotions and personal consultations with ministers and elders, and to maintain the common sense of awakening, collective services of various sorts would be held several times a week. But even though collective awakening was the distinguishing characteristic of a revival season, private devotion and consultation with the pastor retained primacy in the actual event of conversion. In this sense, the revivals of the early decades were harvests of individual converts: conversion took place *during* a revival largely because of the heightened spiritual concern of the church, but it did not really take place *within* the revival. These revivals provided a spiritual atmosphere that helped individuals go through conversion.[16]

During the 1820s, the revival became a special event. With its own particular mechanism and dynamism, it began more abruptly and burned far more intensely for three to six weeks before it burned out. Churchmen of the earlier decades had taken pains to ensure that the emotionality of the revival did not pass from intensity to disorder. They had maintained strict devotional boundaries between church members and those who were unconverted but awakened, gathering the awakened into separate inquiry and anxious meetings while putting the members into prayer meetings where they would pray for God to bestow his grace upon those who were unconverted. By emphasizing personal devotions and associating conversion with a "state of humility" in which the communicant withdrew for private prayer and introspection, they had preserved the privacy and essential individuality of conversion. They kept leadership of the revival and its meetings in the hands of ordinary authorities: the regular minister, or someone he had called in for assistance, presided over all public worship sessions and conducted the inquiry sessions; elders or deacons conducted the prayer meetings; and women did not engage in public prayer. To make certain that mere fervor was not mistaken for genuine piety, they refused to admit the putative convert to church membership until after a period of spiritual probation.[17]

The revivals of the twenties, however, broke down these boundaries and this decorum as they generated their own logic and rules.[18] Smaller devotional sessions and private prayer continued to play a role, but the general assemblage became the driving force of the revival. Using what was referred to as a "protracted meeting," these sessions would go on almost continuously for anywhere from four to twenty days. The regular minister or a visiting preacher, called upon (frequently at the insistence of the congregation) for his reputation as an especially effective preacher, usually presided over these meetings, but ministers from the town and neighborhood and divinity students were needed to help keep the meeting and revival going. The protracted meeting brought together all the different groups and spiritual exercises that traditionalists had labored to keep separate. In what critics condemned as a spiritual three-ring circus, it deployed prayer, exhortation, song, and confession to meld anxious penitents, established church members, men and women, newly saved, and young and old into a fervent community of feeling. In sermon and exhortation preachers addressed the anxious, sometimes even calling upon sinners by name, as they tried to get them to realize the peril of their souls. When the penitents became especially overwrought with a sense of sin, they came forward to what were eventually designated as "anxious benches" to be preached at and prayed over until they cast off sin and surrendered to God. There they would confess and testify to their awful wickedness in open and tearful agony, often punctuating it with "audible groans and boisterous gestures" while those around them beseeched God to grant them grace. When the penitents began to feel a sense of release and deliverance, they frequently went off with a saved Christian to pray in thanksgiving and in praise to God. But soon they would return to the protracted meeting as they themselves now took on the role of evangelist, exhorting those still unsaved to repent and receive the deliverance which they themselves now enjoyed.[19]

Thus did the revivals of the 1820s concentrate and orchestrate emotion, gathering the agony, the beseeching, and the ecstacy into a single emotional force which it turned against the unconverted. If the earlier revivals can be said to have created a spiritual atmosphere that helped conversion take place, these revivals can be said to have assaulted the communicant with collective religious emotion. In the terms of Charles Grandison Finney, they so intensified the "heat" or "temperature" of a church that they "broke down" all resistance to the gospel message.[20] In this sense, the revival itself was *the* extraordinary and transforming event in the communicant's life. Not only did one experience a profound inner change, but it was the revival and the revival alone, with its intense and concentrated emotionality, that wrought the change.

The 1820s revivals, then, were rituals of rebirth in ways that the earlier revivals had not been. The converts coming out of these revivals—having gone into them with the bundle of anxieties described—experienced a dramatic sense that they had surrendered, not just their will, but their whole sinful self, and made themselves a totally "new heart." In its force and dramaturgy, the revival both intensified and objectified the sense of total change, as the communicant went from the terrible bondage of sin and self to the joy of righteousness in a matter of hours or days. The revival heightened the penitent's identity as a depraved sinner almost beyond endurance and then assailed it as sinner and evangelist, assisted by the emotionality of the greater audience, wrestled for the sinner's soul until he finally shed his sinful being, an act symbolized by his movement first to the anxious bench and then to the prayer of the saved. Finally, immediate action sealed the sense of the totality of the change as the convert, transported by the fervor of deliverance, returned to urge those still enslaved in sin to repent and surrender to God. Thus, within the revival itself, communicants moved into a mode of feeling and acting diametrically opposed to the sin and anxiety of their previous life. In place of a posture of alienated and perilous hostility to God, they experienced a reconciliation with God in which they felt themselves become fully dedicated servants of his will. In addition, communicants were drawn into full participation in a community of love. In song, prayer, and exhortation, revivals focused on expressions of love to and from God; but perhaps even more importantly, as a collective ritual, the revival revolved around the active expression of evangelical love and concern. Converts began as the objects of concern of the revival and its professing participants and ended up in a posture of intense solicitude for those around them who remained the victims of sin.[21]

Among certain converts, this intense experience of rebirth and the spiritual activism it fostered created an equally intense sense of spiritual calling. It was certainly not new for a convert to develop a sense that he had been called to the Gospel ministry. Here again, however, the distinguishing feature was the immediacy and intensity of the feeling. A "call" had traditionally grown out of the gradual "growth in grace" by which penitents, after the actual event of conversion, had come to realize that God had indeed bestowed his saving grace upon them. Thus both in time and in character, a call had usually been distinct from conversion itself.[22] It took the form of the realization that God had designated one for the ministry, and recognition and acceptance of the call was the initial step toward the ministry, but a young man did not think of himself as having entered upon his sacred office until he had finished formal preparation and was at least liscensed, if not ordained. Many of the ministerial recruits from the new revivals, however, possessed a far more dramatic and immediate sense of calling. They saw their whole lives as changed, feeling that they must drop what they were doing or had planned to do and dedicate themselves fully to God's service. Moreover, they felt that this life of active consecration and service had begun *now*, even though no specific office had been entered. Indeed, they had acted on this sense in the very revivals that had converted them, leading prayers, counseling the anxious, and exhorting their unconverted friends; and some even went on to assist in other revivals. As Theodore Weld (who became perhaps the most effective apostle of abolitionism in the 1830s) put it, recalling his own conversion by Finney in 1826, conversion "put an end to my studying. I was with him in his meetings, speaking and laboring all that summer."[23] Weld and those like him thus emerged from the revivals that converted them, not only with a sense of rebirth, but with an equally deep sense that God had chosen them as instruments of his purposes and that their agency and duties had already begun. Servants of God was not something they were meant to become but something they already were.[24]

This sense of agency, in turn, fostered a conception of the sacred office that essentially transcended existing clerical offices, even though a pastorate was the eventual goal for which they set about preparing themselves. To some degree, of course, clergymen had always defined their ultimate office in terms that went beyond their specific charge. The architects of the new evangelicalism, men, like Beecher and Finney, who provided the models for this generation, had conducted their careers according to a comprehensive vision of the evangelical cause and had indoctrinated the new generation with the need to evangelize the nation. Moreover, by the late twenties this rhetoric had developed a millennial cast. As Lyman Beecher put it, "It was the opinion of Edwards that the millennium would commence in America. When I first encountered this opinion I thought it chimerical: but all Provident developments since and all existing signs of the times lend corroboration to it."[25] The most significant sign of all, furthermore, was the new revival, whose power and scope had ranged far beyond the simple shower of grace ordinarily associated with a revival. As *The Spirit of the Pilgrims*, the leading New England evangelical journal, put it in 1831, "We can only say, the night is far spent and the day is at hand, 'lo, this is our God, we have waited for him. Joy to the world, the Lord is Come.'"[26] To the older generation, this millennial rhetoric provided a vocabulary that could encompass the evangelical system they had constructed and the unparalleled successes they seemed to be having. The fervent ministerial recruits from the new revivals, however, took their definition of their essential spiritual task from this sense of millennial expectancy. They felt that God had called them to usher in the millennium, and this notion of their millennial agency dominated their subsequent sense of their essential office, even though its specific dimensions were not always very easy to fathom.[27]

On the surface, it was the ardor of their piety and the breadth of their evangelical vision that seemed to distinguish these young men. At the core of this dedication, however, was a rather different style of vocational piety, one characterized by a demanding inner spiritual discipline and an equally compelling need for continuing moral activism. Rebirth had broken their bondage to sin, but continuing triumph over it could only come if their striving toward perfect holiness—a frame free of sin and filled with evangelical concern to redeem the world—was unrelenting. Religious conversion is frequently accompanied by a sense of transcendence over the world, the feeling that one now possesses a timeless relationship to God and has entered a mode of being in which worldly conditions no longer have any real significance.[28] For the recruits from the new revivals, however, rebirth led, not to a transcendent disregard of the world, but to implacable hostility toward it. Their previous ambivalent sense of the world, as at once an emporium for the gratification of their desires and dreams and a treacherous labyrinth, was replaced by the conviction that the world itself was sin and that as Christians born to righteousness they were as much obliged to combat the sinful world as they were to rid themselves of all remnants of sin. Rebirth thus in no way diminished their sense of the reality of sin, but created intense hatred of it as the horrendous bondage from which they had been delivered and against which they had been called to wage unrelenting war. It was in such activism that they both realized and intensified their identity as reborn Christians and agents of God's ultimate millennial purpose. As one evangelical put it, it was not "till we rise into a higher sphere, *the sphere of doing*" that we can "rise to the knowledge of God," for it was in doing that "we give life to our speculations, and substance to our creed, and meaning to our professions."[29] It was when they felt themselves to relent in this activist expression of their piety that they felt themselves bereft of a sense of their reconciliation and closeness to God and felt that they had let their own impurities deflect them from duty.[30]

The inner dynamism of their sense of call and duty was reflected in their spiritual and vocational behavior following conversion.[31] Like Theodore Weld, many immediately expressed their consecration to God by enlisting as assistants in the new revivals before enrolling in the institutions that would give them the formal training they needed to become full-fledged Gospel preachers. In addition, their activities in the colleges, institutes, and seminaries both reflected and intensified the activist imperative within their piety. Their elders, of course, continually subjected them to indoctrination both about the importance of specific tasks and about the urgency of the need to evangelize the nation and convert the world. At Andover, for example, the cause of foreign missions was given particular emphasis, while Oneida Institute in Whitesborough, New York, had been deliberately founded to equip the recruits from the middle and late twenties for full-fledged roles in the new revivals, and Lane Theological Seminary, reorganized in 1832 with Lyman Beecher at its head, was expressly designed to serve as the major training institution for that evangelical cadre which, in the words of the Reverend Thomas Skinner "would bring the millennium to the very door."[32] Most importantly, however, the ministerial students themselves took the initiative in turning the schools into institutions for deepening their piety and consecration. They set up special study groups, organized ad hoc societies for honing their awareness of the sins they had to combat and the duties they had to perform, gave spiritual advice and chastisement to each other, and conducted numerous special prayer and devotional sessions. In addition, they turned the school environs into an arena of practical piety, assisting in revivals in the neighborhood, helping organize auxiliaries of the various benevolent societies, and setting up and conducting Sabbath schools.[33]

The pursuit of formal training, however, also fostered a kind of vocational impatience. A seminary, as the term connotes, was essentially "a peaceful, consecrated" place, "where the wicked . . . trouble not, where the cares of the world oppress not," to which one withdrew to prepare for the ministry by "associating almost exclusively with those who have drunk at the fountains of ancient and modern science, who have also sanctified their literary acquisitions at the altar of heaven."[34] But in becoming ministerial students, these young men had not ceased to be evangelists with a need to maintain their spiritual and vocational witness by doing. Moreover, with the spiritual life style of the seminaries heightening this sense, they frequently began to feel uncomfortable as divinity *students* with a life of mere preparation, which often seemed too far removed physically as well as psychologically from the activism their sense of consecration to God required. While the activities in seminary and its environs provided some outlet for this vocational impatience, many young men found them insufficient and interrupted their formal preparation to enlist as full-time agents with one benevolent enterprise or another, or, if they had had a full year or more of seminary, take on a home missionary assignment.[35]

This activism, however, did not always relieve their spiritual restlessness. Agencies by their very nature were partial and limited: while they provided one with concrete and important tasks to perform, they were still not the same as the full delivery of the Gospel message. They also were not permanent positions but a form of temporary service and thus, for all the sense of purposeful activity they allowed, still represented a delay in attaining the pastoral position to which these young men thought they were headed. In addition, the life of an agent was a difficult and lonely one. It meant a constant sojourn, moving from town to town, meeting with indifference and sometimes with open hostility.[36] But perhaps most importantly, such a life frequently fostered a sense of spiritual malaise and evangelical failure. Cut off from the spiritual communion and fellowship which they had enjoyed in revival, college, and seminary and which had kindled their piety, they felt themselves sliding into spiritual indifference and sloth. Moreover, they attributed the indifference they faced and the lack of progress in their campaigns to their own impurity, and looked upon their hardships as God's punishment for their failure to live up to their vows. Then, for one reason or a combination of them—a sense of delay in becoming a preacher, belief that they did indeed need more spiritual and formal preparation, or a need to regain the spiritual communion and intensity an educational institution could provide—they would re-enroll in a seminary or possibly take on a regular parish.[37]

Such, then, was the spiritual and vocational context out of which evangelical commitment to abolitionism was forged. Abolitionism found its most fertile ground among those evangelicals who were caught in the grip of this new and dynamic form of sacred vocation, but had not yet translated it into a form that matched either the intensity of their inner consecration or the scope of the task to which they had dedicated themselves. They possessed a sense of calling that united a drive for perfect personal holiness with insistent moralism. This spirituality, in turn, was attached to a notion of sacred office that extended well beyond specific tasks and positions to embrace the ultimate millennial cause. In effect, they were caught up in an open-ended spiritual and vocational dialectic: their piety demanded expression in concrete moral activism, pursuit of which fostered a need for even greater holiness, which itself then needed more satisfactory channels of expression. Existing institutional forms, moreover, proved inadequate to contain or express a sense of continuing witness, but the form it took had to satisfy both their millennial purpose and the demands of their perfectionist spirituality. Significantly, very few of the evangelicals who became abolitionist activists in the 1830s had worked out a settled ministerial identity at the time of their adherence to abolitionism. A large majority became abolitionists while they were still ministerial candidates, agents in one of the enterprises, or young preachers who were serving as home missionaries rather than as regular "stated" pastors. Moreover, most of the evangelical abolitionists—men like Beriah Green, Amos A. Phelps, or Elizur Wright—who had been ordained before becoming abolitionists had not really settled upon a pastorate as the essential vehicle for expressing their sense of sacred calling but had moved out of the parish.[38]

Although these were the conditions from which evangelical abolitionism emerged, the commitment itself was formed around a specific idea, namely, the notion that slavery was sin, an idea which grew directly from standard evangelical images of sin. Sin was "a temper of mind," a disposition of heart and will in "obstinate dissent and enmity against God." Churchmen had traditionally considered pride the essential attribute of a sinful frame of mind, but by the early years of the nineteenth century they had come to see selfishness, constant craving for self-gratification, as the fundamental temper of sin.[39] Whatever the particular sin might be, they depicted it as an appetite or craving which eventually became an all-consuming lust, leading to temporal and eternal destruction. This vision of "the nature and consequences of sin" found its fullest expression in the idea of intemperance, which by the 1820s was considered the most heinous example of sin as self-gratification. Intemperance, indeed, gave sin a horrifying tangibility, providing churchmen with a way to depict graphically the course of sin from the initial desire through to the final ruin. Whatever the course of a particular descent into hell, somewhere along the line the sinner usually fell into intemperance, and began to turn his energies to satisfying a thirst that quickly took control of him and led inexorably to the commission of the most horrendous crimes. Indeed, the tableaux depicting intemperance invariably had a final scene in which the opposition between selfishness and benevolence was played out in stark terms: the drunkard not only destroyed himself, but sacrificed the health and well-being of wife and children (usually murdering one of them in a drunken rage), toward whom he was by nature and religion required to exercise the greatest benevolence. The portrait of intemperance as sin went further, furnishing evangelicals with metaphors for describing the world of nineteenth-century America. They used intemperance to depict how the pervasive materialism of American culture enslaved the soul. Indeed, evangelicals invariably pictured intemperance as an intrinsic element of economic life: the strain of competition and the pursuit of gain was either sustained by drink (the excitement of commerce and speculation needing the artificial "stimulus" of alcohol), or drink furnished evening refuge from the market place, or, finally, the only solace for ruin or disappointment.[40]

The attack on slavery appropriated and expanded these images of the nature of sin and the world. Slavery, even more than intemperance, exemplified self-gratification: beyond sacrificing the needs of others, it appropriated the whole human being and turned the slave into an object whose whole purpose was to serve the desires of the master. As Beriah Green, one of the earliest evangelical abolitionists, put it, "His wife, his children, himself, soul and body, another man, under the protection of bloody laws, seizes as his property and turns them to such account as his pampered appetites and inflamed passions demand."[41] The most vivid result of slavery (to which abolitionists turned again and again) was a system of lust, of unleashed, illicit sexuality. Slavery made the female slave the helpless victim of the master's insatiable sexual desires, as, under slavery, one early abolitionist wrote, "the marriage relation, the source of all others, is out of the question. And in its stead is introduced a system of Universal Concubinage."[42]

This portrait of slavery as sin exemplified the general existence and operation of sin in American society. If their conception of intemperance had reflected the evangelical's sense of the nature of the world and how it encased the individual in sin, slavery provided a more systematic and inclusive image of the sinfulness of American society. Slavery was not simply a state of being and behavior, it was also an institution whose tenacles spread throughout the society and implicated everyone, North and South alike. As an economic system, of course, slavery was the opposite of a free-labor system. In this vision, however, slavery in its essence did not differ from the broader American life but seemed to take to its logical end point society's lust for gain and the willingness to sacrifice all to selfish ends. This point was made most vividly in abolitionist portraits of the slave trade: there the slave was dehumanized into a commodity, solely a source of profit for the trader, whose relation to the slave was totally commercial and exploitative, utterly unalloyed with feelings of responsibility or benevolence. Slavery thus captured and objectified the deepest evangelical sense, not only of the nature of sin as lust, but of American society as totally encrusted in sin, as wholly opposite in its structure and modes to the disinterested benevolence of the divine order.[43]

Such unalloyed sinfulness was a powerful and resonant image, one to which young evangelicals laboring under a demanding and expansive sense of spiritual vocation were particularly susceptible. If slavery was the ultimate embodiment of lust and self-gratification, then the "downtrodden, helpless, hopeless" slave would be the ultimate object of genuine benevolent concern.[44] Indeed, as one young evangelical, James Thome, put it, "I know of no subject which takes such strong hold of a man as does abolition. It seizes the conscience with an authoritarian grasp, it runs across the path of the guilty, goads him, haunts him and rings in his ears the cry of blood. It builds up a wall to heaven before and around him! It goes with the eye of God and searches his heart with a scrutiny too strict to be eluded. It writes 'thou art the one' upon the heart of every oppressor."[45] More central, however, than the fact of the discovery of the claims of the slave on evangelical energies and affections was the nature of the recognition of the sin of slavery. In a very specific sense, the evangelical abolitionists of the early thirties were converts. Immediate abolition was at heart a theological conception that united the image of the sin of slavery with the basic evangelical conception of Christian duty toward sin. Moreover, the final step in the making of an evangelical abolitionist was an explicit spiritual experience that fastened the commitment to abolitionism as firmly as their initial conversions had fixed their commitment to God and the Gospel ministry. The insight that slavery was sin hit them with a force comparable to that with which a sense of their own depravity had originally struck. The truth of the doctrine of immediate abolition was accepted in the same way in which a convert was said to have a "saving knowledge" of Christ, and it similarly became the foundation of Christian identity and action.

The conversion to immediatism came in several ways. Some were brought to it by a charismatic figure with whom they had an intimate spiritual relationship. Those in the grip of the millennial spiritual discipline were especially dependent upon and susceptible to the influence of spiritual peers. Institutional decorum and established rituals had played a relatively minor role in shaping their spirituality. Their model of a religious community was less the ordinary church than the new revival, in which intensity of piety, rather than designated position, conferred spiritual authority. Moreover, a particular form of spiritual friendship was an essential part of their religious experience, serving both confessional and vocational functions. They prayed and worshipped together, chastised each other for spiritual failings, discussed the obligations of their common consecration, and spurred each other to greater fidelity to the divine cause. Frequently, a young man looked for direction and spiritual guidance to those he considered more advanced in piety and dedication. A letter from J. L. Tracy to Theodore Weld in 1831 exemplifies this kind of spiritual relationship. Weld wrote to Tracy, suggesting that he had let his trust in God wane, and Tracy replied, assuring Weld that his "kind admonition will not be lost on me," and confessing that "I never expect to find another such friend in this world and I trust I shall so act so much the part of a disciple of Jesus as not to forfeit what I have already received, your own confidence and friendship."[46] Many of the initial leaders of immediatism came to their abolitionism through this kind of relationship. A spiritual exemplar would inundate his "friend" with antislavery tracts and personal letters devoted to the subject and would bombard him with direct personal counsel and prayer sessions until the friend recognized the awful truth of slavery and committed himself to its eradication. Theodore Weld, far and away the most effective apostle of abolitionism, was brought to it by the English emancipationist Charles Stuart, an older man who had long been Weld's confessor, confidant, and closest friend. Weld, in turn, converted Beriah Green, Elizur Wright, James Birney, and H. B. Stanton, among many others.[47]

More systematically organized and collective efforts also converted ardent young evangelicals to the abolitionist cause. These conclaves occurred in the early thirties in many of the colleges and seminaries where Yankee evangelical influence was especially strong. Williams, Western Reserve, Amherst, Bowdoin, Dartmouth, Hamilton, and Union Colleges all had them, as did such institutes and seminaries as Lane, Oneida, Andover, and Bangor. The prototype of the more collective ritual for converting people to immediatism, however, was the famed "Lane Debates," the eighteen-day series of meetings that Weld directed at Lane Theological Seminary in Cincinnati, Ohio, in March 1834.[48] The debates were wildly successful: they converted almost the entire student body to abolitionism and provided the model for the attempt of the next few years to convert the whole evangelical community. The term *debates* is a misnomer. What happened at Lane in March 1834 was really a revival. The sessions were orchestrated as a protracted meeting, designed to establish conviction about slavery in the same way that a revival established conviction of sin, by assaulting the emotions until Truth was felt with such intensity that it became the ground for all subsequent spiritual action. The mechanism for the actual conversion to immediatism, moreover, was "sympathy." The meetings were organized to evoke "an excitement of sympathy" that so deeply involved the students in the plight of the slave that they would *feel* the utter necessity for immediate emancipation and stop tarrying and act.

The sessions devoted an immense amount of time to prayer: prayers opened and closed each session and punctuated each exhortation and confession. Everyone was implored to turn his private prayers to the subject. In no sense were these prayers *pro forma*. Based upon the "prayer of faith" used in revivals, they were meant to cleanse the group's spirit and prepare it for the reception of Truth. Testimony and confession similarly punctuated the sessions as speakers, especially those who had first-hand knowledge of slavery, like William Allen, a Southerner who even stood to inherit slaves, and James Bradley, a former slave and the one black student in the seminary, tried to engender in others a feeling for its horrors. The orchestration of the whole process was very deliberate and very effective. The lectures, confessions, prayers, and exhortation combined to arouse the deepest sympathy for the slave victims as well as deep loathing for the sin itself, and to foster an inescapable inner necessity to act. In Weld's words, "Light was elicited, principles fixed, and action followed."[49] Moreover, just as recruits from the new revivals felt themselves obliged to translate their consecration into immediate action, the Lane students immediately began to put their newly discerned principles into practice. They formed an antislavery society, set up Bible schools and various benevolent agencies among the free blacks of Cincinnati, and enrolled themselves as agents of abolition, traveling around and trying to convert the larger evangelical community. And when the trustees tried to disband the antislavery society, the students withdrew from the seminary, condemning it as un-Christian and unfit to equip them as ministers of the Gospel.[50]

Whether it happened individually through personal charismatic influence or in a more collective ritual, the conversion to abolition elevated one to a new spiritual and vocational plateau. Immediatism was less a program of what to do about slavery than, in evangelical terms, a "disposition," a state of being in which the heart and will were set irrevocably against slavery. In the heartfelt reception of the truth about slavery, immediate abolition was followed by psychological and doctrinal necessity in the same way that hatred of sin followed a saving knowledge of Christ. Indeed, for the abolitionist, the conversion to immediatism bound one's whole sense of identity and esteem as a Christian and an agent of God to antislavery activism, making immediatism the sign of whether or not a person was a saved Christian and a faithful servant. Slavery and the slave provided a unified focus for the two basic emotions around which the sense of Christian being and vocation revolved—the genuine and deeply felt hatred of sin and the equally fervent evangelical love for the victim of sin. Slavery provided a compelling focus for the sense of duty, while the slave became the object of the love by which they marked their sense of distance from the sinfulness of selfish impulses and worldly attachments. For the abolitionist converts, abolition thus became the essential embodiment of their sense of sacred vocation. As the objectification of the sin of the world, slavery became *the* foe to be conquered in the millennial battle to which they had consecrated themselves.[51]

Abolition in a very precise way, then, was a form of evangelicalism, and they were its evangelists. Their mode of persuasion was identical in tone, structure, and epistemology to the address that any evangelical preacher worth his salt would use to break down a sinner's resistance to truth. Slavery was sin and as sin had to be relinquished and fought, just as in a revival a sinner had to repent immediately and turn his energies against sin. Indeed, for the abolitionist activist to insist on anything less was unthinkable. Gerrit Smith put it very explicitly when he challenged Lyman Beecher's refusal to adopt immediatism while he nonetheless avowed that slavery was evil. "Now if I were standing by," Smith wrote, "whilst you were laboring to bring a fellow sinner to repentance, and, instead of countenancing your solemn and urgent exhortation, you should relieve his pressed conscience by telling him, not yet, you would not be likely to number me amongst the advocates of the doctrines of Bible Repentance."[52] The abolitionism of the 1830s, thus, was not simply another in a sequence of evangelical causes. In the words of one critic, it was a "different Gospel," but it was a Gospel nonetheless, one whose challenge to evangelical definitions of what it meant to be a Christian neither Christians nor their ministers could ignore.[53]

6

Abolition and the Crisis
of Public Order

The abolitionist insistence that church and clergy bear full and immediate witness against slavery was an extension of Christian guardianship to which most of the clergy and most of the public at large
proved powerfully resistant. Among the American public, abolitionism quickly met an opposition whose intensity and fervor matched its
own, as "abolitionist" became a dreaded epithet and abolitionists
became victims of vituperation, mob violence, and legislative and
judicial suppression. This, moreover, was not simply the response of
a vocal and vehement few. By mid-decade, public spokesmen from
President Jackson down to fourth of July orators on the "perils to
the Republic" were blending their voices in firm denunciation of
abolitionism. Even within the broader evangelical and clerical community, abolitionists met with intense hostility. Even as they came to
accept the condemnation of slavery as sin, most evangelical clergymen, and especially those in positions of ministerial leadership, perceived immediate abolitionism as a perversion of clerical public
guardianship, a misappropriation of evangelical ideas and institutions
in ways that disrupted social order rather than buttressed it.[1]

The abolitionists' style and method was an immediate source of
alarm. The abolitionists did, indeed, press their case with single-
minded fervor. They flooded the country with inflammatory tracts
designed to provoke hatred of slavery and sympathy for the slave.
They sent agents into communities to organize antislavery societies,
and they insisted upon forcing discussion of the issue into local

churches, voluntary associations, and ecclesiastical bodies in their attempts to get the churches to bar slaveholders from true Christian fellowship.[2] They brooked no compromise and denounced not only the slaveholder as a "manstealer" guilt of heinous sin, but also all who differed from them as participants in the sin. It did not seem to matter whether a person had been a faithful Christian all his life or had acted out of benevolent motives: if a professing churchman or Christian did not embrace and practice immediatism, he was guilty of promoting the cause of slavery. Lewis Tappen, for example, condemned Finney for cowardice and "sinning against conviction," because Finney refused to devote his public prayer to slavery rather than to conversion.[3]

But it was the abolitionists' intensity or even the extreme imagery of their portrait of slavery as sin alone that ultimately disturbed their evangelical critics. Evangelicals had long used the same imagery to condemn intemperance and sin in general and were always trying to push communicants and colleagues to greater ardor in their devotions and campaigns against vice. What was most disconcerting about abolitionist fervor was their failure to observe the procedures by which New England evangelicals distinguished genuine religious emotion from natural, or "animal," feelings. The confusion between animal zeal and religious affections had vexed New England evangelicals for a long time. During the early decades of the Second Great Awakening, churchmen had worked out several devices for guaranteeing that their revivals did not develop the excesses that had eventually destroyed the First Great Awakening.[4] They looked less to the depth than to the kind of emotion to discern genuine religious affections, and judged a true conversion by the absence of self-righteousness or censoriousness. Feelings grounded in grace rather than mere animal "excitement" were expressed initially in deep and prayerful "humility" and were witnessed in the convert's acceptance of established procedures, decorum, and authority. The form and intensity of the new revivals of the 1820s and early 1830s had further intensified these concerns about the quality of religious feelings. Many evangelicals, in fact, had, in the words of one, "rejoiced with trembling" when the new revivals flared up. By moving the convert suddenly from penitent to evangelist, the new revivals practically obliterated the period of humility that had been used to authenticate conversion. In addition, the zealous converts in these revivals frequently skirted self-righteousness in their impatience with older, but less wrought-up, church members. They even sometimes turned their enthusiasm against authority when they attacked pastors who had reservations about some of the measures the new revivals employed.[5]

Many clergymen thus almost automatically recoiled from the initial blasts of abolitionist fervor. To them, the vehement denunciation of sincere, professing Christians and clergymen with long personal histories of exemplary Christian carriage and benevolence was sheer fanaticism. And the abolitionists' insistence upon forcing discussion of slavery into every Christian institution appeared the essence of monomania. One critic, for example, condemned the Lane episodes "as an eminent instance of the monomania, which not infrequently is the result of the concentration of a powerful intellect and burning zeal upon any one momentous subject to the exclusion of others."[6] What was even more troubling about this fanaticism was that it appeared to be an uncontrollable force of enormous power. Antiabolitionist evangelicals, indeed, drew upon many of the same images to depict the abolitionist as fanatic that abolitionists themselves used to depict the sin of slavery. Abolitionists were not the only ones to appropriate the image of the drunkard. Just as craving for drink possessed the drunkard, so too was the fanatic dominated by the lust for excitement; and just as the inebriate sacrificed everything to his lust for drink so too did the fanatic accept no limits on the "demonic" pursuit of his cause. As the Lane Theological Seminary applied this image to the Lane students:

All men, and especially the young, partake of the enthusiasm of agitated minds around them, and those whose judgements are not settled too often become intoxicated with the powerful stimulus. The mind so delights in this kind of excitement, that it can hardly forsake it for the business of secluded study; the relish for it becomes too much like that for cold water compared with the burning cup of the drunkard.[7]

The abolitionist thus appeared to be a fanatic, beyond any inner control and impervious to any form of external restraint. The consternation over this apparent fanaticism, however, was shaped by a larger set of assumptions about the nature of social order. Evangelicals traditionally had associated public order with harmony, and their social outlook contained a deeply antipolitical strain, a distrust of organized political conflict, and a fear of collective political mobilization. In addition, the increasing democratization of American public culture during the 1820s and 1830s greatly intensified these longstanding fears. To some clerics, of course, the advent of Jacksonian politics represented a further transfer of political power from a wise and learned elite to the tumultuous, unlettered lower classes. But the changes in the political culture went beyond this to include a broad transformation of the character and modes of public life. In the first place, the very character of the public as a public was changing. As electoral politics, more than anything else, began to provide the central symbols and values governing national public life, politics became the central public ritual of American life. It was the one institution that seemed to encompass the far-flung diversity and separation of American society and to provide the American people with a sense of Americanness as well as a sense of common participation in the same political community. Participation, indeed, was broad and varied, as the democratic electorate joined in public not only at the polls, but also at rallies, conventions, parades, and barbecues. As electoral combat increased and intensified around two emerging national parties, complete with symbols, slogans, and songs, a constant barrage of political oratory inundated the American public, no longer discernable as a recognizable set of ranks and orders but only as a vast and homogeneous mass.[8]

The rhetorical surface of politics riveted the attention of most commentators. The innumerable sermons, addresses, lectures, editorials, and orations devoted to the "signs of the times" and to what was variously referred to as the "character," "spirit," or "tendency" of the age invariably used terms like "hubbub" or "frenzy" to capture what they found most characteristic and battling about the new democratic political culture.[9] By the thirties, moreover, a number of new agencies of public sentiment and opinion were further intensifying the tumult of public life. Societies for this and that, lecturers and publicists of every sort, self-appointed "prophets" and "reformers" were beginning to add their "nostrums" and "schemes" to the public clamor. The public—"the all powerful sovereign"[10] of American life—was not only engulfed in the conflicts of party, but also swamped in a hubbub of voices "crying lo here, and lo there," as self-selected spokesmen of dubious legitimacy threatened to drown out the voices of those who had traditionally taken the lead in forming public sentiment.[11] Thus in various ways was the public, this vast and somewhat mysterious force, in a volatile and unstable state. As James Hall, a Cincinnati editor, prominent evangelical layman, and the first man to speak out publically against the Lane Debates, expressed the problem: "in a republican government, where discourse is free, and where all great measures are to be decided by popular suffrage, there will often be violent conflicts of opinion, nor will any department of society or class of men escape the occasional visitation of a storm of passion."[12]

Democracy had not only turned the public into a volatile mass, but also seemed to many spokesmen to have weakened the agencies of intellectual and moral authority that had traditionally formed and restrained public opinion. As Hall's strictures implied, public discourse was no longer the monopoly of such long-established and legitimate public spokesmen as officeholders, press, and clergy. But, in addition, the broader democratization of American life had made individual self-determination the overriding principle for judging institutions and measures. At the very least, it seemed that the society had no real intellectual center, as neither officeholders, the clergy, nor any of the self-appointed spokesmen seemed able to command general respect. At its worst, this rampant self-determinism degenerated into a spirit of anarchy and nullification as it elevated "individual notions" above all authority. As the Lane Seminary board put it: "It is evident to all who are accustomed to observe the signs of the times, that there is at present in our country among all classes and departments of the community, a strong and growing propensity to insubordination—a disposition to set up individual notions or constructions in opposition to lawful authority, to justify resistance to law by private opinion."[13]

It was within this context that opponents of immediatism equated it not only with fanaticism but with disorder. Aside from the merits of the issue, and even in spite of the considerable acceptance of the notion that slavery was sin, the abolitionists themselves were seen as a threat to social order. The issue itself, of course, was about as explosive as any the republic could possibly face. As Jefferson had warned as early as 1820, slavery was the "firebell in the night" of the American Republic, and organized abolitionism threatened the power and interest of the South and fanned the racial fears of Northerners. As James Hall put it, "It connects itself with religion and government—it involves the industry and prosperity of the country—it has a near relation to the public morals—it concerns the consciences and pecuniary interests of many of our fellow citizens."[14] Moreover, the public mind by its very nature was vulnerable to a "storm of passion" on such an issue. And the abolitionists not only had access to the public mind, they insisted upon plying it unceasingly with abolitionist tracts and agitation, even though much of the public did not want to be plied with the subject and expressed their opposition in mob violence. By the late thirties, indeed, the spector of disorder was such that many feared that the Republic would not survive, that it could not withstand the public passion that abolition and the opposition to it had wrought, and that it would succumb to some form of despotism. In January 1838, just a few months after an antiabolitionist mob had murdered the Reverend Elijah Lovejoy, a young Whig from Illinois, Abraham Lincoln, issued such a warning in an address to the Young Men's Lyceum of Springfield, Illinois. Pointing to the combination of public passion and the disrespect for law, Lincoln warned that the Republic was ripe for plucking by a Napoleon-like demagogue, who would use the popular fear and passion to gain despotic power.[15] Just a little more than a year earlier, Charles Grandison Finney (a man unlike Lincoln in most ways) had expressed a similar fear in a letter to Weld:

> *Br. Weld is it not true, at least do you not fear it is, that we are in our present course going fast into a civil war? Will not our present movements in abolition result in that? Shall we not ere long be obliged to take refuge in a military despotism? Have you no fear of this? If not, why have you not? Nothing is more manifest to me than that the present movements will result in this, unless your mode of abolitionizing the country be greatly modified.[16]*

The disordering impact of abolitionism, moreover, went well beyond its capacity to arouse violent opposition. Ultimately, immediate abolitionism appeared to be subversive because it seemed to undermine the structure of order. In the first place, it seemed to trample the boundaries between church and state and between religion and politics, boundaries thought to lie at the foundation of public order. The constitutionally enforced separation of church and state was grounded in a particularly American notion of religious freedom. Strict separation was not only necessary to secure freedom of conscience, but it had a more positive public dimension as well. The United States was thought to be a Christian nation, and its religion was considered fundamental to its preservation. Moreover, it was axiomatic that its ability to perform this function depended upon the separation of Church and State and religion and politics.[17] Indeed, the whole edifice of evangelical public guardianship had been built around this separation. The great task of a republic was to foster liberty without jeopardizing order and, conversely, to maintain order without encroaching on liberty. The public order, correspondingly, was thought to be composed of two distinct but complementary realms. Politics and government, grounded in popular sovereignty and occupied with the day-to-day conflicts of interest and opinion and the ongoing pursuit of power, was the realm of liberty. But to balance the turmoil of republican politics and the anarchic potential of an increasingly democratic and individualistic society, there was a realm of order, composed of the broader public culture, beyond private opinion and distinct from partisan or sectarian doctrine, and housed in agencies like home, school, and church.[18]

It was to this realm of order that the social leaven of religion and the legitimate public role of the clergy belonged. To evangelicals, of course, ultimately only the restraints of religious conviction and institutions could provide the individual morality and self-restraint that made liberty possible. The United States, moreover, was a Christian nation in ways that went well beyond the private devotion of much of its people. Much of its public culture—its essentially undisputed "higher" precepts and symbols of order—derived from Protestant Christianity and from the belief that the America Republic was sustained by special providential oversight. This higher public culture existed outside the realm of day-to-day political conflict and, indeed, was thought to be able to sustain the public order only if it remained free from the contamination of politics and partisanship. The clergy was among the accepted public spokesmen of this culture. Thus both the formal separation of church and state and the informal, but no less important, distinction between the political and the nonpolitical public realms set the legitimate boundaries of clerical public spokesmanship. The clergy dealt not with "measures" but with principles and problems of personal and public morality, interpreting public problems in light of basic Christian beliefs rather than promoting particular programs. The boundary between legitimate clerical public address and illegitimate "priestcraft" was fixed at partisanship—advocacy of a measure before a formal political or governmental body, or alliance with a political group. The distinction, to be sure, was never terribly precise, and, as the controversy over the campaign to halt the Sabbath mails indicated, the definitions were open to a variety of interpretations. Nonetheless, that a distinction existed and that it was of crucial importance to the public order were ideas beyond dispute.[19]

Because of its notion of slavery and its own characteristics, however, immediate abolitionism violated these precepts and boundaries in a number of ways. Indeed, whether viewed from the political side or the religious side, immediatism was an anomalous public force. Initially, evangelical abolitionists insisted that their efforts were wholly religious and deliberately nonpolitical. Their starting point, after all, was the notion that slavery was sin, and they addressed themselves to the formation of the Christian commitment that they took to be antecedent to political redress. As they saw it at first (the opposition, especially in the South, quickly forced some modifications in their thinking), their special task was to set moral conviction aright: it was then up to that sentiment to find the political means to implement its insistence that slavery come to an immediate end.[20]

The problem, however, was that, unlike intemperance, slavery was not simply a matter of behavior, but an institution with legal and even constitutional legitimacy, which, if it was to be abolished, would ultimately have to be removed through political and governmental agencies. Thus, no matter what theological meaning immediatists might give to it, abolitionism was inherently a political matter, at once a religious doctrine and a public program. Their advocacy of abolition was hence perceived as an attempt to push a specific public measure, an illegitimate attempt to intrude themselves and their religious views into the political and governmental realm. In addition, they seemed essentially political in their modus operandi, even though their model was the evangelical benevolent society. Rather than confine themselves to trying to gain voluntary assent to their beliefs, their antislavery societies, especially in the petition campaigns, seemed designed to mobilize public opinion and then use it to pressure political institutions to act against the interests of others.[21] In this sense, organized abolitionism seemed not only partisan, but essentially a kind of political party, and the abolitionists seemed guilty of the very worst form of "political priestcraft." In addition, the abolitionist campaign to get the churches to make abolition a confessional requirement seemed both a political encroachment onto the domain of religious devotion and a violation of freedom of conscience, an attempt to force "a different Gospel" onto religious bodies that had been bound together by voluntary assent to the "whole Gospel."[22]

In addition, organized immediatism seemed to violate the democratic and procedural values that kept ordinary conflicts of political interest and opinion within acceptable bounds. In the growing democratization of their society, Americans had increasingly demanded equal access to whatever position in life they wished and could attain by their talents and efforts. A corollary of the idea of equal opportunity was the insistence that no individual, group, or institution possess the power or privilege that could hamper their legitimate efforts or interests. Indeed, even while Americans were joining voluntary associations by the hundreds, they were becoming deeply suspicious of "combination," ever ready to perceive monopoly, privilege, aristocracy, or conspiracy in the concerted behavior of others. Moreover, this new democracy was increasingly vehement in its insistence that democratic process determine the conduct of public life, that public measures be determined by democratic opinion and through procedures that were subject to popular control and sovereignty.[23]

Both in form and force, immediate abolitionism seemed to violate these values and procedures. In form, the antislavery societies were "voluntary associations." Though cooperative and collective and sometimes engaged in what might be characterized as public activities, voluntary associations were nonetheless fundamentally private organizations. Voluntarily joined or quit and dependent upon no legal sanction or collective public consent, they engaged only those who chose to be addressed by them and were expected to refrain from encroaching on the rights or interests of others.[24] It was just this noncoercive "voluntary principle" that the antislavery societies, for all their possession of the familiar characteristics of the voluntary association, seemed to violate. In some ways, this was the ultimate source of outrage. For a variety of reasons—deep-seated prejudice and hatred of the blacks, fear of abolitionism's effect upon law and order, concern that antislavery agitation would provoke a political crisis that would destroy the union—most Americans were deeply fearful of the manner and measures of the immediatists. But equally importantly, abolitionism was a powerful public force which they seemed powerless to thwart or avoid, since it neither possessed built-in limits nor recognized any restraints outside itself. The abolitionists insisted upon playing a public role, affecting fundamental interests, beliefs, and institutions, but appeared to operate wholly beyond ordinary means of democratic control: intent on pushing a clear-cut public measure and interjecting themselves forcibly into the public process, they operated outside the reach of electoral sanction and seemed impervious to, if not actually defiant of, the overwhelming public sentiment against them. Local communities, for example, seemed helpless against the assault of the traveling agents of the American Anti-Slavery Society, who, appearing as a species of alien agitator, entered a community and tried to organize an antislavery affiliate. Even when such communities tried to use office and democratic machinery to pass and enforce ordinances prohibiting antislavery agitation and organizing, it seemed of little avail. The abolitionists came on anyway: they had a higher call to duty, one which enabled them to endure opposition and risk personal danger.[25]

Fanaticism, disorder, subversion—though abolitionism might appear to be any or all of these, the inescapable fact remained that it had emerged from firmly within evangelicalism. It derived its doctrine from evangelical theology, took its tactics and organization from revivalism and the benevolent empire, and drew its concept of duty from traditions of clerical public guardianship that the clergy at large still embraced. Indeed, the evangelical abolitionists themselves insisted that they were not departing from these traditions but were the only ones capable of perfectly fulfilling them. Thus, for all their abhorrence of the abolitionist call and all the pressures to resist it, the challenge was unavoidable. The larger clerical community was highly susceptible to the claims of the slave on their evangelical sympathies, and in fact most evangelicals of the New England strain fairly quickly embraced the notion that slavery was a sin.[26] But once that notion was accepted, slavery unavoidably fell within the purview of clerical public guardianship. On almost every level, for the individual pastor no less than for evangelical leaders, and in almost every forum, the clerical community was forced to grapple with how to respond to the abolitionists in their midst as they tried to work out the problem of how the machinery of Christian influence should be brought to bear on slavery. The Reverend Parsons Cooke put it well. "Never," he asserted, "was it more difficult to ascertain what is duty, in relation to the use of our public responsibilities than it now is. . . . Reflecting minds are in a maze of perplexity. And this age of discovery would do enough for one age, if it could discover to us the path of duty, and lay open the channel in which the quickened energies of the public mind may most safely and beneficiently flow forth for reform and human improvement."[27]

Essentially, finding the path of duty involved a search for distinctions and rules by which the antiabolitionist evangelicals could isolate the sources of abolitionist excess and thereby exclude it from legitimate Christian endeavor. They insisted that the principle that slavery was a moral evil be applied in a tone and with methods that took account of the particular and existing circumstances of the community. They pointed out that the notion of slavery as sin was a "new view" which many long-standing and sincere Christians might have difficulty accepting at first. They argued that slavery was a complicated phenomenon, which might be a sin but was nonetheless a legally constituted institution, established generations earlier, sustained by the United States Constitution, and affecting the interests and fortunes of much of the nation. Thus, the argument went, good and wise men would differ over how to rid the society of the evil, and disagreement with immediate emancipation could well stem not from any lack of Christian conviction, but from benevolent worry over the readiness of the slaves for freedom and from patriotic concern over the fate of the union. Finally, they warned that denunciation of Christian slave-holders as sinners would only harden them against the exertion of any Christian influence against slavery. To the antiabolitionist evan-gelical, indeed, by both its substance and its style, immediatism threatened to destroy all hopes of effective use of Christian influence to end slavery. It divided and weakened the overall evangelical com-munity and was driving the Christian South outside the reach of the evangelical empire.[28]

The antiabolitionist evangelicals tried to derive rules for addressing Christians on slavery from what was referred to as "the whole Gos-pel." In effect, they reversed the immediatist attempt to make abolition the center of Christian witness and repudiated the demand that slave-holders be excluded from Christian fellowship. To them, the first step was to make people Christians and get them into the church and allied evangelical institutions. In its more conservative form, the argu-ment asserted that if the churches pointed out that slavery was wrong but stopped short of denouncing Christians as sinners, public senti-ment would grow, and that in God's appointed time the evil would be eradicated. Essentially this was the colonization position. With the colonization plan, James Hall asserted, "the calm wisdom of the nation has long since settled down in the opinion that this subject should be left to the Providence of God, to the matured decision of time and public sentiment."[29] In its most pointed form, best exempli-fied by Charles Grandison Finney, the "whole Gospel" argument held that the first commitment of an evangelical abolitionist should be the revival. Here, indeed, Finney drew directly upon the analogy with intemperance and from his experiences in the famous Rochester, New York, revival of 1830, which had not only converted hundreds but had also dried out the town.[30] Once people were genuinely reborn as true Christians, Finney insisted, they would of necessity become abolitionists because slavery was sin. As J. W. Alvord, a Lane aboli-tionist whom Finney was trying to persuade, repeated Finney's points in a letter to Theodore Weld:

Is not the necessity laid on us to preach the whole Gospel? Must not the work of Emancipation after all be performed by the church? i.e.—must not she be the Prominent Agent? In order to win God's favor is it not necessary that abolition efforts should be imbued with more of the spirit of God and of prayer? Would not abolition revivalists win to our cause those parts of the church (by no means contemptible in piety or moral worth) who are either timid, or stubborn, or afraid of ultraism? If God

was with us by his converting power would they longer stand back? In
a word, can we not have souls, and save the slave too? and do it as
rapidly?[31]

The anti-immediatist evangelicals also tried to sort out the appropriate agencies for Christian antislavery action. Nothing, in fact, is
quite so revealing of the difficulty of the problem of Christian duty
as the torturous attempts of evangelicals to find a legitimate form of
Christian action, one which could foster the proper moral sentiment
against slavery but which would do so without unduly enflaming
public opinion or illegitimately intruding into the political sphere.
During the Lane "imbroglio," for example, the Lane Faculty issued a
"declaration of sentiment" that tried to establish a distinction between
"associations for 'free inquiry' " and "voluntary public action," and
those which sought "social public action." (The declaration was
written by Calvin Stowe and Lyman Beecher, both of whom were
sufficiently imbued with antislavery sentiments that abolitionists
hoped soon to include them in their ranks.) By associations for "free
inquiry" they meant those like the traditional debating and literary
societies, which were organized for discussion rather than action and
which did not formally advocate any particular position.[32]

The distinction between "voluntary" and "social" public action
reflected the common insistence upon the separation of politics and
religion and was used to argue that the seminary's Colonization Society was voluntary and legitimate, while the Anti-Slavery Society was
"social" and should be disbanded. The precise nature of the distinction, however, was ambiguous, especially since the authors insisted
that they in no way intended to hamper legitimate Christian action
against slavery. If "social" referred to the abolitionists' substantive
goal of ridding the nation of the institution of slavery, then was not
the Colonization Society equally illegitimate if, as its Northern de-
fenders avowed, its ultimate goal was the same? (This, in fact, was
the Lane Board of Trustees' position when it tried to ban both societies as illegitimate incursions in a "social" matter.)[33] If, on the other
hand, "voluntary" referred to the fact that colonization called only
for individual acts and did not directly address the institution, then
the society was not really dedicated to emancipation, a position which
supported the abolitionist contention that colonization actually
strengthened slavery because it "duped the conscience" with the
delusion that individual acts which did not challenge its existence as
a legal institution constituted Christian action against slavery.[34]

Others sought to distinguish ordinary moral machinery from imme-

diatism by describing antislavery societies as "public opinion societies" rather than "benevolent associations," a distinction about method
rather than goals. The goals of the abolitionists were admitted to be
benevolent, but the instrument they used was "public sentiment."
They worked upon "the sinner through the medium of others' indignation, first wrought for that purpose."[35] This, it was argued, had
transformed antislavery societies into partisan instruments, if not
technically, at least in essence, coercive and political. "Public opinion," however, was a very broad category. It was, after all, the function of Christian leadership to form the "public sentiment" that "the
perpetuity of [American] republican institutions" demanded,[36] and
even tract societies were specifically intended to foster opinion about
particular social problems. Moreover, the temperance and Sabbatarian
societies tried to arouse "indignation" and then use it to prohibit
practices that others engaged in.

Efforts were also made to place the antislavery societies themselves,
not simply their methods, beyond the pale by defining them in such
a way as to challenge their claim to be legitimate representatives of
Christian influence in society. This argument insisted that no matter
how Christian the professed origins of their doctrines, the abolitionists' claims upon the Christian public were "unwarranted" because
the societies themselves were not genuine, selectively screened, and
doctrinally pure Christian bodies. In other words, they were not
churches, or the direct instrument of churches, but were "promiscuous
combinations of men of all characters," which were bound together
not by a common soul-felt reception of the "whole Gospel," but only
"by opposition to one specific sin."[37] Such societies, being false Christian instruments, could make no just or effective claim upon the
Christian slaveholder's conscience. This distinction did indeed put the
abolition societies well outside the Christian pale, but at the risk of
throwing out the baby with the bath, since it also undercut the
legitimacy of many of the evangelical societies.

The sticking point, of course, was the abolitionist doctrine of the
sin of slavery. As for the argument about prudence and circumstance,
the abolitionists argued that precisely because slavery—like sin in
the unregenerate will—was so deeply embedded in Southern society,
the only way to get the Southern Christian to overcome the power of
selfish interest and act against slavery was to smite his conscience
with the enormity of the sin in the same way that a revival smote a
sinner with his own depravity and broke down his resistance to truth.
Moreover, if slavery was sin, and if repentance and immediate cessa-
tion from sin were at the core of evangelical Christianity, immediatism

likewise was at the center of "the whole Gospel." And how, if slavery was a sin identical in character to adultery or intemperance, could evangelicals justify not applying ordinary doctrines of guilt and repentance to it? Further still, how could they justify withholding from the slaveholder the sanction of breaking fellowship that they applied to any recalcitrant Christian who persisted in sin after the truth of its nature and of his duty toward it had been made clear to him?[38]

To escape the conundrum, the anti-immediatist evangelicals worked out some distinctions as to the nature of the sinfulness of slavery. They argued that, while slavery was in some respects identical to adultery and intemperance, it did not in all cases so implicate the Christian slaveholder in the guilt of "manstealing" as to warrant breaking off all Christian fellowship with him. The various definitions behind this argument—that slavery was a "social sin," an "organic sin," or an "organic social wrong"—centered on the undeniable fact that slavery, unlike other sins whose character it shared, was sanctioned by the "organic law" of American society and that in many instances the slaveholder did not have the legal power to emancipate his slaves.[39] Establishing degrees of sinfulness so as to set up degrees of guilt, this definition was intended to marshal sufficient Christian pressure to get the Christian Southerner to act, but not so much or in such a way as to drive him away by automatically denying him legitimate title to the Christian label. Though this line of argument with its institutional emphasis and its organic social values has been accurately categorized as "conservative abolitionism," it nonetheless carried some fairly radical implications. If the ultimate evil was organic, then the kind of change demanded was surely drastic. (Indeed, though the position was meant to counter Garrisonism, the logic of the idea was not terribly far removed from Garrison's assertion that the Constitution, because of its sanction of slavery, was an "unholy document" that had to be overthrown.) Moreover, while it might let the slaveholder off the hook of damnation, it clearly asserted the ultimate political dimension of the problem, opening the door for charges that such a posture violated the separation of the public and religious spheres.[40]

By the end of the thirties, then, the structure of evangelical public guardianship was in a state of collapse. Intellectual coherence and consensus had been irretrievably lost; vehement controversy racked its institutions, turning, in the Reverend Leonard Bacon's words, "the very temple of our religious anniversaries into a scene of clamor and violence."[41] By 1835, in fact, evangelicalism was both polarized and fragmented. At the poles were two warring groups of clergymen. Though both sides drew upon the doctrines and experiences of early nineteenth-century evangelicalism, each regarded the other as the champion of false and perverted forms of Christianity. The abolitionists, meeting rebuff after rebuff in their attempts to persuade seminaries, associations, and synods to bear formal witness against slavery, had begun to condemn the clergy and its ecclesiastical institutions as the "bulwarks of Slavery."[42] Their most vehement opponents, trying to protect the purity of church and devotion, stepped up their withdrawal from evangelical activism and tried to raise firm barriers against any form of alien influence. Caught in the middle, of course, were those—like Lyman Beecher—who sought a middle way, a path of duty by which the evangelical empire could fulfill its earlier promise to reclaim and reconstitute American society.

Indeed, what happened to Lyman Beecher's career and reputation in this tumultuous decade provides as good an indication as anything else of the state to which evangelical guardianship had fallen. In 1830, Beecher was the acknowledged leader of evangelicalism, and in 1832, following his pattern of moving wherever he thought the center of evangelical action lay, he went to Cincinnati, Ohio, to head Lane Theological Seminary and crown his career by training the generation that would bring the millennium to America. By 1835, his career lay in shreds. Fifty-one of his best students had withdrawn from his seminary. He also caught it from the other side: in November 1834, while he was in the midst of the imbroglio over slavery at Lane, the Reverend Joshua Wilson, pastor of Cincinnati's oldest evangelical church, brought formal charges of heresy and hypocrisy against him.[43] But his reputation suffered even more than his career. He had dedicated his whole professional life to building the evangelical empire; he had been in the forefront of its most ardent campaigns; and he had consistently devoted his enormous energies and skill to holding its diverse strands together. But the traits and vision which had earlier made him the lauded and acknowledged architect and leader of the evangelical empire now seemed to condemn him as a "trimmer," a wily and scheming opportunist. Many of his oldest associates—colleagues of his Connecticut years like Asahel Nettleton and Bennet Tyler—now spread the charge that Beecher was an ambitious hypocrite whose whole career had been marked by expediency rather than constancy in protecting truth.[44] And from the other side, the young antislavery evangelicals, who had once looked to him for leadership, now condemned him for a lack of courage and fidelity. As John Jay Shipherd wrote of the "collapse" of Dr. Beecher: "Oh, why did he confer with flesh and blood! Why not dare to do what he acknowl-edged to be right! He has evidently been guilty of duplicity, and his sun which I hoped would enlighten the valley and set serenely in the West, will I fear go down in a cloud. Cease ye from men!"[45]

Abolitionism, as both an intrinsic and an extrinsic force, was the precipitating cause of the chaos. But at the same time, abolitionism had exposed and inflamed a set of longer-range tensions which had developed within the evangelical structure over the preceding three decades. Second Great Awakening evangelicalism contained both an institutional and what might be termed an antinomian conception of order.[46] Its revivals and institutions such as mission, bible, and educa-tion societies were conceived as instruments for churching the Ameri-can people, for bringing them into a structure of order that combined the inner restraints of conversion with a protective fabric of societies and associations. At the same time, the new revivals and the translocal ministerial and evangelical institutions fostered a more ideological conception of order, which equated it with a sense of the divine cause that transcended institutional patterns. Second, there was the tension between religion as a force in the world and as a domain apart from it. The concept of disinterested benevolence as the mode of being of the genuine Christian united piety and moralism; but the evangelical communicant still experienced grace as both dominion over the world and as peaceful transcendence of it. Indeed, the institutions of the churches pointed in both directions at once: various societies reached outward in activist engagement with the world while Sabbath and sanctuary pointed toward disengagement and refuge from it. Finally, developments on both ends of the professional structure had created a tension between the minister as a guardian of public order and the minister as pastor to a particular devotional community. On the one hand, the definition of his guardianship and his ultimate commitments as a minister derived increasingly from translocal institutions. At the same time, evangelicalism had altered the character of his ties to his congregation, forcing him to be more responsive to the particular needs and demands of his parishioners while rendering him more vulnerable to their opposition.

These tensions constituted a kind of geological fault stretching beneath the surface of evangelicalism. They transmitted the aboli-tionist shock throughout the whole and shattered the synthesis be-tween private devotion and public duty, between religion as conduct of life and religion as transcendence, and between the minister as public guardian and the minister as guardian of souls, which had held evangelicalism together as a balanced whole. Evangelical disarray thus did not stop with its public facet. The unsettling of notions of public duty mirrored a corresponding disorder in the private dimensions of Christianity. In almost every town and congregation, there were those who demanded different styles of devotion, some finding the measure of their piety in public commitment and others seeking in their religion the tranquility that transcended the chaos of public life. By 1840, the chaos had spread to church and doctrine and to the day-to-day needs of Christian communicants, as it reached beyond assembly and association to individual towns and congregations, powerfully affecting the place of religion and the role of the minister in public and private life.

7

The Crisis of the Pastoral Clergy

The local pastor felt the full brunt of the chaos of the 1830s and 1840s, for, perhaps more than anyone else, he was caught in the middle of the conflicts that plagued evangelicalism. It would probably be hard to find many congregations that were in agreement either about the public purposes of evangelicalism or about the style of preaching they expected from their pastor. Local congregations were filled with different factions, each of which, it seemed, demanded a "different Gospel," as the Reverend E. D. Moore, a particularly battered victim of the process, put it.[1] If a minister had become alarmed over the apparently unsettling effects of various "enthusiasms" and responded by preaching highly doctrinal sermons which stressed man's inability to work toward his own salvation, some of his parishioners might consider him "cold," lacking in "piety and feeling," a sure sign that he had "lost his effectiveness."[2] Even if he resolved simply to "preach religion" and bypass the doctrinal squabbles that the turmoil of the thirties had provoked, there was no guarantee that he would stay clear of opposition. Conflicts within his congregation often were expressed in terms of doctrinal preferences, and each side would demand to know where the minister stood.[3] Similarly, if a minister, whether an abolitionist or not, argued that slavery was an issue of evangelical responsibility, he was bound to be attacked for "political preaching." If he ignored the slavery question, there was no certainty that he would fare better. His parish was bound to have in it a small group of fervent antislavery Christians who would attack their

112

minister's refusal to condemn slavery as a "time-serving" compromise with sin.[4] The Reverend Milton Bramen summed the matter up nicely: "Now what are the clergy to do? To cooperate with all they can not, for some of them are directly hostile to others. Incur obloquy from some quarter they must. If they take one side the other is upon them." Indeed, the situation was so desperate that "between the palmer worm and the locust and the canker worm and the caterpillar the poor clergy are in danger of having their reputation entirely devoured."[5]

The 1840s and 1850s thus mark a nadir for the pastoral clergy. One index of their plight is ministerial compensation. Although precise figures are impossible to obtain, it is clear that a substantial portion of the clergy found itself severely underpaid, both in absolute terms and in comparison with ministerial salaries through the 1830s. In 1854, the Society for the Relief of Aged and Destitute Clergymen estimated that an annual salary of $800 to $900 was needed in the larger towns and cities, while $450 to $500 was needed in most small towns and country parishes. Although the top tier of pastors made between $1200 and $2000, and a large portion of the clergy made enough to get by if they were prudent, at least one-third of the clergy, and possibly more than two-fifths, found itself severely strapped. One association reported that of its sixteen pastors, four made between $700 and $1500, while the remaining twelve averaged only $460; and the Franklin Association in Massachusetts reported that seven of its pastors received from $600 to $700, seven received between $400 and $600, and more than twenty had salaries of $400 or less.[6] Although there are a number of reasons for this situation, one thing that contributed to it was the refusal of parishioners who opposed or were indifferent to their pastor to contribute to his salary. Another index of the difficulties facing pastors in these years is the rate of pastoral turnover. For example, from 1800 to 1810 almost 60 percent of the Congregational churches in Connecticut went without a change of pastors, while only 5 percent had two or three changes. In contrast, only about 32 percent of the Connecticut churches passed through the 1840s without a change, while almost as many, about 31 percent, had two, three, or four changes during the decade.[7]

Pastoral tenure had been steadily diminishing throughout the century, of course, and many clergymen had welcomed the mobility and flexibility that a loosening of the bonds of pastoral permanence had brought about. By the 1840s this flexibility no longer appeared to be such an unmixed blessing. Many clergymen were moving from post to post because the hostility and niggardliness of their parishioners had driven them out of their pulpits. The buffeting John Todd took in these years is perhaps typical. It is difficult to imagine a more prudent and cautious man than Todd. Whenever he entered a situation, he quickly figured out the potential sources of difficulty and worked carefully to overcome or neutralize them. He avoided controversy whenever possible, rarely preached heavily doctrinal sermons, and confined his publications to devotional pieces which were unlikely to provoke controversy. (When Todd was a student at Andover in 1824, he gave such a good critique of Baptist ideas that his instructor, Leonard Woods, suggested its publication. But Todd demurred because he thought it might prove "injurious" to publish a controversial piece at such an early stage in his career.)[8] In addition, Todd was a good preacher and an attentive pastor who worked diligently to cultivate the support and affection of his people. Yet from 1833 to 1840, Todd was forced by his parishioners to change pulpits three times. In Philadelphia in 1840, Todd lost his church, even though he was at the height of his career and possessed the firm support of most of his parishioners. One powerful group was so opposed to him, however, that during the depression of the late 1830s they bought up the mortgages of the church building and literally evicted him.[9]

This buffeting shows up equally dramatically in a more collective perspective. Of the matriculants of Andover Theological Seminary from 1815 through 1835, only 48 of 631, or 6 percent, held a single clerical post of any kind for their entire clerical career, and about 40 percent of these were nonpastoral positions, particularly professorships and foreign missionary assignments. But it is the other end of the spectrum that is most indicative of the turmoil: over 30 percent of the 631 Andover matriculants held between six and twelve positions during their career.[10] In addition, several new and alarming clerical figures made their appearance in these years. First, there were those, usually in their thirties, who after a trying experience or two left the ministry entirely, even though they had undergone two or three years of formal theological training. Second, there were those who remained in the ministry filling a succession of posts but went through periods when they were unable to find a pastorate that could support them. These men (amounting to almost 30 percent of the Andoverians entering the clergy between 1815 and 1835) either spent these periods without a clerical post or took on an agency or a chaplaincy or taught school until they found another pastorate.[11] The Reverend Charles Rockwell, for example, an 1834 graduate of Andover, spent his first three years as a chaplain in the Navy. In 1838 he took on a pastorate in Chatham, Massachusetts, which he held for seven years. In 1845 he moved to Pontiac, Michigan, and two years later moved on to Kentucky. For the next six years, he served in a succession of pastorates in Connecticut, then Pennsylvania, then Maine, followed by New Hampshire and Massachusetts. In 1856 he is found teaching for a period of four years, before entering another succession of pastorates.[12]

Perhaps the most poignant victims of this pastoral chaos were those men in their late forties to late fifties who lost pastorates and were unable to secure another position and spent their remaining ten to twenty years "without charge." How they supported themselves is unclear. A good many probably found a job of one kind or another (postmasterships and clerkships, for example), but the rise of special societies for "aged and destitute clergymen" attests that some of them had to rely upon charity. Though these men could not find clerical employment, they still clung to their ministerial identity and affiliations, maintaining active membership in their local ministerial associations even though they could not regularly practice their profession. This not only gave them a form of professional activity and comradeship, but also provided them with the formal standing to perform for a fee various clerical functions like substitute preaching or performing marriages.[13] A little more than one out of every four of the Andover matriculants from 1815 to 1835 found themselves in this position during their forties or fifties. For the New England clergy as a whole, the figure might well be closer to one in three, since Daniel Calhoun found that, in New Hampshire, those with formal seminary training enjoyed greater stability and security than those who had not received formal theological training.[14]

A sense of crisis and depression gripped much of the clergy. The document produced by the Society for the Relief of Aged and Destitute Clergymen is particularly revealing. It was the result of a systematic effort to collect information about ministerial salaries and communicate it to the Christian public. The committee, composed of three clergymen and three prominent laymen, sent a "circular" to "each clergyman in Massachusetts, to each bishop of the Protestant Episcopal and Methodist Churches, and to . . . many other Ministerial Associations, Theological Seminaries, and Presidents of Colleges, in other states."[15] The report contained a good deal of concrete data on ministerial salaries and the effects of inadequate salaries on pastoral careers and the churches, as well as individual cries of bitterness— "Eight young salesmen in one furniture warehouse in Boston have each the same salary as myself!"—and desperation—"I am growing old; I am very poor; I may lose my parish. What is to become of me."[16] Equally revealing, however, is the sense of the precariousness of the ministry's reputation and position conveyed by the diffidence of the committee's presentation of its case. Salary was an awkward subject for the clergy, especially when it was under assault. The statement of one anonymous pastor suggests the dimensions of the rhetorical problem. "I am not properly supported; but I cannot say a word about it, because it would re-act destructively upon me."[17] Essentially, the committee confronted the task of appealing for money without arousing any further hostility against individual clergymen or against the ministry generally. As one association put the common axiom: "Were the question between a rich and a poor ministry, we should vote for the latter. Woe the day when the pulpits of New England become rich berths, when they afford any *pecuniary* temptation to candidates."[18] Indeed an essential badge of a true minister was his detachment from concern about his worldly portion. Not only was he under a call in which he had trusted himself wholly to God's care, but his essential task was to transmit the message that taught people to store up their treasure in heaven. Thus the committee proceeded with great circumspection, lest it give malcontents any ammunition to use against their pastors. First, it tried to make it absolutely clear that "no forced measures, *in any form*, are for one moment dreamed of by the clergy."[19] It strove mightily for a tone of impartiality: the survey was conducted by a philanthropic society composed of laity and clergy rather than by any particular denomination or exclusively ministerial group, and it printed a wide array of data, including notices of high salaries and cases of dramatic increase in salary. Finally, it took extreme care to avoid any impression that it was attacking communicants. Instead, it adopted the posture that it was simply ignorance of the true facts and conditions that had prevented congregations from giving pastors a just compensation and that, once this ignorance was remedied, communicants would "respond like Christian men." To the letter, the committee followed one seminary professor's advice: "1. To avoid a begging spirit on the part of the clergy. . . . 2. To avoid an *apparent* want of candor in the selection of the facts. . . . 3. To avoid by all means an *apparent* want of confidence in the justness and generosity of our churches."[20]

But perhaps the most anguished cry of beleaguerment came in some of the farewell sermons of ministers who had been driven from their pulpits. The tone of most earlier farewell sermons—at least most of the published ones—was usually celebrational or dedicatory. If conflict had not caused the minister's departure, a conventional farewell sermon usually expressed both congratulation and thanksgiving for a harmonious and beneficial ministry. Even if there had been conflict, the farewell sermon was ordinarily conciliatory. Though it might gently scold the congregation in suitably general terms, its delivery was a ritual designed to restore the foundations of pastoral felicity, and its publication was a formal testament to the ideal of harmony. The sermons of the ousted ministers of the 1840s and 1850s, however, were frequently accusatory, bitter, and desperate.[21] They were intended to vindicate the minister and chastise his opposition, and they dwelt upon such things as "ministerial freedom." They rebuked the "aggression" congregations perpetrated on their ministers, warned of the "spirit of competition and rivalry," deplored the "espionage" by which some parishioners sought to "destroy the reputations" of their ministers, warned of the "tyranny of minorities," and pleaded for the "freeborn rights" of the ministers.[22] Such was the parting shot of the Reverend William Barrows to the Norton, Massachusetts, parish that had ousted him. Suggesting both the impossibility of permanence and the desire for it, he bitterly declared that "the minister is not permitted to have any permanent home. The frequent removal of ministers has become proverbial; and they may well say to their people, '. . . we are strangers before thee and sojourners.' " The minister's plight was so bad, he concluded, that "to act as a pastor and at the same time have assurance of a permanent home has become an impossibility."[23]

The plight of the pastoral clergy was not solely the result of the conflicting and often contradictory demands that communicants placed upon their pastors. It stemmed equally from the fact that clergymen had become increasingly vulnerable to the opposition of their people. Pastoral permanence, of course, had been the principal foundation of a minister's authority and security. With its careful rituals and vows, the ordination ceremony had established a set of vitally important, if not almost sacred, bonds between pastor and people, which only death or the most extraordinary circumstances should break. A felicitous community and a stable and pious church needed a "settled" minister, one who was not a "sojourner" but a full-fledged and permanent member of the community. Over the course of the nineteenth century, however, as the fact of permanence declined, ministers and congregations alike had weakened their attachment to the ideal of permanence, even though a settled ministry remained the dominant form, and even though ordination and installation sermons as well as ex parte councils continued to pay formal obeisance to the ideal. Partly, of course, permanence had reflected the organicism of the eighteenth-century New England town, and the erosion of the ideal of permanence was part of a broader breakdown of the values of rank, familiarity, and place.

But there were also more immediate sources. The new ministerial and evangelical structure had created and applauded a number of nonpastoral posts and had fostered a sense of sacred cause and office that transcended the ordinary pastorate. As a result, styles of career-ism had arisen within the ministry which equated clerical success with various kind of activism and professional advancement rather than with faithful and permanent service to a single parish. There appear to have been three rather distinct types of clerical aspiration that were particularly corrosive to pastoral permanence. First, of course, there were those, like the abolitionists, whose demanding sense of calling and cause had made them uneasy with ordinary pastoral labor. Fre-quently, out of guilt over pastoral failure and a need for more imme-diate service to the larger cause, such ministers would leave a parish to take on missions or agencies.[24]

Second, there were those who entered the clergy, not with a deep need for self-denial and self-abasement, but with a firm sense of per-sonal aspiration. With its machinery for recruiting and educating "indigent young men," the ministry provided a far more coherent path than any other occupation or profession for the aspiring and energetic young men whom the declining New England towns could no longer sustain. Moreover, the ease with which a young man of determination could avail himself of this structure meant that many young men who had not been thrust into the ministry by a cataclysmic conversion experience had entered it as an instrument with which, in the words John Todd applied to himself, "to rise above [their] circumstances."[25] (In fact, when a number of its beneficiaries failed to go into the min-istry after using AES funds to get a college education, the AES was heavily criticized for opening the sacred office up to secular ambi-tion.)[26] This does not necessarily mean that their dedication to the ministry was half-hearted, that they lacked piety or sacrificed duty to ambition. (Those who in this sense lacked commitment to the ministry were quickly driven out by the conditions of the 1840s.) Rather, the ministry provided the form for their desires to move beyond their circumstances. For them ministerial fidelity lay less in the suppression of personal aspiration than in the choice of a profession which, in Todd's words, involved "doing good for others"; and they equated personal success with what their profession labeled as clerical success: the occupancy of a more important post or the move to a larger con-gregation from which one could reach more people by preaching or writing.[27]

Finally, there was the style of aspiration of those who looked at the ministry less in pastoral or ideological terms than as an intellectual profession and source of intellectual leadership for the society. A good number (though not all) of this type appear to have been sons of clergymen and prominent laymen.[28] Although they did not look upon the ministry as an instrument of social mobility, they too possessed a sense of personal aspiration. Nurtured in an intellectual environment, they frequently developed intellectual and aesthetic tastes beyond, though not necessarily opposed to, evangelicalism. In the end, however, the ministry was frequently the only available profession for these men to enter. Their taste for ideas and their aptitude for study singled them out for intellectual life, and their elders presented the ministry to them as a duty imposed upon them by their talents, piety, and family traditions. Moreover, like their colleagues from the "cottages of the poor," the young men of such inclination and traditions did not relinquish their intellectual tastes when they entered the ministry, but looked to it as a career for satisfying them. This attraction, moreover, frequently proved far stronger than the traditional attachments to permanence for its own sake, and many of them eventually found their way into the more purely intellectual posts, like college professorships and editorships, that the ministry now provided.[29]

On the other side, congregations frequently exhibited a similar wish to be free of the constraints of permanence. With its emphasis upon sustaining a personal and emotional relationship to God, evangelicalism was a pastoral and prophetic religion in which the minister was not expected to perform sacred rituals but to move his congregation. And by the nineteenth century, congregations had begun to place far greater value on a clergyman's performance as a preacher than upon the benefits to be gained by the simple presence of a settled minister. No longer were many congregations willing to endure dullness for the sake of unity and permanence. In addition, they made "edification," the capacity to arouse their emotions, quicken their piety, and convert their children, the essential yardstick of pastoral effectiveness. Revivals, moreover, increasingly set the standard parishioners expected of their preachers. Indeed, one objection raised against the use of visiting evangelists and protracted meetings was that they established models of intensity and effectiveness that the regular stated pastor could not maintain. Settled pastors frequently fell into difficulty with their congregations after periods of revival, when it was likely to appear that they had "lost their effectiveness." In the 1830s, ministerial associations even set up committees to "inquire into the causes which so often occasion difficulties in churches and societies soon after seasons of revival, and which sometimes lead to dismission of the pastor."[30] Thus, just as young ministers were quick to move on to better opportunities, congregations were quick to rid themselves of a clergyman whose preaching did not live up to their notions of edification. Moreover, they did not hesitate to raid churches which were thought to have a particularly effective preacher.

Various devices were improvised for getting around the constraints of ordination and permanence. Breaking full ordination bonds was seldom easy, even though it was being done with increasing frequency. The process was doubly trying if one side did not really want dismission, for then the other side was forced to launch a campaign of ploy and counterploy to try to push the issue to a point that made dismission unavoidable, if only for the sake of peace. Such struggles, indeed, frequently left a legacy of factionalism and bitterness that led to stormy pastoral relations for years. When, for example, the Middletown, Connecticut, church dismissed its minister in 1812, it was unable to agree upon another for four years, and even then changed ministers four times in the next decade.[31] And when the Bethany Church dismissed Nathaniel Huntington in 1823 after a particularly bitter fight, it went through fourteen pastors in the next twenty years.[32] In addition, in congregationalist usage, dismission ordinarily required the action of an ex parte council, which often refused requests for dismission because it did not consider the reasons given compelling enough to warrant inflicting the damage to the church that disruption of ordination bonds was thought to entail. By the 1830s, however, evangelicals had adapted several forms for avoiding the problems caused by such restraints.[33] One fairly broadly used device was to keep the minister as a "stated supply," a state beyond trial preaching but short of ordination or installation, which could endure for any length of time. Until 1820 the device was used only under special circumstances. (For example, in Connecticut during the entire decade from 1810 to 1820, only about 1 percent of the pastors were on stated supply.) In contrast, in 1858, almost 30 percent (321 of 1118) of the New England clergymen serving Congregationalist pastorates were on stated supply. In this respect, there was a marked difference between upper New England (New Hampshire, Maine, and Vermont), where almost half the ministers were on stated supply, and lower New England (Connecticut, Rhode Island, and Massachusetts), where 16 percent were on stated supply, although in 1861, 26 percent were.[34] In addition, even when they went through the forms of ordination and installation, churches and ministers had found it mutually advantageous to specify their obligations in clear, formal contractual terms. One variant placed ministers on an annual, renewable contract, while the other major variant, reflecting both the ideal of permanence and the desire for a simple escape hatch, was a contract of indefinite tenure that specified that either side was free to break the agreement with the simple condition of adequate notice.[35]

The erosion of the ideal of permanence, however, was not the only source of the pastoral clergy's vulnerability to congregational opposition. The fundamental nature of the pastoral relationship had changed in ways that were, of course, related to the end of permanence. In the eighteenth century, the relation had been essentially an authoritarian one. As the magisterial analogy suggested, the church selected its own pastor, but once they had chosen him they were expected to subordinate themselves to him so long as he did not violate the nature of the office.[36] Thus, the ordained public nature of the office and the social position of the clergyman had combined to give the minister essential dominion over the content of devotion and the exercise of his ministry. As the Reverend Dr. Enoch Pond put it in his 1844 manual, *The Young Pastor's Guide,* "Formerly, ministers were more distinguished than they now are by the peculiarities of their dress, and of their general appearance. They were less familiar and sociable with their people; kept them at a greater distance; and were regarded, often, with a reverence bordering on fear."[37]

During the early decades of the nineteenth century, this authoritarianism and deference disappeared as the relationship became less formal and more immediate and personal. To again quote Pond's highly idealized portrait in his *Guide,* the older reverence had been replaced by the "influence which one pious, intelligent, familiar, devoted *friend* may be supposed to possess over another. Minister and people are accustomed to live together, now, on terms of intimacy and equality."[38] This change in the pastoral relationship was partly a function of the character of evangelical devotion and communion. But in addition it reflected the altered and intensified demands that parishioners had come to place upon their pastors. Not only did they want to be edified, they also demanded considerable personal and individual attention. Communicants expected their ministers to pay regular personal and spiritual visits to them, attend to their illnesses and sorrows, preach a sermon or two on Sunday, give the traditional Thursday address, and conduct extra services such as concerts of prayer for revivals, or various bible study and inquiry meetings.

Such attentiveness could certainly be a source of pastoral security— one ordination sermon went so far as to suggest that no bonds were stronger than those that a faithful pastor could establish with "the yoke of affection."[39] At the same time, however, as the relationship became more informal and personal and the service more emotional and immediate, the ties became more fragile and precarious. For affection to give a minister much security, certain conditions had to obtain: there had to be considerable harmony within the congregation, near unanimity as to what was expected of a preacher, and a willingness to subordinate personal tastes and petty grievances to the greater good to be gained from a regular, stated pastor. In the chaotic 1830s, 1840s and 1850s, these conditions were hard to find. Even more importantly, however, the individual members of the congregation each had a strong sense of personal stake in their minister's effectiveness. In short, they looked upon the pastor less as the town's or church's minister than as *their* own minister and counselor, to be judged and retained according to his performance in meeting *their* particular spiritual needs. Indeed, what characterizes the 1830s and 1840s is not only the pervasiveness of conflict, but also the intensity and vindictiveness with which opponents frequently assaulted their pastors. Opponents often developed such a high personal or ideological investment in their grievance as to place it beyond any possible compromise. They would stop at very little in their attempt to alienate the minister's support, finding in almost any act or statement a fruitful source for an attack on his effectiveness, piety, morality, or integrity. The Reverend E. D. Moore's opponents even went so far as to forge a hotel register in an attempt to prove adultery between Moore's wife and a parishioner the Moores had befriended without knowing to which faction in the church he belonged.[40] Sooner or later such determination usually drove the minister away, either by making conditions intolerable for him or by driving even the minister's supporters to urge him to leave so that peace might be restored to the church. One council, lamenting that the pastoral office was becoming the "sport of ignorance or caprice," described the process succinctly. "A man, wearing the livery of a Christian, may conceive a most unreasonable prejudice against his pastor, [and] by dint of most ingenious and unwearied effort, he infuses the leaven of his own bad feelings into the minds of others." This accomplished, he would then "be able to make a plausible show of extensive disaffection and then demand, on the *ground of existing circumstances*, the removal of the pastor."[41]

By the 1840s, then, the relationship between a pastor and his people had become essentially a client relationship. In their laments about the local pastor's plight, in fact, clergymen complained that the ministry was losing its character as an office. Instead, the plaint ran, the minister had been reduced to a "mere hireling," as the fact or spirit of the contract replaced the "sacred bonds" that had once tied pastor to people so firmly.[42] Indeed, even pastors and congregations which had not adopted the newer contractual forms operated according to contract-like assumptions in which both sides were essentially equal. The clergyman, no matter how long he might actually stay in a particular post and whatever the outer form, no longer really "settled" into an office to "unite" permanently with the people of a congregation. Rather, he was perceived as someone who offered a service to a set of clients who demanded continuing performance and who would not hesitate to dismiss him if his performance fell below standards which they had given themselves the power to set.

The advice elders tendered young clergymen provides a telling indication of both the precariousness of the pastor's position and the need to protect his job by tailoring his pastorate to the particular condition and needs of his people. Although Samuel Miller's, *Letters on Clerical Manners* (1829), Heman Humphrey's, *Thirty-four Letters to a Son in the Ministry* (1842), and Enoch Pond's, *Young Pastor's Guide* (1844) did not always give the same advice, their purposes were identical and unmistakable—survival. These manuals were explicitly designed to brief the young clergyman on the operation, character, and pitfalls of a pastorate. Particularly revealing in Pond's and Humphrey's volumes are the precautions which they urge young men to take to immunize themselves against later opposition. They urge the candidate to seek out intelligence about the exact state of the congregation: how it treated previous ministers, what conflicts there had been in the past, how readily they paid their ministers. It was suggested that a young man discretely inquire about the costs of supporting a family in that town so that he would ask for an adequate beginning salary and thereby avoid the trouble that asking for more money frequently caused.[43] Heman Humphrey even told the young minister not to preach all his best, most carefully worked-out sermons in his attempt to win over a congregation that was considering him. Humphrey advised writing a number of sermons on the spot, under the ordinary, day-to-day pressures that a pastor faced, so that the congregation would not form expectations which he would be unable to satisfy once he had run through his stock of polished sermons. In addition, the tactic would help secure him against a feeling that he had lost his effectiveness, which opponents would use to try to oust him.[44] Finally, both Pond and Humphrey warned that if there was some opposition or lukewarmness to a call a young man received, he should make sure to "consider who they are, what is their standing, what is their influence, what are the grounds of their opposition, and what are the possibilities of its gaining strength or being overcome,"[45] before he accepted the post.

The manuals were equally full of advice on how to survive once one had taken a pastorate. Miller, for example, devoted almost half of his volume to "conversation" in an attempt to help the young pastor avoid entanglement in controversy by giving him detailed instructions on how to talk on different subjects and how to address the various social types he would encounter. Among his maxims were these: as a learned man, a minister was expected to have opinions on the topics of the day, but he should studiously avoid seeming opinionated and develop "judiciousness" and "circumspection" in talking on such matters; he should avoid becoming a raconteur, because humor was bound to strike some as inappropriate for a clergyman; he should never get drawn into argument in public; he should never engage in gossip and should take special pains to ensure that his wife and family never repeated his private comments or assessments to anyone else.[46] But in addition to protection, a pastor needed to build support and affection. He was told to be especially attentive to his parishioners in times of illness, sorrow, and distress. Home visits were portrayed as especially valuable devices, which should be paid to each parishioner at least twice a year, once as a friendly call and once to provide spiritual counsel. These visits not only enabled the pastor to build up a network of personal ties and foster a sense of direct personal concern, but they also provided a kind of spiritual intelligence that helped him preach and pray in ways suited to his communicants' particular spiritual condition. Indeed, Pond suggested, with a little luck and much hard work a young man might even succeed in establishing himself as both an effective preacher and an indispensable spiritual "friend."[47]

Another source of pastoral conflict stemmed from the gap between profession and parish which had been brought about by the changes in the overall structure of the ministry. Until the first decades of the nineteenth century, all but a handful of clergymen had occupied pastorates, and most professional activities, from the production of theological and controversial literature to the training of ministers, had been done by men who at the same time served a particular church. But with the creation of the evangelical empire, many of the leaders who articulated the goals of evangelicalism and set the priorities of the profession were no longer connected with particular congregations but had moved into the associations, colleges, and

seminaries. Moreover, by 1830 most of the Congregational-Presbyterian ministers (as well as many New England Baptists) were being
trained in the theological seminaries.[48] Though the divinity student
might gain some experience as a substitute or an agent, he still went
into the field with little knowledge of what were called the "practical"
aspects of a pastoral ministry. (It was to fill this gap that Miller,
Humphrey, and Pond wrote their pastoral guidebooks.) In addition,
though the divinity student took courses in pastoral rhetoric and
homiletics, his training tended to be highly formulaic. It provided the
doctrinal system he was to transmit to his audience and formal models
and rules for the construction of his sermons. Thus, at a time when
pastoral survival demanded extraordinary sensitivity to local conditions and to parishioners' particular needs and views, a clergyman's
training and many of the notions he received about his broader professional duties militated against the development of such sensitivity.

The gulf between profession and parish could lead to trouble in
several ways. While most parishioners were interested mainly in conversion, edification, and personal attention, many clergymen emerged
from seminary with a somewhat broader notion of their clerical responsibilities. Seminaries were also bastions of orthodoxy, designed
to furnish their products with the sound and pure doctrine with which
to protect the churches from error and heresy, and they tended to be
organized around a particular theological emphasis and frequently
stamped their students with a sense of doctrinal, factional, or denominational loyalty.[49] Various kinds of evidence, however—laments of
ousted ministers, the obiter dicta of ex parte councils, and the simple
behavior of congregations—make it clear that many church members
were becoming less and less patient with doctrinal exposition and
denominational combat. When, for example, John Todd, one of
Andover's most highly prized products, took his first pastorate, he
entered it strictly as a doctrinal partisan. His elders chose him for the
church in Dedham, Massachusetts, which was embroiled in legal controversy with the Unitarians and was considered a key battleground
in the struggle between Evangelicalism and Unitarianism. But when
the immediate crisis ebbed, Todd, still imbued with the importance of
the campaign, faced opposition from some of his communicants who,
though firm evangelicals, were uninterested in continuing the warfare
against the Unitarians in Dedham.[50] Though the discontent did not
actually drive Todd from his pulpit, it did help persuade him to take
the offer that the Edwards Church in Northampton, Massachusetts,
offered him.[51] Here, too, he ran into similar difficulties, and when he
moved on in three years to a large church in Philadelphia, he resolved

to avoid doctrinal partisanship. In other words, it took Todd eight years and two troubled pastorships to rid himself of notions of ministerial duty and doctrinal loyalty that Andover and his elders had instilled in him.

Similarly, when Henry Ward Beecher took on his first pulpit, he was imbued with a sense of the importance of the New School/Old School conflict that was splintering Congregational-Presbyterianism and of the competition with Methodists for adherents. But within little more than a year he ran into trouble with his congregation. He started out preaching solid New School divinity and gave his congregation the system of sermons he had sketched out while in seminary. Even to himself, his sermons seemed cold and "unfeeling," and from his notations in his *Sermon Book* it is clear they left his congregation equally uninspired.[52] When he tried to join the church with a New School Presbytery, they rebelled and chose to become an "independent" presbyterian church, unaffiliated with either side. And when it became clear that he was trying "to preach down the Methodists," his church presented him with a formal list of complaints—that he fomented religious "partisanship," that he neglected home visits because of "too great a sense of himself," and that his "credit was exercised too freely."[53] Moreover, they made it clear to Beecher that they expected him to correct these faults if he wished to remain as their preacher.

In addition, ministers imbued with the importance of one or another of the campaigns against vice frequently aroused vehement opposition when they tried to impose strict new standards of behavior on their churches. Not only could this spark the ire of people who had long thought themselves upright citizens and good Christians but now felt themselves under direct personal attack as sinners, but it also frequently excacerbated underlying sources of community tension and conflict. One of the things that provoked E. D. Moore's opponents to such fury as to forge the hotel register was his launching of a temperance campaign in the town; and Todd's Philadelphia opponents, some of whom were businessmen caught in a tough competitive situation, bitterly resented his condemnation of Sunday business enterprize.[54] And the Reverend David Oliphant found this his temperance advocacy opened a Pandora's box in what for ten years had been a peaceable Beverly, Massachusetts, parish. In 1832, in keeping with the growing temperance sentiments within evangelicalism and with the support of many of his parishioners, Oliphant began to urge the necessity of total abstinence for any who would be considered genuine Christians and to argue that the town's taverns should be closed down. There quickly rained down upon him a torrent of opposition, centered among an apparently well-respected and extensive Beverly family, the Trasks, who considered their reputations assaulted and their position within church and community at stake. Soon the whole town was embroiled in a series of petitions and counterpetitions, condemning or supporting Oliphant. At one point the church burned down, and Oliphant and his supporters were convinced that persons opposed to their temperance campaign had set the fire. Eventually, after two councils, Oliphant was left with no alternative but to leave, for only his departure, his supporters agreed, would let the church return to even a semblance of normal devotion.[55]

Not surprisingly, the clergy tried in a number of ways to protect themselves against their capricious parishioners. Some Massachusetts associations, for example, suggested instituting consociations on the Connecticut model in order to place the power of arbitration in cases involving "ministerial character and conduct" in the hands of an agency, beyond local community and neighboring council, which would be more sympathetic to the pastor's plight.[56] There was, in addition, a firm reassertion of the ideal of permanence. Ordination and installation sermons as well as more explicitly historical pieces extolled the virtues of permanence by invoking a mythical past marked by harmony in the community and by pervasive pastoral influence. Congregations were warned against letting themselves become enamored of "popularity," of preaching which was merely eloquent and which provoked only the most ephemeral of feelings. Clergymen urged them to take the longer view, to realize that sound and lasting faith came only through a long and careful course of indoctrination and that their spiritual interests were better served by a pastoral friend who would succor their daily needs than by a minister whose superficial eloquence might provide momentary "excitement."[57] Moreover, there is some evidence that ministers were deciding to forego the risks involved in pursuit of broad professional success and choosing situations with prospects of long-range stability. During the years of his Philadelphia pastorate, for example, John Todd nostalgically and idyllically contrasted the virtues of a "quiet ministry" in a small New England town with his pastorate in a major church in a center of national evangelical activity. And when he ran into troubles in 1840, Todd did in fact return to a small New England town, rejecting offers which he earlier would have preferred. He accepted a pastorate in Pittsfield, Massachusetts, where he served for the remaining thirty years of his professional life.[58]

The most far-reaching response to the crisis of the pastoral clergy, however, involved a change in the way the clergy itself was construed. Earlier evangelicals had insisted that the ministry was a calling that was totally different in character from any secular profession. Insofar as they had applied the term to the clergy, they had used it to refer to the character of a minister's commitment and had spoken of the quality of his "profession." Moreover, they had defined the ministry more in terms of its nature as a sacred and public office than in terms of any specific training it required. During the 1840s, however, in a new and self-conscious way, evangelicals began to refer to the clergyman as a professional in the same way they applied the term to a doctor or a lawyer, to denote a special area of circumscribed competence which required specific and rigorous formal training. Churchmen now argued that the clergyman's special task was "the cure of souls" and that to perform this service effectively required extensive formal training.[59] This portrait of the clergyman as a professional was partly a codification of the changes that had taken place in the organization of the ministry over the preceding thirty years. Though they would not have admitted it in quite so many words, this construction amounted to an acceptance of the idea that "edification" was the essential job of the minister and of a client-oriented notion of the ties between a pastor and his people. But what had precipitated the conscious articulation of the new conception of the minister was the need to re-establish the pastor's control over the devotion he dispensed and give him at least some measure of personal and professional security.

The new conception of the minister set up boundaries of pastoral duty that essentially removed the major sources of controversy and conflict—social activism, uninspiring theological disquisition, and doctrinal partisanship—from explicit pastoral responsibility. Under the older, more public conception of the ministerial office, of course, the local preacher had also been an agent of evangelical public purposes, a denominational or doctrinal warrior, and sometimes a theologian and trainer of pastors. Most of these functions had moved away from the parish to the new specialized institutions, and, increasingly, doctrinal controversy was carried out by "learned Doctors" writing from the seminary and in religious journals rather than from the parish. But perhaps most importantly, the conception of the pastor as essentially a physician of the soul involved a change in the character of the pastor's intellectual role. Earlier, a minister had been expected to provide his congregation with a comprehensive intellectual system rather than simply to supply the particular message that would immediately move them or directly aid them in "the conduct of life."

Theology and moral and natural philosophy had provided the broader intellectual framework, and its language had been comprehensible to laity and clergy alike. The notion of edification and soul cure—the idea that a minister should "preach religion rather than about it"—however, represented a separation of pastoral rhetoric from this larger framework. By 1850, in fact, both churchmen and congregations increasingly considered good (that is, effective and popular) preaching to be largely devoid of theological and philosophical terms and to rely instead upon the direct words of the scripture or apt and homely illustrations of Gospel precepts.[60] In fact, theology and moral and natural philosophy were transformed into technical tools, special subjects taken in seminary which were necessary to make a minister a sound and orthodox preacher but which did not provide the substantive ingredients of his preaching. This can be seen particularly clearly in the specialization of religious periodicals. The journals of the first two decades of the nineteenth century, such as *The Panoplist, The Connecticut Missionary Magazine, The Christian Disciple,* or *The Christian Spectator,* contained a wide range of doctrinal, reportorial, controversial, and devotional pieces and were directed to profession and parish alike. Increasingly, however, evangelicals directed religious weeklies like *The Boston Recorder* or *The Independent,* with their short, nondoctrinal, hortatory, and devotional articles, to the laity, while they turned the monthly and quarterly journals like *The American Biblical Repository* (founded in 1838) into almost purely professional journals directed primarily to the ministry.

The conception of the pastor as a professional also served to circumscribe the limits of his responsibilities as a minister so as to secure him against the effects of social issues and contention. First, there was the argument that religion itself was not directly related to matters of the secular world. When they were constructing the evangelical empire, churchmen had stressed the overall social significance of evangelicalism. Revivals, to adapt the title of an 1831 piece in *The Spirit of the Pilgrims,* were "a necessity to the perpetuity of our institutions." Only evangelical religion, the argument had run, could provide the self-government that would keep America's democratic spirit from degenerating into anarchy and mob tyranny and its wealth and enterprise from sinking into "voluptuousness and depravity."[61] By 1840, however, a number of churchmen had begun to have second thoughts about the entire rhetoric of the direct social significance of evangelicalism. Such notions, they argued, amounted to a tacit acceptance of secularism and diminished the sense of the sacred and eternal, which, they insisted, was the only real concern of evangelicalism. Religion, having "no necessary connection with . . . influence in the surrounding world," the argument went, should not be concerned with social purposes or the prosperity of secular institutions.[62] The Reverend Milton Bramen argued, moreover, that the attempts to "trace the abundance and wealth and political advancement of the nation to the Gospel" hindered conversions and revivals.[63] Essentially, this defined the sacred sphere as a totally private one, utterly separate from any direct public responsibilities. And, indeed, in his appropriate sphere, the pastor was distinguished both from a public official and from the ordinary citizen in his relation to "matters not directly religious."[64] Any public responsibilities a minister might have stemmed from his status as a citizen, not from the nature of his office and profession. As one clergyman argued, a pastor's congregation "may not begrudge him his opinion on matters not directly religious, whether they be expressed in the street or in the drawing room or at the ballot box, any more than he may arraign them in the sanctuary for theirs. He has duties to perform as a neighbor and as a member of the body politic, from which he is not exempt because he is called to preach the Gospel."[65] Essentially, then, the minister was seen as one who offered a private service to a specific clientele; and beyond this, his clerical function and responsibilities did not extend. As one minister argued, the nature of the profession "leaves the ordained man without his title, office and official obligations in political, civic, and social matters. . . . When he steps aside from the place and claims of his office, he is as the lawyer out of the courtroom, the judge off the bench, or as the physician away from the sick bed. He is a man untitled, and has common lot with the multitude."[66] It was a figure far removed from the earlier one of the pastor as a "watchman on the walls of Zion."

In addition to circumscribing the pastoral function so as to remove various forms of controversial advocacy from it, the new conception provided a measure of authority and control over this domain. The New England clergy, of course, had never been a priesthood, a separate spiritual caste whose unique powers granted it almost exclusive authority over religious matters. Moreover, the reduction of the pastoral office to a client relationship had stripped away much of the authority that in eighteenth-century New England had come from the general reverence for public office per se and from the minister's place in the upper rank of a social structure rationalized by a culture of deference. By the forties, however, churchmen had begun to use a notion of ministerial training and expertise in ways that were functionally comparable to a Roman Catholic priest's capacity to perform the miracle of transubstantiation. As someone formally educated in the various theological and biblical "sciences" in ways that no layman (no matter how learned) could be, the minister possessed knowledge that distinguished him from the laity in the same way that possession of the requisite "science" distinguished the lawyer and doctor from the nonpractitioner.[67] Clerical advice manuals, in fact, urged the young minister to set aside the time (and to let his parishioners know that he had set it aside)—mornings, and all of Fridays and Saturdays—for the study and meditation he needed to prepare effective lectures, prayers, and sermons. Charges to congregations warned them to be sure to respect the minister's time in the study. And pastors and churches were urged to make special financial arrangements upon settling a minister just to enable him to maintain a professional library.[68]

In addition, churchmen elaborated the notion that there existed a professional decorum uniquely appropriate to the minister. First, the advice contained in the advice manuals as well as in installation and ordination sermons represented the invention of new codes for regulating general relations with one's parishioners. It was pointed out in chapter 4 that the idea of unique clerical manners reflected the emergence of a new ministerial consciousness which distinguished the clergyman from the social class with which he had been identified. This detachment, however, extended to all ordinary social relationships. The minister was portrayed as one who properly ought to preserve a special disengagement in which he was the spiritual friend of all but the social friend of none. Such a stance, at once aloof from his people and involved with them, served both to preserve the pastor from feuds and entanglements that had no direct bearing on his office and function and to foster among his parishioners a sense of personal spiritual dependence upon him.[69]

In addition, the delineation of a code of pastoral decorum represented, in Erving Goffman's phrase, the construction of a formula for the minister's "presentation of self" in ways which would give him the bearing that immediately stamped him as a true minister.[70] Essentially this bearing consisted of manifest Christian piety and decorum: the good and faithful minister exemplified not only the morality expected of a clergyman but also the tranquility that a life in Christ's bosom brought to one. He displayed a general bearing beyond anxiety, a detachment that signaled not disdain but freedom from the bondage of worldliness, and a frame of charity exempt from anger and contentiousness. At the same time, however, a minister's decorum had to stop short of sanctimoniousness. His bearing should not communicate any sense that he thought himself superior to his parishioners. If he was different, it was not because he was better, but because he was a Christian and because being a faithful pastor demanded a more strenuous and persistently successful attempt to live one's Christianity. (Some ministers, in fact, avoided sanctimoniousness by coming before their flock not as a superior and stern judge, but as one who was also a man, one who had experienced and understood their temptations and anxieties.) The new conception of the pastor, then, surrounded the minister with an aura of professional expertise and Christian character that enforced deference to him in matters touching upon his carefully circumscribed sphere. It served to preserve him from any implication in the ordinary life of his community that might jeopardize his position, and it restored a form of authority that simple occupancy of the office had once provided.[71]

8

From Reform to Refuge: The Devotional Transformation

The chaos of the thirties and forties unsettled the local communion. Churches confronted innumerable claims on their time, energy, and resources; communicants found themselves forced to grapple with new demands on their conscience and devotion; dissension and factionalism wracked many churches. This sheer turmoil, moreover, created a growing suspicion that somehow the central character of the church as a sanctuary had been violated. One of the things that had characterized the devotional style of Second Great Awakening evangelicalism was its translation of personal devotion into a direct sense of public responsibility. But many evangelicals increasingly came to believe that the emphasis had been distorted. As one cleric lamented, "professing Christians of the present have so many objects of *public* enterprise and exertion to occupy their time and engage their attention that they are often tempted to slight the more *private* and less attractive duties of retirement and devotion."[1] It seemed, indeed, that the public dimensions "not directly religious" had so encroached upon the sanctuary as to undermine its character as the domain of the sacred, the place to which Christians could repair to renew their sense of the promise of salvation and of the immediacy of the divine presence in their lives.[2]

Church and clergy responded to this situation in various ways. They set about restoring the capacity of churches to protect themselves against outside forces. They tried to expunge the discordant and the impure. And they tried to strengthen the boundaries between the church and the world, the sacred and the profane. By 1850 these efforts to restore the sanctuary added up to a far-reaching reorientation of the style and focus of evangelical devotion.

The campaign to protect the individual churches from disruptive external influences took several forms. There was first a clarification of the precise nature of the translocal evangelical institutions and their relation to the individual communion. Although the churches had been the focal point of the broader evangelical campaigns, directors and agents of them had frequently treated the churches as units in the larger network of organization. By the late thirties, however, churchmen had begun to insist upon carefully distinguishing the local communion from all the other institutions. Ministerial and denominational associations and the benevolent societies served significant ends, but, it was insisted, they were not part of the church and possessed neither ordained status nor authority over the individual churches. As Leonard Woods put it in 1838 in an article defending the legitimacy of benevolent associations, the term "church" could only "properly signify a particular society or congregation of Christians, united together for the worship of God in one place."[3]

Evangelicals also set up rules governing the conduct of outside agencies. They insisted that no matter how benevolent or praiseworthy its goals might be, an outside agency should not impinge upon local routines and that local pastors and ministerial associations should determine whether, when, and how the agencies operated in local areas. Some Massachusetts associations instituted a calendar of specified times when all the churches in the association would take up a collection for each of the broader benevolent causes, thereby obviating the need for agents to appear on the scene and try to rally local Christians to their particular cause.[4] Many associations put forth guidelines for the conduct of revivals and the use of outside assistants, so that control of them would remain firmly in the hands of the stated pastor.[5] Associations also tried to tighten the procedures for selecting and controlling the licentiate pastor. This "anomaly in ecclesiastical jurisprudence" had initially been used simply as a temporary grant which let a young man preach the Gospel while he was seeking a pastorate. In the twenties and thirties, however, it had been used as a more general license to work as an itinerant evangelist, and much of the behavior that had alarmed many churchmen was done by licentiate pastors. Consequently, the Suffolk South Association, for example, insisted that a young man be licensed to preach only within the geographical confines of the association that licensed him and that the association itself retain and exert strict control over him.[6] Moreover, in 1836 the general associations of both Connecticut and Massachusetts passed resolutions that barred itinerant preachers and agents from the societies from entering local churches unless expressly invited by the local minister or the neighborhood ministerial association.[7]

Evangelicals of various persuasions went to great lengths both to restore harmony to the churches and to preserve the purity of their doctrine and devotion. Ultimately, they believed, conflict was traceable to impurity. "Peace is the *result*, not the *precursor* of purity," the Reverend David Grosvenor declared, adding that "the wisdom that is from above is *first* pure, and then peaceable."[8] The Old School faction of Presbyterianism, indeed, reacted so vehemently to the immediatism that had provoked the new revivals of the late twenties and to the antislavery agitation that they traced to it that in 1837 they exscinded all the Presbyteries that were dominated by Beecherite and Finneyite "revival men." They made a literal and unambiguous interpretation of the Westminster Confession the basis for enforcing doctrinal conformity and strengthened the power of the General Assembly to safeguard the local churches from the intrusion of unsettling elements. In addition, they abrogated the Plan of Union of 1801, under which the Congregational-Presbyterian alliance had constructed the benevolent empire. Moreover, they withdrew their sanction from the American Education Society, condemning it as a conspiracy of New Divinity activism, and transferred all their benevolent activities away from nonecclesiastical voluntary societies to agencies under direct control of the General Assembly.[9] Many of their Congregationalist counterparts similarly tried to strengthen the barriers against false doctrine and practice. They set up more systematic and rigorous screening procedures for candidates for the ministry.[10] Even those at the opposite end of the spectrum—the antislavery and abolitionist evangelicals—went as far in their efforts to construct harmonious spiritual communities out of pre-existing purity. Many antislavery and abolitionist churches operated as independent churches. Some stayed with the New School faction of the Presbyterians, which was more Congregational than Presbyterian in its conception and exertion of ecclesiastical authority.[11] Moreover, many newly gathered abolitionist churches eventually became Congregationalist churches. The abolitionists, with their strong sense of a church as a community of feeling, were drawn to congregational notions of internal organization. Furthermore, they needed doctrinal autonomy in order to enforce abolition as a confessional requirement for church membership. Excluding at the outset all sources of conflict over doctrine or duty, they established a harmony built upon common social opinion as well as common spiritual experience.[12]

It was not only external agitation that had brought discord and impurity to the churches: false conversion, with its confusion of mere excitement for genuine religious emotion and its false and excessive zeal, was equally a source of contamination and disorder. These years saw a remarkable outpouring of literature about revivals. There had been, of course, a prolific revival literature for almost forty years, but the writings of the 1830s and 1840s stood in relation to the revivals of the late 1820s and early 1830s as Jonathan Edwards' *Thoughts on Revivals of Religion* stood to the First Great Awakening. In that work Edwards had tried to clarify and preserve what had been good in the Awakening while discarding the excessive and detrimental.[13] Similarly, the volumes by Finney, Sprague, Porter, Barnes, and Tyler sought to distill the experience of the 1820s into a set of practical or cautionary precepts. Whether they were inspired by fear of the zeal, as were Porter's, Sprague's, and Tyler's, or by disappointment over the wane of the 1830–32 revivals, as was Finney's, the manuals all tried to restore order and harmony to revivals.[14]

Those who associated impurity and conflict with the excessive zeal of the new revivals tried to establish pre-1820 forms of piety as the model of genuine spirituality. They resurrected an insistence that "humility," guaged by deference to pastoral judgment and uncontentious carriage, be the absolute criterion for a genuine conversion.[15] They stressed the importance of a careful course of previous indoctrination and urged ministers to devote their energies to the educational institutions—bible classes, inquiry sessions, young person's study associations, Sabbath schools—which would establish sound doctrine and gradually nourish communicants toward salvation.[16] Second, they tried to regulate the use of the various "measures" that the new revivals had employed. These writers, in fact, were particularly concerned that the "new measures," especially the anxious bench and the protracted meeting, had made revivals "mechanical." Revivals, it seemed, had become human contrivances rather than outpourings of divine grace, and the feelings they "artificially" provoked were those of mere natural emotion rather than genuine religious affection.[17] The Suffolk South Association, for example, urged that anxious meetings be carefully separated from other meetings and that they should not be a "mixed assemblage for counsel and exhortation" but should contain only people who were under "pungent conviction of sin." Although they did not altogether repudiate protracted meetings, they did suggest that churches use them very sparingly and rely mainly on "ordinary means of grace."[18] Even Charles Finney had become less enamored of them. He now argued that it was a mistake of "morbid sensitivity" to consider such meetings essential to a revival and insisted that they never be given precedence over private devotion.[19] Finally, they urged setting up "probationer's classes," a sort of spiritual half-way house where the genuineness of piety could be tested after the tumult of the revival had passed.[20]

Men like Finney, Beecher, and Barnes, who had been among the most ardent revival men of the twenties, were equally eager to make revivals more harmonious and predictable. This can be seen most clearly perhaps in the shift in Finney's views. He fretted no less than any other evangelical at how discord had affected revivalism. While his 1835 *Lectures on Revivals of Religion* was an urgent plea for revivals, he nonetheless came close to embracing the notion of evangelical decorum that many of his earlier opponents had held. His Oneida revivals in 1826 and his famous 1830 Rochester revival had been insistently aggressive in their proselytism, and Finney had had little patience with the criticism of the forms of his revival. He insisted that a revival had to be free to work according to its own emotional momentum, and that fastidiousness about form simply hindered a revival.[21] Now, however, Finney warned churches and pastors to take particular care to avoid anything that might disturb the unity and tranquility of the churches. He warned that censoriousness and contentiousness, particularly among the new converts and the most ardent promoters of a revival, could destroy it. He also argued that the revival should not interrupt the "necessary business" of everyday life or unduly disrupt daily routines.[22] (This was a far cry from the sense in the Oneida revivals that the revival transcended all. In those revivals, businesses frequently closed, and meetings carried on with little heed to such interruptions as regular meals.) Equally muted was Finney's idea of the emotional tone of a revival. His notion of a revival or a church (in the *Lectures*, the two were almost coterminus) as a community of feeling remained intact. But Finney spoke of the emotional tone as much in terms of unity and harmony as he did in terms of "temperature" and "warmth." In 1837, in *Christian Affinity*, Finney had portrayed a revival as working through a form of emotional warfare in which the righteous labored to raise anyone with "a lower degree of heat" to their own high level by assaulting them with their own superior fervor. The vision of emotional accord in the *Lectures*, however, was one with which few evangelicals would quarrel. He roundly condemned contention, discord, invidious spiritual comparison, and any expression of self-righteousness as hindrances which would "grieve the spirit."[23]

In addition, evangelicals increasingly emphasized the importance of revivals as instruments for improving the quality of their communicant's piety. As early as 1833, Ebenezar Porter had warned that "the strength of a church consists not in the *number* but in the *character* of those who belong to it." "Any skillful commander," he analogized, "would choose to rely on a select band of soldiers to possess true hearts . . . instead of ten times the number of recent and promiscuous volunteers." In fact, he concluded, "of many a church it may be said as to all purposes of unity, and stability, and moral strength, the people are *TOO MANY*."[24] Indeed, the vision of the good revival that became dominant was almost indistinguishable from what evangelicals wanted everyday devotion to be. Many, like Beecher and Finney, in fact, spoke of "perpetual revivals." But what they meant—and intended their manuals to produce—hardly differed from what other evangelicals called a consistently spiritual church: a steady but moderate zeal, not so high as to consume itself, exhausting church and pastor, but not so low as to drift toward indifference.[25] Moreover, though evangelicals in the forties still worked to expand the evangelical domain, they looked far less to mighty conquests than to steady, almost natural accretion. The reconstituted perpetual revival was really directed as much to Christians already inside the door as to the sinner outside. To be sure, the unregenerate were not neglected, but the sinners to whom a revival was directed were family members of regenerate church members or regularly attending, but not yet converted, members of the congregation. Moreover, in the *Lectures* Finney gave a good deal of attention to what he called "reconversion" and to "backsliders," terms referring to those previously converted whose piety had lapsed. A revival, indeed, was to be directed as much toward them as to the as yet unsaved.[26] (This attentiveness to the devotional needs of the convert is reflected in Finney's subsequent career. When he became professor of theology at Oberlin College, his preoccupation became sanctification—what happened to the Christian in conversion and how he could grow spiritually *after* he received divine grace.)

In addition to these attempts to protect doctrine and devotion from external influences and provide more orderly and consistent emotion, there was a change in the character of evangelical devotion and its accompanying affections. By the 1840s preaching and worship increasingly centered on the figure of Christ. Though most discussions of conversion and good Christian character still began with the familiar ideas of submission and duty, focus turned more often to Christ's love than to God's command as sermons began to dwell more on the atoning and forgiving Son than upon the ruling and demanding Father. The life and character of Christ, his suffering and patience, his meekness and forgiveness amidst unspeakable trials and against implacable foes, became one of the most fetching pulpit topics. Heaven was another highly popular pulpit theme. In what sometimes amounted to a species of utopian fantasy, preachers depicted its joys, beatitudes, and especially the intimate warmth of existence in that other realm.[27] Many ministers described Christ's love and Christianity as a "system" or "law" of love rather than of moral government. Indeed, the shift in metaphors from government to love is indicative of the broader devotional transformation. The moral government scheme of divinity, which had informed most New England evangelical preaching in the early decades of the century, had centered upon the image of God as a perfectly just and perfectly merciful governor who demanded repentance and obedience and who in return provided a structure of order and security.[28] The outer framework of divine rule remained unaltered: conversion continued to be construed as a surrender to God. But clergymen, especially younger ones, it seems, increasingly muted their use of the notion of obligation in leading the Christian to surrender to God. Instead, they adopted the theme of "Christ's love sufficient to all things" as the "motive" (to use their language) with which to draw their communicants toward salvation.[29] George Beecher put it very revealingly in a letter to another young minister, who was as prone as was George himself to dwelling on the "darker side" of his character. He warned him not to read Finney's *Sinners Bound to Change Their Own Hearts,* because it was "too harsh." Instead, he argued that although "the Bible requires you to do duties, it at the same time tells you that God's grace shall be sufficient to you, and that His strength shall be perfected in your weakness." Most wonderful of all, he pleaded, the Bible "brings before you the Lord Jesus, as your friend and intercessor, and the high priest of our profession; and thus relieves the distress of conscious weakness and guilt, by encouraging assurance of assistance, forgiveness, and love." Finally George implored his young colleague to dwell less upon his "sins and deficiencies" and to think "more of Christ, his character, his love, his suffering."[30]

The image of Christ also informed notions about regenerate Christian character. Evangelical preaching addressed to the convert had always been designed to nourish what were referred to as the Christian graces. Dwelling on themes of duty and responsibility, evangelicals had usually addressed the regenerate in terms of an outwardly directed benevolence. Godliness was perceived and Christian character developed, the communicant was told, in acts of benevolence. But increasingly evangelicals began to employ a rather different term to characterize a frame of benevolence. They spoke of "eminent holiness," a notion that referred most specifically to the inner state rather than to the outward expression of grace. Churchmen urged Christians to cultivate holiness, to purge themselves of all remnants of sinfulness and all unhallowed feelings.[31] Christ, moreover, was the model of holiness to which they turned with recurrent and loving frequency. But it was as much his personality as his action that they pointed to for emulation. They urged their communicants, and they themselves tried, to become ever more Christlike, to turn their personal devotions, their Christian fellowship, and various devotional exercises to efforts to attain a love like his—gentle, meek, forgiving, and humble. Only such an inner state could render the Christian's carriage toward others truly benevolent and bring one spiritual peace. As George Beecher confided to his journal in 1838, "I desire more and more earnestly to imitate *perfectly* the meek and gentle and lovely spirit of Christ; so humble, so unostentatious, so irregardless of his own interests and reputation, so unwearied and constant in his labors." He especially desired to "become more meek," declaring that "my impetuosity of feeling and nervous irritability can never be overcome, but by a more diligent and unwearied course of self-government and watchfulness and prayer."[32]

The use of Christ as motive and model involved a transformation in what was accepted as genuine religious emotion. It established a clear and definite style of feeling that was identifiably and unmistakably religious by strengthening the boundaries between animal passions and the feelings provoked by worldly endeavors on the one hand, and the affections inspired by Christ and marking the gracious heart on the other. Essentially, fixing upon Christ as both source and exemplar for genuine religious feelings represented a retreat from passion and fervor. Indeed, evangelicals, like most middle-class Americans, were increasingly terrified of passion, fearful of any form of strong emotion in themselves or in others that was not "safe."[33] Particularly revealing is an episode Henry Ward Beecher recounted in 1837 in the journal he was keeping to help him gain perspective on "feelings, feelings, feelings," as he put it. Beecher noted an episode in which he and a young woman on an outing to a museum came across a painting with some apparently erotic content. At least

Beecher's own response had been erotic, and the journal entry was a clear attempt to deal with the storm of sexual feeling that had come over him. He expressed deep mortification at the very thought that the young lady might have realized what had gone through his mind, and he glossed the account of the episode by angrily asserting that museums should not be permitted to display such paintings where unmarried young men and women might see them. Then, he launched into a prolonged discussion of Byron and the evils of uncontrollable passion.[34] The intensity of such fears is exemplified in the Reverend Sylvester Graham's portrait of human sexual nature. In his *Lecture to Young Men on Chastity*, Graham conjured up a nightmare of how the human passions could be transformed into an uncontrolable engine of destruction by the slightest stimulus. "It is by abusing his organs," Graham wrote, "and depraving his instinctive appetites, through the devices of his rational powers, that the body of man has become a living volcano of unclean propensities and passions."[35] And he spoke equally graphically of what happened to a young man addicted to masturbation: "when he had reached the age of twenty, with a broken down constitution, with a body full of disease, and with a mind in ruins, the loathsome habit still tyrannized over him, with the inexorable imperiousness of a fiend of darkness."[36] Though Graham's imagery was perhaps extreme, his fears were typical, as childrearing manuals and dietary and health regimes designed to protect the body and soul from artificial stimulation all attest.[37]

The feelings associated with Christ, however, were very different from natural or animal passions. First, the experience of saving grace became less emotionally tumultuous, though Christ-inspired piety could be just as deep. In some ways invoking Christ as the "motive" for conversion represented a very different use of emotion as a tool of religious exhortation from the new revivals' use of it. Preaching the love of Christ did not assault the penitent's identity in an attempt to provoke such feelings of self-loathing, guilt, and hatred of sin as to lead to abject surrender to God's will. (Some evangelicals, in fact, had become fearful of such strong emotions, worrying that they might lead to "melancholy," madness, or suicide. Indeed, the newly established insane asylums had a separate category for religious madness.)[38] Christ was a gentler persuader, coaxing the penitent toward conversion by awakening "a very tender and affecting dependence upon Christ, a leaning upon him, a feeling of his infinite goodness, and suitableness to every specific want and the graciousness of his mercy, so free from reproach, so gentle."[39] Conversions were no longer a struggle waged between a stern and damning Father and a defiant son until the son surrendered. Instead, they were more like the reclamation by a friend of one who had been lost, for, as Henry Fowler put it in his diary: "There is one friend at least who sticketh closer than a brother, who has promised to share our burdens and comfort us in our sorrows, to whom earthly friends in comparison are as nothing, who is always nigh at hand & whose compassions fail not. Yes happiness is ours if we will only keep near *Christ.*"[40]

The religious affections Christ inspired, moreover, were directly the opposite in kind as well as intensity to human passions. They were totally unaggressive and nonviolent, and partook not of force or power but of gentleness and tranquility. Indeed, the terms employed to describe such feelings are revealing: meek, gentle, humble, sweet, tender, unreproachful, forgiving. Rather than "zealous," the watchword for this new mode of religious feeling would have to be "sentimental." And when churchmen wished to portray the Christian graces in a human frame they frequently used feminine examples. The love of Christ as well as Christian love was warm and caring, best exemplified by the selfless and sometimes suffering, but always receiving and forgiving, mother and the pure succoring and pacific, but nonsensual, love of the true wife.[41] Thus, genuine religious feelings were not only wholly different in kind from the emotions of natural and worldly life, but they provided the antidote to them. For as one received and emulated Christ's love one became less aggressive, spiteful, and contentious toward others, taking on instead the peace of his all-sufficient love and the forbearance of Christian forgiveness.

This shift in the style and content of evangelical emotion and worship accentuated the sense of the church as a sanctuary for the sacred and a refuge against the world. The resurgence of Sabbatarianism served to dramatize the distance between sacred and profane. Maintaining the purity of the Sabbath by consecrating it to worship and abstaining from secular activity not only honored God; it also heightened the contrast with the world. Sabbath thus was the time apart— "the single day of the week in which no tide of business rises and no storms blow."[42] And the church was the place apart—where communicants experienced communion and sentiment, feelings of caring and being cared for directly opposite to the anxieties, contentiousness, irritation, and passions of daily life.

This is seen most clearly in the rituals of evangelical worship. The 1830s and 1840s saw the emergence of music as a major component of evangelical devotion. Following the precepts of Lowell Mason and others, word and tune were carefully united so as to clearly and effectively communicate evangelical ideas and sentiments. As H. Crosby Englizian has put it, "Church music was not to be an interlude, a temporary expedient. Neither was it a preparation for worship; proper psalmody was to be worship."[43] Moreover, the themes of many of the most widely used Gospel hymns of these years stressed Christ as the unreproachful redeemer:

> *Just as I am—Thou wilt receive;*
> *Wilt welcome, pardon, cleanse, relieve,*
> *Because thy promise I believe,*
> *O Lamb of God, I come, I come.*[44]

Hymns depicting heaven not as the opposite of hellfire and damnation, but as home and refuge and a place of reconciliation and reunion with loved ones, were especially popular. In addition, churches increasingly used carefully trained choirs to direct these sentiments to the communicant's heart and arouse the requisite religious emotions.[45] Pastoral prayer also took on particular importance as a means for bringing a sense of the reality and immediacy of Christ's presence to communicants. Indeed, the institution of businessmen's prayer meetings during the revivals of 1858 suggests the desire for and effectiveness of this kind of edification. As Henry Fowler, asserting that "a prayer is often more powerful in its influence than a sermon," put it in his diary, "How much one is affected by a good prayer! How it directs one's thoughts right up to God, and heaven and makes one feel that God is near, even in the midst of us."[46]

The sermon, however, remained the core of the evangelical service. But increasingly the preacher had become a performer, and the sermon itself less a formal exposition or even an exhortation than a special kind of performance, which engulfed an audience much as the performance of a good actor or musician would. Following the notion that the minister's function was to transmit truth in pure and orthodox form to his congregation, the traditional sermon had operated according to a set of clear rhetorical constraints. Essentially, the traditional sermon had been a formal argument: it moved from the biblical grounding of the particular doctrine to be inculcated, through the exposition (organized into a logical sequence of "heads"), which proved the doctrine, to the application of it to the particular audience and situation. Moreover, the sermon ordinarily confined its language to the Bible and the idiom of the evangelical system. Since the Bible contained both the revealed word of God and a type for all human experience and behavior, sermons customarily drew metaphors for dramatizing doctrine and exemplifying its aptness to contemporary life from the Bible.[47]

The manifest evangelical content of the sermons of the 1840s and 1850s differed very little from earlier sermons. Man as sinner, salvation by faith alone through the intercession of Christ's atonement, and conversion as an event in time achieved by the action of the Holy Spirit working through the affections of the heart remained the underlying ideas of evangelical preaching. What had begun to change, however, was the structure and language of the sermon, how it operated as a rhetorical event.[48] Confining preaching to edification involved a loosening of some of the traditional constraints on sermon making, even though some ministers retained the shell of the earlier formalism. There was a broadening of the range of available rhetorical devices, as modes of personal address previously confined to prayer and examples of peril and anguish drawn from the ministers' experience and from situations of contemporary life began to find their way into pulpit sermons. There was a similar broadening of the language. Doctrinal and theological vocabulary became much less predominant. Although the Bible remained a mine of imagery and metaphor, preachers increasingly employed domestic and naturalistic metaphors and drew upon sentimental and didactic literature as they stretched for what Henry Ward Beecher referred to as "home-bred words"—"those which people are used to and suggest something to them." These words, he went on, "that we heard in our childhood store up in themselves the sweetness and flavor that make them precious."[49] Finally, the sermons of these years were much less likely to proceed as formal argumentation than to move through a sequence of images or impressions designed to fuse idea and feeling into an "elevating" thought, or into Christian "sentiment," to use the contemporary word that captures both the ideational and the emotional dimensions.

Behind these changes in rhetorical strategy and idiom, moreover, was a change in how Gospel preaching operated as a devotional ritual. This can be seen most clearly in the bonds that sermons established between preacher and people, and in the roles the preacher adopted in the sermon itself. The minister remained, of course, an "ambassador" of God, but increasingly this task was construed as the act of bringing "the *true* power of the Gospel—the love of Christ" to his hearers.[50] The focus thus was as much on the medium, the preacher, as the message, the love of Christ. At the heart of this conception was the idea that edifying preaching of Christ's love ultimately came from its power over the minister's own life. It was this idea that lay behind the insistence that a preacher had to strive above all else for "eminent holiness," that he had to build a Christian personality fully attuned to experiencing and observing life in terms of the law of Christ's love, and that with this foundation he could construct sermons that effectively brought Christ to his hearers.[51]

Under this style of preaching, then, the performance itself also communicated the Gospel message. Ministers usually adopted a gentle tone, concerned rather than reproachful, forgiving rather than angry. Moreover, in his sermon a minister frequently assumed the mantle of a special friend to his hearers. He established bonds of understanding and sympathy by conjuring up touching images of the anxieties and temptations of life, and by portraying himself as a fellow human being, equally subject to the sorrows, cares and temptations that troubled them. This bond of sympathy and concern was then deepened in ways that stemmed from his office and bearing as a Gospel preacher, caring went beyond sympathy to help, becoming almost Christ-like in the end as he took on Christ's saving love and brought it to them.[52] Henry Ward Beecher referred to this pulpit style as "natural" preaching and the "living Gospel," by which he meant a genuine soul-felt preaching that was devoid of artifice but was consummate in its artistry—an artistry, he insisted, that required training, discipline, skill, continuing preparation, and a vast repertory of rhetorical tools. "When the hand of the Lord is laid upon the heart," Beecher declared, "from the formative power of inward truth the outward form may be generated as in the language of a poem."[53] Interestingly, in fact, an almost identical conception was applied in 1850 to Jenny Lind, the Swedish Nightingale, of whom Henry Tuckerman wrote, "so directly from the heart of nature springs her melody, and so beyond the reach of art is the simple grace of her air and manners, that we associate her with the opera only through the consummate skill—the result of scientific training—manifested in her vocalism." He concluded that "Nature in her seems to have taken Art to her bosom, and assimilated it, through love, with herself, until the identity of each is lost in the other."[54] And Neil Harris summarized her tour in terms equally applicable to the new pulpit style: "every step of the way was prepared, every feature planned, every reaction nurtured. But his [Barnum's] star was presented as the quintessence of spontaneity, lacking affectation or contrivance."[55]

As good an example as any of the sermon as performance in this sense can be found in a sermon, *How To Become a Christian*, which Henry Ward Beecher, who was the most effective preacher of his generation and who more than anyone else made the sentimental sermon an art form, preached at Burton's theater in New York City during the revival of 1858.[56] The sermon was explicitly a conversion sermon; moreover, its implicit doctrinal structure was very similar to Finney's 1830 sermon, *Sinners Bound to Change Their Own Hearts*, namely, that they should turn immediately against sin and through Christ's atonement give themselves wholly to God.

He portrayed conversion as a simple step that needed no doctrinal knowledge or assent. It was Christ the Savior, he made clear, not creeds or doctrines, who was the object of belief. Indeed, at the very beginning he told his hearers to "get rid of" all their "false notions" about the need for long doctrinal preparations.[57] He flatly asserted that there was no person in the room (almost all of whom were strangers to him) who was not "abundantly qualified today, before the sun goes down to become a true Christian in the spiritual and experimental sense of the term."[58] Having portrayed conversion as a simple matter of choice, Beecher then set about leading his audience to that choice by fashioning an extended analogy between Christ's love and a feast. He developed the image of an establishment in New York City, "an eating place, free to the hungry." His focus was a man "from genteel society," who had fallen on difficult times and exhausted all possibilities of borrowing money and dining with friends. (His audience was composed mainly of businessmen, some of whom must have been a bit anxious about the recent depression.) The man knew of the "dining saloon where there is plenty of good to be had for nothing," but even with a "gnawing stomach" he felt "too proud to go as a beggar." Still, his hunger led him reluctantly but surely to the door, where he saw the riches. He waited, fearing that someone would "recognize him and know him," but "the attraction is so great he goes in, . . . nobody sees him and nobody seems surprised." He grasps a crust of bread and then "sits right down and makes a feast," wondering how he had been such a fool as to linger. Beecher next asked the obvious question: "are there not such fools in this congregation?" and declared that "if there are any in this congregation that have seen the bounty spread forth in the love of Christ, that they can have without money and without price . . . don't let them wait for somebody to explain it any more. Try it yourself today."[59]

As he built his efforts to persuade his hearers to "try it," Beecher switched to a personal form of address, forging a bond of intimate—almost private—ministration. He exuded a deep sympathy and identity with his communicant's plight, declaring that "I always feel most for those who are farthest from grace, perhaps because I see in them some likeness to myself." Then, analogizing from Christ's ministry among those "most wretched," he assured his listeners that "whenever I know a man that nobody else prays for, it seems as if my heart would break for him."[60] Having established a bond of intimate personal concern, Beecher then gave a catalogue of all the wickednesses, petty and great, to which men were drawn, from rum-selling ("that is about as bad as a man can be in this world"), to gaming, and stealing, both outright and through the "genteel way so-called honest men steal and call it financeering."[61] But rather than push this vivid catalogue to a choice between repentance or exclusion from Christian comfort and fellowship, Beecher used it to bring his penitents the sufficiency of Christ's love by taking on Christ's caring as his own. Instead of his father's or Charles Finney's "repent, repent," he asked his congregation "to give me your hand for you are my brethren," and exclaimed:

> *He sends me here to say to some man who is on the point of decision, but who thinks it is of no use to try to be good any longer—drink, perhaps may be taking you down; or your passions are dragging you down, and you don't know how to resist the insidious pleasures which surround you; or your companions are taking you down, and nobody, as you think, cares for you—nobody prays for you or gives you instruction. Yes there is one man who does—I care for you; not out of my own nature, but because the spirit of my Master makes me thus care for your soul . . . saying "take care of that man, and bear him up, lest at any time he dush his foot against a stone!"*[62]

Such concern and comfort—and Christian love—were of a sort that few evangelical communicants of the 1850s could resist, and it is little wonder that Beecher was the most popular and highly remunerated pastor of his day. For what the Christ-centered, edifying sermon at its most effective did was create in and for evangelical communicants an experience of Christ's embrace in which the anxieties of sin and the world faded into insignificance, at least for the Sabbath. By 1850, then, the churches had become protected and withdrawn islands of piety. Rather than provide communicants with the discipline for coping with the world or organize their responsibilities toward it, they sheltered them from the world and brought them the transcending comforts of Christ's atonement and love.

9

Office to Profession

Out of the intellectual, institutional, and devotional chaos of the 1830s and 1840s came a new kind of equilibrium.[1] The application of a notion of profession to the clergy and the isolation and protection of the sanctuary were part of a larger clarification of the place and role of church and clergy in society. Eighteenth-century New England had possessed what might be termed a theocentric culture, in which the individual's relationship to God, the ordination of its institutions, the explanation of its history, and the norms governing manners, morals, and public obligations all derived from the word and will of God. New Englanders had derived their sense that their lives conformed to an ultimate order from their own personal relationship to God and from their assurance of God's sovereign presence in the world. Believers not only monitored their standing with God by their conformity to the God-given rules of faith and conduct, but also derived a sense of earthly order and security from confidence that their community was a Godly one, ordered according to divine law and sustained by the active exertion of God's sovereignty.[2]

This theocentric communalism had given the eighteenth-century ministry its essential character as a public office. Public moneys had paid the minister, and the polity had taken part in his selection. Most importantly, however, the sacred office had defined and sustained the community as a public. The minister conducted what was referred to as "public worship," performing the rituals and delivering the Word that ordered the community as an organic whole. In this sense the minister belonged to the town. It was above all else his enduring presence in the community—gathering a church and settling a minister transformed a mere settlement into a community—that was of greatest significance, and it was largely through this presence that a minister was of importance to the individual.[3]

This communalism did not survive the eighteenth century, and by the 1850s church and clergy were stationed very differently in society. In one sense, the church can be said to have moved from the center of the social order to one of its poles. This is not to say that the importance of the church had diminished. One could argue that the church per se was a more ubiquitous presence in the life of the mid-nineteenth-century communicant than it had been in the life of the eighteenth-century believer. In the eighteenth century, the church had anchored the town, but the town had framed and contained its inhabitants' lives. But when in the nineteenth century the town had atrophied as the frame of order, the church took on a new kind of primacy. Towns became structureless, less places to which people belonged than places where they resided for a time. In this context, the local church itself had become perhaps the most important social institution for its communicants, providing forms of communion and a sense of belonging and inducting its people into a dense fabric of organizations and associations. Moreover, the broader structure it directed communicants into was not the secular community but the denomination. When communicants moved to a new town, they found in the evangelical church a ready-made community of like-minded and like-believing, in which they could immediately establish a sense of belonging and enter a network of trustworthy acquaintances and safe institutions.

Furthermore, while religion continued to provide believers with their sense of ultimate well-being, it gave them a rather different sense of order. In the eighteenth century, the devotional idiom governing the relationship between God and the individual had also governed one's place and demeanor in the larger social order. By the 1850s, however, the salvational bond was experienced as the antidote to secular existence. A believer's deepest sense of personal security and order—now anchored in the love of the Son more than in the governance of the Father—came less from a sense that God's direct sovereign presence sustained life and its institutions than from the enjoyment of a sentimental relationship with Christ that transcended the chaos, loneliness, and hostility of the secular world.

By the mid-nineteenth century, then, the church had become almost exclusively a devotional center. No longer was it a public institution. As a structure it did not belong to the polity as it had under establishment. Nor did it have any explicit public or civil function or presence, and it did not address its communicants as citizens of any particular polity. It was purely a voluntary association, supported by private donation, and an exclusive one, serving and superintending only those who wished to join it. In short, the mid-nineteenth-century church was solely a private organization for the nurture and worship of a self-selected group of Christian believers.

The transformation of the church into a citadel of devotion, withdrawn from and protected against the outer world, did not mean that religion shed its civil dimension or that the clergy had abandoned clerical guardianship. In fact, as Timothy Smith has argued, the 1850s witnessed vehement expressions of clerical social concern and a renewed insistence that the United States was fundamentally a Christian nation.[4] The clergy's recovery of its public voice, however, rested upon a firm separation between the devotional and the public dimensions of religion. In the eighteenth century, of course, a common idiom and discipline had united devotion and citizenship, and the evangelicalism fashioned in the first quarter of the nineteenth century had preserved this unity by making moral activism the sign and witness of salvation. By the 1850s, however, few churchmen insisted upon a direct connection between piety and moralism, between a communicant's personal relationship to God and the articulation of Christian views on public issues. In part, this separation between devotion and citizenship reflected the belief that in the 1830s and 1840s the public realm had violated the devotional sphere, that in giving such primacy to the impact of religion on this world, abolitionists and others had lost sight of the ultimate significance of Christianity as a plan of salvation.

The insistence upon maintaining clear boundaries between the devotional and the public dimensions of Christianity had, however, a more positive aspect. By the mid-fifties it had become axiomatic that the capacity of religion to sustain an inner sense of order and nurture inner moral restraints depended upon keeping the churches free from contamination by the world. Most importantly, however, the separation of the two dimensions of religion reflected a conception of social order very different from the communalism of the eighteenth century or the evangelicalism of the first third of the nineteenth century. Rather than construe the social order as an organic whole, the mid-nineteenth century tended to view it as a set of separate domains. In this context, the isolation of the devotional realm can be seen as part of a broader segmenting of life, as distinctions between sacred and secular, domestic and economic, masculine and feminine, private and

public took on an indelibility and significance they had not possessed
in the eighteenth century. The social order thus was seen as a kind of
equilibrium in which opposite, but equally necessary and desirable,
aspects of life and society, each in its "appropriate sphere," balanced
each other. Moreover, social order, in this view, was seen to depend
upon the preservation of the boundaries between the different spheres
of life. In fact, the way nineteenth-century Americans organized and
distinguished space reflected this sense of a social order.[5] The house,
for example, separated its internal spaces in new ways according to
function and sphere and, as a whole, increasingly became solely a
private and domestic arena, cut off from and protected against public
and economic functions and activities. The church, moreover, was no
longer the kind of public space it had been in the eighteenth century.
Then, while containing the sacred space where public worship took
place, it had provided the arena for a wide variety of other public
activities, frequently serving as the place where the broader citizenry
gathered as a public. But by the mid-nineteenth century, churches
rarely served as gathering places for general or, to use the nineteenth
century term, "promiscuous" assemblages. Instead, a series of new
structures—lecture halls, opera houses, libraries, town halls—had
been constructed as public places. Indeed, even forms of religiously
based activism, such as temperance exhortation and organization, had
moved into separate organizations, which met in special temperance
halls and lycea rather than in churches.

The social significance of religion was not confined, however, to its
character as ballast and antidote to secular existence. As it had earlier,
organized Christianity continued to provide a moral vocabulary for
national life. Here too, by the 1850s, there was a clarification of the
boundaries that distinguished clerical public guardianship from other
forms of public discourse and activity. The recovery of a clerical public voice in the 1850s built upon the distinction between the political
and moral spheres of the public culture. In the eighteenth century, the
clergy had articulated the nature of public office and authority and
popular obedience and obligation. Now, however, the procedures of
governance and the selection of civil officeholders were considered
clearly beyond the scope of clerical public concern. Even churchmen
rarely discussed political institutions in terms of divine ordination;
instead, they were defined in terms of secularized democratic theory
and commitments. The role of religion in sustaining the broader public culture consisted in laying out the Christian dimensions of public
issues. Moreover, the public opinion for which the clergy was particularly responsible was thought to be neither partisan nor sectarian, but

common and universal, and to lie at the foundation of order. In this sense, it was the clergy's task to articulate a particular body of public opinion rather than to organize public action.

This clarification of legitimate clerical punditry can be seen in the clerical address to the problem of slavery, which, by the fifties, had again become the focal point of clerical public discourse. In some ways this was unavoidable: as the conflict between North and South over slavery intensified and eventually escalated into civil war, believers expected the clergy to apply Christianity to the issue and to find some providential meaning and design in the trials they and the Republic were enduring. In fact, to some extent the conflict may well have provided the occasion for the clergy to reassert the leadership that had been uncertain and compromised during the 1830s and 1840s.[6] The discourse on slavery, however, was very different from that of the thirties and took place within a very different climate of opinion. Though firmly antislavery, few churchmen of the fifties were immediate abolitionists. Though condemning slavery and calling for its eventual end, organized Christian antislavery opinion contained neither a program nor a direct strategy for abolishing slavery in the South. In addition, while they denounced slavery as a moral evil, few churchmen of the New England strain tied antislavery opinion to the problem of one's personal standing with God. Finally, with the emergence of antislavery politics and the rise of the Republican Party, the publication of *Uncle Tom's Cabin*, and the separation of the denominations into Northern and Southern branches, the clergy's nonprogrammatic denunciation of slavery became far less divisive than the abolitionism of the thirties had been. In fact, clerical attentiveness to the issue of slavery in the fifties helped contribute to the emergence in the North of a general moral consensus against slavery.[7] In this sense, the Northern clergy came before the public to address slavery, not in the guise of agitators or reformers, but in that of the upholders of common, universal truths.[8]

In the 1850s, then, the role of the clergy remained much as it had been. As the body charged with the care and application of the Christian Gospel in society, it still nurtured communicants in their devotion to God, and it still articulated a body of Christian social doctrine. But the clergy's position in society and its character as a social institution had changed in ways that reflected the changes in society and the new definition of that society as an order. The eighteenth-century clergy had been above all else a local institution. The ministry had scarcely any translocal, corporate structure or identity. All but a handful of clergymen had been more or less permanently settled in particular parishes, and the term "minister" and "clergyman" (essentially synonymous) referred only to those who were situated in pastorates.[9] Almost all the services the clergy provided to society were done by the parish clergy. The general public it served, moreover, had been organized into a series of identical constituencies served in a variety of ways by a single clergyman.

By the 1850s, of course, all of this had changed. In the first place, the pastorate was no longer in the eighteenth-century sense a public office. In no sense was the mid-nineteenth-century minister a town pastor, and no civil jurisdiction had any role, or even any stake, in his selection or presence. Ordinarily one of several preachers from his own or other denominations, he served only his specific spiritual constituency. He was not in any necessary way integrated into the social structure of the town, rarely thought of himself as belonging to it, and rarely remained in a single town for much of his professional career. Moreover, it was no longer his primary function to define and superintend the place and obligations people had in the larger polity, nor was he expected to articulate a general intellectual structure by which life in all its facets could be comprehended. The pastoral role had become almost exclusively a devotional and confessional one. Above all else, a minister's communicants expected him to sustain their sense of an immediate bond with Christ, to personally attend their afflictions with comforting counsel, and to preach and pray in ways that provoked sentiments appropriate to those seeking or enjoying Christ's all-sufficient love.

Second, many of the services and functions performed in the parish by the local minister during the eighteenth century were now performed by specialized institutions that were unconnected to the local churches and conducted by clergymen with no pastoral position or responsibilities. In addition to the colleges and seminaries staffed and headed by clergymen, there was a vast and well-organized structure of Christian philanthropy. By the mid-fifties, many of the evangelical, humanitarian, and benevolent associations which the past decades had spawned had developed into well-organized bureaucracies. Headquartered in the major cities, they had state or regional auxiliaries, were administered by a full-time secretary and his staff of assistants and agents, and had well-worked-out techniques for raising funds from local churches or prosperous individual donors. Much of this philanthrophy was devoted to the support and spread of religious nurture and institutions, and many of the associations were the eleemosynary institutions by which the "voluntary system" of the American Church operated. In addition, city missions, pauper, orphan, and charity societies, and such institutions as the YMCA applied Christian social ethics to the victims of misfortune and vice. Though men like Henry Gallaudet, with his Hartford School for the Deaf, and Charles Loring Brace, with his Children's Aid Society, stand out, dozens of other clergymen also made service in one of the charity or mission societies their clerical vocation.[10]

Finally, although some ministers might occasionally address public concerns from their Sunday pulpits, the essential locus of clerical public guardianship had moved beyond the parish to nonpastoral and translocal agencies. This, of course, reflected changes in the character of the public as well as changes in the organization of the clergy. The clergy no longer addressed a communal public, but a dispersed, anonymous, and national one, composed of diverse denominational and doctrinal strands, differing political affiliations, and various regional identities and social interests. Clerical public guardianship thus resided in the body of generalized, nonsectarian, nonpartisan opinion formulated by clergymen who, whether they occupied a pastorate, editorship, or professorship, self-consciously addressed this broader national public. Moreover, this opinion was promulgated through such translocal agencies as the lecture and lyceum circuit, the religious press, and the American Tract Society. Especially, as Wilson Smith pointed out in his *Professors and Public Ethics*, had many college presidents and professors assumed the mantle of Christian guardianship. They saw themselves as public men in much the same way as the eighteenth-century pastor had considered himself "a watchman on the walls of Zion." They taught moral philosophy—the capstone of the traditional liberal arts curriculum—which was intended to give their students the preparation they needed for citizenship and social leadership. In addition, they wrote treatises on public ethics and lectured on the lyceum circuit, maintaining a visible and articulate presence as the shapers of Christian social doctrine.[11]

By the 1850s the clergy was no longer framed by its role and position in the local community but was shaped by a new kind of translocal structure and professional consciousness. For the eighteenth century *the clergy* properly refers to the aggregate of individual ministers. But for the mid-nineteenth century, the term accurately connotes a collective and self-conscious body of which the parish clergy was simply one part. *The ministry* referred to those holding pastoral posts, while the more inclusive term, *the clergy*, referred to the whole corpus of trained and certified men of God filling a variety of positions and performing a variety of nonpastoral tasks. In short, by the 1850s, in institutional terms, the clergy had become a profession, a coherent, self-conscious occupational body, organized and defined by a set of institutions which were outside lay or public control, which controlled the special learning needed to become a clergyman, and which possessed the power to determine who could enter the clerical ranks. But *profession*, like *office* in the eighteenth century, was not simply a matter of structure: it contained as well what might be called a social grammar. For the eighteenth century, the term *office* not only denoted the formal position the minister occupied in church and community, but also connoted the full dimensions of his role. In addition, it captured the nature of his authority, conveying legitimacy as an ambassador of God and placing him in the appropriate station in his community. By the 1850s, what Burton Bledstein has referred to as a "culture of professionalism" was forming an equally comprehensive social code.[12] Whether a pastor or not, the clergyman's essential orientation, to use Daniel Calhoun's term, was now toward the profession.[13] It created him, sustained his sense of himself as a clergyman, defined his role and provided the most important community of which he felt himself a part and by which he distinguished himself from other groups in the society. In addition, it was as a "professional" clergyman that one gained the standing to represent organized Christianity and convey it to whatever constituencies one might serve. Moreover, its character as a profession enhanced the clergy's collective legitimacy as the overall guardian and definer of God's word and presence in society. Under the culture of professionalism, monopoly over the appropriate lore and authority to control and dispense it properly belonged to the collective body of certified practitioners, those who had gone through the rituals and training (which only those already through them could define and control) that made one a "professional" rather than a layman or amateur.

The United States on the eve of the Civil War, then, was probably not less religious, but differently religious than eighteenth-century New England. The clergy was probably not dramatically less influential and important in the culture, but it deployed its influence differently. For during the first half of the nineteenth century, the relationship of the parts—of church to community, of Christian devotion to public duty, of pastor to church and community, and of clergy to the public—had changed, transforming the whole just as the twist of a kaleidoscope shuffles the same bits of glass into an entirely different design.

Notes

Chapter 1

1. Since this chapter is intended to provide the backdrop for developments at the end of the eighteenth century and the early nineteenth century, the focus has been placed upon the more general characteristics rather than upon local and temporal variations. Much has been written about the American ministry, particularly the New England ministry. The works of Perry Miller, though concerned with the larger intellectual and social edifice of New England Puritanism, tell a good deal about the ministry: *Orthodoxy in Massachusetts, 1630–1650* (Cambridge, Mass., 1933); *The New England Mind: The Seventeenth Century* (Cambridge, Mass., 1954); *The New England Mind: From Colony to Province* (Cambridge, Mass., 1953). See also Alan Heimert, *Religion and the American Mind: From the Great Awakening to the Revolution* (Cambridge, Mass., 1966). A crucial essay for any discussion of the ministry in America is Sidney Mead, "The Rise of the Evangelical Conception of the Ministry in America, 1607–1850," in H. Richard Niebuhr and Daniel Williams, eds., *The Ministry in Historical Perspective* (New York, 1956). David Hall, *The Faithful Shepherd* (Chapel Hill, 1973) challenges Mead's interpretation and is far and away the best analysis of the clerical office for seventeenth-century New England. In many ways, the ministry that Hall suggests emerged by the end of the seventeenth century endured throughout much of the eighteenth, and the discussion in this chapter is heavily indebted to Hall's work. A difficult but provocative discussion of the ministry is contained in Daniel Calhoun, *Professional Lives in America* (Cambridge, Mass., 1965). Two recent dissertations are also valuable: John William Youngs, Jr., "God's Messengers: Religious Leadership

in Colonial New England, 1700–1750" (Ph.D. diss., University of California, Berkeley, 1970), and James Schmotter, "Provincial Professionalism: The New England Ministry, 1692–1745" (Ph.D. diss., Northwestern University, 1973). Williston Walker's *Creeds and Platforms of Congregationalism* (New York, 1893) and *The Congregationalists* (New York, 1894) are also very useful.

2. Hall, *The Faithful Shepherd*, pp. 72–92; Walker, *The Congregationalists*, pp. 76–124. See also Edmund Morgan, *Visible Saints: The History of a Puritan Idea* (New York, 1963).

3. Morgan, *Visible Saints*, pp. 17–37; Hall, *The Faithful Shepherd*, pp. 75–78, 102–4; Darrett B. Rutman, *Winthrop's Boston, A Portrait of a Puritan Town, 1630–1649* (Chapel Hill, 1965).

4. Walker, *Creeds and Platforms*, p. 215.

5. Hall, *The Faithful Shepherd*, pp. 102–6, 220–22; Walker, *The Congregationalists*, pp. 222–26; Walker, *Creeds and Platforms*, pp. 214–16. Ordination and installation sermons are particularly good sources for conceptions of the ministerial office and the relationship between pastor and people and between pastor and profession. See, for example, Freegrace Leavitt, *The Ministerial Office a Good Work* (New Haven, 1762); Levi Hart, *The Christian Minister, or Faithful Preacher of the Gospel Described* (New London, 1771); Robert Breck, *Sermon Preached at the Ordination of the Reverend Mr. David Parsons* (Springfield, Mass., 1783); and Timothy Hilliard, *A Sermon Delivered at the Ordination of the Rev. John Andrews* (Newburyport, Mass., 1789).

6. Miller, *From Colony to Province*, pp. 248–69; Walker, *The Congregationalists*, pp. 200–14; Alonzo Quint, "The Origins of Ministerial Associations in New England," *The Congregationalist* 2 (1860): 203–12; Alonzo Quint, "Some Account of Ministerial Associations (Congregational) in Massachusetts," *The Congregationalist* 5 (1863): 293–304.

7. Walker, *The Congregationalists*, pp. 230–36.

8. See Clarence C. Goen, *Revivalism and Separatism in New England, 1740–1800: Strict Congregationalists and Separate Baptists in the Great Awakening* (New Haven, 1962), and William McLoughlin, *New England Dissent, 1630–1833: The Baptists and the Separation of Church and State* (Cambridge, Mass., 1971).

9. Walker, *Creeds and Platforms*, p. 274.

10. See Calhoun, *Professional Lives*, pp. 88–177.

11. These figures are taken from a complete and systematic examination of the six volumes of Franklin B. Dexter, *Biographical Sketches of the Graduates of Yale College* (New York, 1885–1912). These volumes contain a mine of material about ministerial practices, careers, and lives. Moreover, since the overwhelming portion of the established ministers of eighteenth-century New England were college educated,

the Yale lists provide a "representative" sample. Although the sketches are not as complete as those in Sibley's *Harvard Graduates,* the Dexter volumes have the advantage of spanning the entire century. James Schmotter, "Provincial Professionalism" and "Ministerial Careers in Eighteenth Century New England: The Social Context, 1700–1760," *The Journal of Social History* 9 (1975): 249–67, also examines pastoral tenure. Although his portrait generally comports with mine, he draws some different conclusions. Looking at the first half of the eighteenth century from the standpoint of the even more stable late seventeenth century, he emphasizes the comparative disorderliness, while I, looking from the standpoint of the extraordinary rate of pastoral turnover of the early nineteenth century, emphasize the comparative stability of the eighteenth century.

12. Dexter, *Biographical Sketches,* is an especially rich source for information about the process by which churches and pastors selected each other. See, for example, Dexter, *Biographical Sketches,* 1: 41–42; 5: 590–617.

13. Lyman Beecher, *Autobiography,* ed. Barbara Cross (Cambridge, Mass., 1962), 1: 70. The life and letter biographies of clergymen, most of which quote extensively from letters and diaries, are a particularly good source for monitoring clergymen's responses to the strains of pastoral life. William Mathews, *American Diaries: An Annotated Bibliography of American Diaries Prior to 1861* (Berkeley, 1945), gives a list of published diaries and memoirs and autobiographies with printed selections from diaries and journals. See, for example, Francis Wayland, *Memoir of the Life and Labor of Adoniram Judson, D.D.* (Boston, 1853), pp. 17–45; Cyrus Yale, *The Life of Rev. Jeremiah Hallock* (New York, 1828), pp. 17–69; Jotham Sewall, *A Memoir of Rev. Jotham Sewall* (Boston, 1853); Asa Cummings, *A Memoir of Edward Payson* (New York, 1830), pp. 26–46, 78–108.

14. See, for example, Dexter, *Biographical Sketches,* 1: 107–8.

15. Dexter describes a larger number of instances in which the man who first occupied a newly created pulpit had an enduring and stable pastorate. A more collective portrait of the durability of the first ministry in a church's history can be found in the histories of the individual churches of Connecticut contained in *Contributions to the Ecclesiastical History of Connecticut, prepared under the direction of the General Association* (New Haven, 1861), pp. 344–516.

16. Isaac Parsons, *Memoir of the Life and Character of the Rev. John Vaill, Late Pastor of the Church of Christ in Hadlyme* (New York, 1839), p. 40.

17. Beecher, *Autobiography,* 1: 70.

18. Walker, *The Congregationalists,* p. 225; Henry Martyn Dexter, *American Congregationalism, as it Is, as it Was, as it Should Be* (Boston, 1856); Dexter, *Biographical Sketches,* 1: 514.

19. There was considerable litigation between clergymen and towns and pastors and churches. See Calhoun, *Professional Lives,* pp. 94–107; Dexter, *Biographical Sketches,* 1: 36–37, 58.

20. Dexter, *Biographical Sketches,* 1: 514; and pp. 74, 361, 679, 759.

21. Dexter, *Biographical Sketches,* 1: 287. See pages 119–121.

22. Dexter, *Biographical Sketches,* 3: 371.

23. See Stephen Foster, *Their Solitary Way: The Puritan Social Ethic in the First Century of Settlement in New England* (New Haven, 1971), pp. 99–127, for a good discussion of the notion of calling.

24. Ordination sermons and dismissal controversies are a particularly good source for the ideals of pastoral conduct and bearing. See also Hall, *The Faithful Shepherd,* pp. 65–66, 174–80; and Calhoun, *Professional Lives,* pp. 108–9.

25. The outcry against an unconverted ministry during the Great Awakening suggests that ministerial piety might well have declined in the early decades of the eighteenth century. Schmotter, "Provincial Professionalism," and "Ministerial Careers in Eighteenth Century New England," indicates that in the 1720s and 1730s there was an increase in the number of younger sons and poorer youths entering the clergy as an occupation.

26. See, for example, Cummings, *Memoir of Edward Payson;* Yale, *Life of Rev. Jeremiah Hallock;* Parsons, *Memoir of the Rev. John Vaill;* Beecher, *Autobiography;* Joseph Furgeson, *Memoir of the Life and Character of the Rev. Samuel Hopkins, D.D.* (Boston, 1830).

27. "Careers," *International Encyclopedia of the Social Sciences* (New York, 1968), 2: 252–53.

28. See note 11 above. See, for example, the accounts in Dexter, *Biographical Sketches,* 1: 212–13, 551–55, 681–82.

29. See also Timothy Breen, *The Character of a Good Ruler* (New Haven, 1970). A particularly good source for the notion of magistracy is the election sermon. See, for example, Andrew Lee, *The Origins and Ends of Civil Government with Reflections on the Distinguished Happiness of the United States* (Hartford, 1795); and Joseph McKeen, *A Sermon Delivered at the Annual Election* (Boston, 1800).

30. Walker, *Creeds and Platforms,* p. 214.

31. Edward M. Cook, "The Fathers of the Towns: Leadership and Community Structure in Eighteenth Century New England" (Ph.D. diss., Johns Hopkins University, 1972), which analyzes officers from seventy New England towns, is an important study of eighteenth-century office holding, and I have drawn upon it heavily.

32. Cook, "Fathers of the Towns," pp. 271–321.

33. Eighteenth-century New Englanders were highly conscious of gradations in social rank and standing. Yet status was an extremely complex and subtle matter, drawing upon family reputation and duration in the community, formal or official position in the colony, wealth, and learn-

ing. There was a provincial elite at the top, but the individual communities also had a system of recognized gradations, which was frequently separate from the provincial hierarchy and which varied according to the age, location, and type of town. Edward Cook's study provides the most sophisticated and subtle description of status in eighteenth-century New England. David F. Allmendinger, *Paupers and Scholars: The Transformations of Student Life in Nineteenth Century New England* (New York, 1975), pp. 45–54, contains an important account of the "poor" at eighteenth-century Harvard and Yale. Schmotter, "Provincial Professionalism" contains a systematic description of the social origins of clergymen, using occupational categories as designations of status. His study focuses on the period before the Great Awakening when, it appears, a greater portion of the clergy came from the lower orders than in the last two-thirds of the century. Even according to his figures, however, the vast bulk of the clergy came from upper or middling rank, rather than from lower ranks. My examination of eighteenth-century Yale graduates indicates that for the second half of the century, with the exception of the cohorts from 1720 to 1740, when slightly over half came from clerical families or were sons of at least local respectables (as indicated by a formal designation of respect), more than two-thirds came from these sources. Moreover, probably no more than about 10 percent were "poor" boys. See Chapter 4 for a fuller discussion of recruitment of indigent young men into the clergy.

34. Dexter, *Biographical Sketches,* 1: 523, 559, 649.
35. This can be seen by looking at the class rank (through the first two-thirds of the eighteenth century, Harvard and Yale ranked their matriculants according to family standing) of those men who filled the pulpits in the "first" churches in the major towns or churches near one of the metropolitan centers, from which they could be expected to exert clerical leadership. See Dexter, *Biographical Sketches*; and *Contributions to the Ecclesiastical History of Connecticut.*
36. See Parsons, *Memoir of the Rev. John Vaill*; see also Dexter, *Biographical Sketches, passim.*
37. Much has been written in recent years about New England communalism. Some historians have emphasized the organic stability of the New England town, while others have stressed the factiousness and individual bickering to which New Englanders were prone. For the purposes of this chapter, I have stressed the ideal of a well-ordered community which defined the minister's role as a guardian of order, even though the reality did not always conform to the norm. In addition to Cook, "Fathers of the Towns," see John Demos, *A Little Commonwealth: Family Life in Plymouth Colony* (New York, 1970); Charles Grant, *Democracy in the Connecticut Frontier Town of Kent* (New York, 1961); Philip Greven, *Four Generations: Population, Land,*

and Family in Colonial Andover, Massachusetts (Ithaca, 1970); Kenneth Lockridge, *A New England Town: The First Hundred Years* (New York, 1970); Michael Zuckerman, *Peaceable Kingdoms: New England Towns in the Eighteenth Century* (New York, 1970); Richard Bushman, *Puritan Yankee: Character and the Social Order in Connecticut, 1690–1765* (Cambridge, Mass., 1976); John M. Murrin, "Essay Review," *History and Theory* 11 (1972): 226–75.

38. The character of colonial New England as a culture still heavily dependent upon oral discourse has not been given much attention. Daniel Calhoun, *The Intelligence of a People* (Princeton, 1973), pp. 210–29, contains a very suggestive analysis of colonial preaching. For the fast days, see William DeLoss Love, *The Fast and Thanksgiving Days of New England* (Boston, 1895). Discussions of clerical public leadership can be found in various places. See, for example, Perry Miller, "From the Covenant to the Revival," in Perry Miller, *Nature's Nation* (Cambridge, Mass., 1967), pp. 90–120; and Edmund Morgan, "The Revolution Considered as an Intellectual Movement," in Morton White and Arthur Schlesinger, eds., *Paths of American Thought* (Boston, 1963), pp. 11–33.

39. Perry Miller, of course, has provided the classic exposition of the jeremiad. See Miller, *From Colony to Province*, pp. 19–40, and Perry Miller, "Declension in a Bible Commonwealth," in Miller, *Nature's Nation*, pp. 14–49.

40. Miller, "Declension in a Bible Commonwealth," pp. 35–47.

41. The exertion of church discipline also frequently followed periods of revivals, when the reinvigorated church would cleanse itself of impurities.

42. See Emil Oberholzer, *Delinquent Saints: Disciplinary Actions in the Early Congregational Churches of New England* (New York, 1956).

43. Kai Erikson, *Wayward Puritans: A Study in the Sociology of Deviance* (New York, 1966) is a highly suggestive study of how Puritans dealt with deviance.

44. Azel Backus, *Absalom's Conspiracy, A Sermon Preached at the Annual Election* (Hartford, 1798), p. 52.

45. Dexter, *Biographical Sketches*, 1: 475. I am indebted to Calhoun, *Professional Lives*, pp. 92–93, for this formulation of how a people united in their pastor.

Chapter 2

1. David Hackett Fischer, *The Revolution of American Conservatism: The Federalist Party in the Era of Jeffersonian Democracy* (New York, 1965), p. 191. There is a rich, voluminous, and growing literature on the development of America's "first party system." See, in addition to Fischer, Joseph Charles, *The Origins of the American Party System*

(New York, 1956); William Nisbet Chambers, *Political Parties in a New Nation, 1776–1809* (New York, 1963); Noble Cunningham, *The Jeffersonian Republicans: The Formation of Party Organization, 1789–1801* (Chapel Hill, 1957), and *The Jeffersonian Republicans in Power: Party Operations, 1801–1809* (Chapel Hill, 1963); James M. Banner, *To the Hartford Convention: The Federalists and the Origins of Party Politics in Massachusetts, 1789–1815* (New York, 1970); and Paul Goodman, *The Democratic-Republicans of Massachusetts* (Cambridge, Mass., 1964). William Nisbet Chambers, *The First Party System: Federalists and Republicans* (New York, 1972) is a useful collection from the vast monographic and article literature.

2. Fischer, *Revolution of American Conservatism*, pp. 50–54; Goodman, *The Democratic-Republicans*, pp. 62–74; Chambers, *First Party System*, pp. 45–50.

3. See Zuckerman, *Peaceable Kingdoms*, and Cook, "Fathers of the Towns," for full discussions of local electoral contests in eighteenth-century New England.

4. Cook, "Fathers of the Towns," p. 307.

5. Fischer, *Revolution of American Conservatism*, pp. 50–72; Charles, *Origins of the American Party System*, pp. 7–37, 91–103; Banner, *To the Hartford Convention*, pp. 216–37.

6. For a somewhat different view, which emphasizes the newness and coherence of the Hamiltonian structure but which still agrees that it did not develop modern party machinery, see Chambers, *Political Parties in a New Nation*, pp. 24–53; and Chambers, *First Party System*, pp. 45–57.

7. Cunningham, *Jeffersonian Republicans*; Goodman, *The Democratic-Republicans*; and Eugene Link, *Democratic-Republican Societies, 1790–1800* (New York, 1942).

8. See Fischer, *Revolution of American Conservatism*, pp. 1–28; Banner, *To the Hartford Convention*, pp. 3–53; and Linda Kerber, *Federalists in Dissent: Imagery and Ideology* (Ithaca, 1970).

9. Fischer, *Revolution of American Conservatism*, pp. 41–45.

10. Ibid., p. 45.

11. Ibid., p. 107.

12. Ibid., pp. 110–28.

13. Cunningham, *Jeffersonian Republicans in Power*, p. 125.

14. See Banner, *To the Hartford Convention*, pp. 268–94; Goodman, *The Democratic-Republicans*, pp. 127–56; Cunningham, *Jeffersonian Republicans in Power*, pp. 125–47; Fischer, *Revolution of American Conservatism*, pp. 182–201; Edmund Purcell, *Connecticut in Transition* (New York, 1902).

15. See, for example, Jonathan Edwards, Jr., *The Necessity of the Belief of Christianity by the Citizens of the State in Order [sic] to Our Political Prosperity* (Hartford, 1794); Aaron Bancroft, *A Sermon Preached before His Excellency, Caleb Strong* (Boston, 1801).

16. Backus, *Absalom's Conspiracy,* p. 40.

17. John Smalley, *The Evils of a Weak Government* (Hartford, 1800), pp. 25–32.

18. Strictures against electioneering can be found in almost any election sermon of these years. See, for example, Jonathan Edwards, Jr., *Necessity of the Belief of Christianity;* Isaac Lewis, *The Political Advantages of Godliness, a sermon preached at Hartford on the anniversary election* (Hartford, 1797); Nathanael Emmons, "Prayer for the Defeat of those Who Attempt to Subvert Good Government," *Works* (Boston, 1842), 2: 96–112. See also, Richard Hofstadter, *The Idea of a Party System* (Berkeley, 1965).

19. Backus, *Absalom's Conspiracy,* p. 40; see also Bancroft, *A Sermon,* pp. 9–29; Lee, *Origins and Ends of Civil Government,* pp. 12–20; Cyprian Strong, *The Kingdom is the Lord's* (Hartford, 1799), pp. 39–41; Lewis, *Political Advantages of Godliness,* pp. 12–20.

20. Emmons, *Works,* 2: 59–72; McKeen, *A Sermon,* pp. 10–12; Lewis, *Political Advantages of Godliness,* pp. 18–19; see, for example, Lee, *Origins and Ends of Civil Government,* pp. 27–37; Backus, *Absalom's Conspiracy,* pp. 29–30; Bancroft, *A Sermon,* pp. 12–16.

21. Backus, *Absalom's Conspiracy,* p. 29.

22. For the intensity and extremism of the political rhetoric of these years see Marshall Smelzer, "The Jacobin Phrenzy: Federalism and the Menace of Liberty, Equality, and Fraternity," *Review of Politics* 13 (1951): 457–82; Marshall Smelzer, "The Federalist Period as an Age of Passion," *American Quarterly* 10 (1958): 391–419; John R. Howe, "Republican Thought and the Political Violence of the 1790's," *American Quarterly* 19 (1967): 149–64.

23. See Banner, *To the Hartford Convention,* pp. 122–68; Purcell, *Connecticut in Transition.*

24. Quoted in Cunningham, *Jeffersonian Republicans in Power,* p. 125.

25. For analysis of this cluster of ideas see Kerber, *Federalists in Dissent;* Fischer, *Revolution of American Conservatism;* Banner, *To the Hartford Convention;* and Gordon Wood, *The Creation of the American Republic, 1776–1787* (Chapel Hill, 1969).

26. See Bernard Bailyn, *The Ideological Origins of the American Revolution* (Cambridge, Mass., 1967), and Wood, *Creation of the American Republic* for extensive treatments of the ideology of power and liberty that underlay the Revolution and the politics of the Federalist era.

27. Wood, *Creation of the American Republic,* pp. 427–86; Charles, *Origins of the American Party System,* pp. 122–41; Goodman, *The Democratic-Republicans.*

28. See Gary B. Nash, "American Clergy and the French Revolution," *William and Mary Quarterly* 22 (1965): 397–98.

29. Lewis, *Political Advantages of Godliness,* p. 24.

30. Backus, *Absalom's Conspiracy,* p. 46.

31. Quoted in Fischer, *Revolution of American Conservatism,* p. 285.

32. See Banner, *To the Hartford Convention*, pp. 119–215; Goodman, *The Democratic-Republicans*, pp. 85–96; Purcell, *Connecticut in Transition*.
33. Purcell, *Connecticut in Transition*, pp. 227–89; Goodman, *The Democratic-Republicans*, pp. 93–98.
34. Banner, *To the Hartford Convention*, p. 143.
35. The orientation of these "young Federalists" is brilliantly analyzed in Fischer, *Revolution of American Conservatism*, pp. 29–50, 182–201.
36. See, for example, the comments on politics that Thomas Robbins committed to his diary in these years. Increase N. Tarbox, ed., *The Diary of Thomas Robbins* (Boston, 1886–87), 1: 472–77.
37. See Banner, *To the Hartford Convention*, pp. 158–67; Beecher, *Autobiography*, 1: 190–300 is a superb source for the clergy's outlook, as are the election sermons of these years and the moral society sermons cited in note 49 below.
38. For the Griswold affair, see Purcell, *Connecticut in Transition*, pp. 282–97; and Beecher, *Autobiography*, 1: 188–90.
39. Emmons, "Sinful Customs," *Works*, 2: 81–82.
40. Emmons, "Example," *Works*, 2: 66–67.
41. See William Nelson, *Americanization of the Canon Law* (Cambridge, Mass., 1975).
42. Lyman Beecher, *The Remedy for Dueling* (Sag Harbor, New York, 1806), p. 8; Aaron Dutton, *The Importance of a Faithful Execution of Law* (New Haven, 1815), p. 22.
43. See Purcell, *Connecticut in Transition*, pp. 280–314; and Beecher, *Autobiography*, 1: 260–300.
44. Historians have paid little attention to the early, local moral societies. Charles Keller, *The Second Great Awakening in Connecticut* (New Haven, 1942), pp. 41, 136–38, has a description of the Yale College moral society. Contemporary descriptions can be found in several places, particularly in the sermons delivered at their founding and at their regular meetings. See, for example, Emmons, "The Evil Effects of Sin," "Example," "Sinful Customs," which were delivered to the local society he founded. See also, Lyman Beecher, *The Practicability of Suppressing Vice, by Means of Societies Instituted for the Purpose* (New London, 1804), and Beecher's *Reformation of Morals, Practicable and Indispensable* (Hartford, 1812) for descriptions of various precedents for the moral societies.
45. Emmons, "Sinful Customs," pp. 73–78; Beecher, *Reformation of Morals*, p. 13.
46. Beecher, *Reformation of Morals*, pp. 34–38.
47. Beecher, *Autobiography*, 1: 188.
48. Beecher, *Reformation of Morals*, p. 14.
49. The Connecticut Moral Society is treated in Sidney Mead, *Nathaniel Taylor, 1786–1856: A Connecticut Liberal* (Chicago, 1942), pp. 79–83; Edmund Purcell, *Connecticut in Transition*, pp. 324–26; Keller, *The*

Second Great Awakening in Connecticut, pp. 41, 136–38. All of these accounts, as does the one that follows, rely heavily upon the correspondence and recollections in Beecher's *Autobiography*. Other sources for the society are the reports in *The Connecticut Evangelical Magazine and Religious Intelligencer* 10 (1815): 80, 225–29, 257–64; and the sermons delivered at its regular meetings each year, beginning with Lyman Beecher, *Reformation of Morals*; Heman Humphrey, *The Efficacy and Importance of Combined and Persevering Action* (New Haven, 1815); Dutton, *Faithful Execution of Law* (New Haven, 1815); Noah Porter, *A Sermon delivered at the Meeting of the Connecticut Society for the Promotion of Good Morals* (New Haven, 1816).

50. Beecher, *Reformation of Morals*, p. 21.

51. Dutton, *Faithful Execution of the Law*, pp. 11–12.

52. "Formation and Constitution of the Columbia Moral Society," in Gordon Wood, ed., *The Rising Glory of America, 1760–1820* (New York, 1971), p. 93.

53. "Connecticut Moral Society," *The Connecticut Evangelical Magazine* 15 (1815): 80, 225–29, 257–64.

54. This interpretation of the emergence and significance of the moral societies (and, by extension, of the evangelical and benevolent societies that grew out of them) departs from existing accounts. The standard interpretation of clerical public activism in this period is contained in John Bodo, *The Protestant Clergy and Public Issues, 1812–1848* (Princeton, 1954); Charles C. Cole, Jr., *The Social Ideas of the Northern Evangelicals, 1820–1860* (New York, 1954); Clifford S. Griffin, *Their Brothers' Keepers: Moral Stewardship in the United States, 1800–1865* (New Brunswick, 1960); Charles I. Foster, *An Errand of Mercy: The Evangelical United Front, 1790–1837* (Chapel Hill, 1960); W. David Lewis, "The Reformer as Conservative: Protestant Counter-Subversion in the Early Republic," in Stanley Coben and Lorman Ratner, eds., *The Development of an American Culture* (Englewood Cliffs, 1970); and Clifford S. Griffin, "Religious Benevolence as Social Control, 1815–1860," *Mississippi Valley Historical Review* 44 (1957): 423–44. These works construe the clergy as a conservative elite that saw its status and influence challenged by democracy and secularism and interpret the moral and benevolent societies as instruments of social control and the restoration of clerical influence. Lois Banner, "Religious Benevolence as Social Control: A Critique of an Interpretation," *Journal of American History* 60 (1973): 23–41, challenges this interpretation, arguing that their religious motivations are more important than status anxieties and that religious benevolence is best understood as a form of humanitarian reform rather than as an attempt to retain elite domination. My approach, however, is more structural: rather than address the question of whether clerical motives were conservative or humanitarian and focus simply on what

the societies did, I have asked what kind of social institutions they were, how as public agencies they differed from other public instruments, and where in the social order they placed the clergy. It is from this perspective that I have interpreted them as a new public institution and as part of the emergence of a different kind of public order, serving a rapidly changing society.

Chapter 3

1. The revivalism in New England during the early decades of the nineteenth century has been given less attention than later revivalism. See Keller, *The Second Great Awakening in Connecticut,* and Sidney Mead, *Nathaniel William Taylor.* Donald G. Mathews, "The Second Great Awakening as an Organizing Process, 1780–1930: An Hypothesis," *American Quarterly* 21 (1969): 23–43 is an enormously suggestive study.

2. The best sources for the activism and energy of this generation of ministers are their diaries and letters. See, for example, Tarbox, *The Diary of Thomas Robbins,* and Beecher, *Autobiography.* The religious intelligence and miscellany sections of the new evangelical journals such as *The Panoplist, The Connecticut Evangelical Magazine,* and *The Spirit of the Pilgrims* are also a revealing index of the organizational energies of the clergy.

3. *The Connecticut Evangelical Magazine* is a good source for the revivalism of these years, since it regularly printed accounts of local revivals. Bennett Tyler, *New England Revivals* (New York, 1846) is a collection of most of the articles which appeared between 1796 and 1815. See also, Ebenezar Porter, *Letters on Revivals of Religion* (Boston, 1833), and Beecher, *Autobiography,* 2: 39–57, 119–54.

4. Clarence Faust and Thomas Johnson, eds., *Jonathan Edwards, Representative Selections* (New York, 1962), pp. 73–84.

5. Ibid., pp. 340–72. See also Heimert, *Religion and the American Mind* and Ernest Tuveson, *Redeemer Nation: The Idea of America's Millennial Role* (Chicago, 1968).

6. A good source for the social instrumentalism of revivals in these years is the moral society sermon. See Humphrey, *Efficacy and Importance of Combined and Persevering Action;* Porter, *Sermon Delivered at the Meeting of the Connecticut Society;* and Beecher, *Reformation of Morals.*

7. Barbara Soloman, ed., Timothy Dwight, *Travels in New England* (Cambridge, Mass., 1969), p. xxxiv.

8. Ibid., pp. xxxiv–xxxvi; Beecher, *Reformation of Morals,* pp. 26–28; Dutton, *Faithful Execution of Law,* pp. 11–12.

9. Beecher, *Reformation of Morals,* p. 6.

10. Ibid., p. 29.

11. Wood, *Rising Glory*, p. 11.
12. For the persistence of eighteenth-century attitudes, even amidst these social changes, see, for example, Lewis, *Political Advantages of Godliness*; Beecher, *Remedy for Dueling*; Emmons, "Jereboam," *Works*, 2: 196–212. See also Kerber, *Federalists in Dissent*, pp. 173–215; Fischer, *Revolution of American Conservatism*, pp. 1–28; Banner, *To the Hartford Convention*, pp. 3–83; Wood, *Creation of the American Republic*, pp. 593–619.
13. See, for example, Dutton, *Faithful Execution of Law*, pp. 7–23; Emmons, "Jereboam," pp. 196–202; Porter, *Sermon Delivered at the Meeting of the Connecticut Society*, pp. 11–17.
14. Humphrey, *Efficacy and Importance of Combined and Persevering Action*, pp. 17–28; Beecher, *Reformation of Morals*, pp. 19–24.
15. Personal documents such as letters, diaries, and journals are the best sources for the conversion process. Mathews, *American Diaries*, lists hundreds of spiritual diaries, and the various life and letter biographies of ministers also contain accounts of conversion experiences. The evangelical press, especially *The Connecticut Evangelical Magazine*, *The Christian Spectator*, and *The Spirit of the Pilgrims*, contains accounts of conversions as well as various delineations of the process. A particularly rich source is Lyman Beecher's correspondence with his children, particularly Catharine, as he tried to lead them to conversion, and his argument with Ebenezar Porter over what procedures to use in securing conversions: see Beecher, *Autobiography*, 1: 340–407; 2: 119–54. See also Kathryn Kish Sklar, *Catharine Beecher: A Study in American Domesticity* (New Haven, 1973), pp. 20–59.
16. "A Popular Objection to Revivals, Considered and Rejected," *The Spirit of the Pilgrims* 1 (1828): 398–407; "Thoughts on Revivals," *The Spirit of the Pilgrims* 1 (1828): 38–42, 73–82, 144–49, 354–57.
17. My own approach to religious organizations is very similar to Donald Mathews, "Second Great Awakening as an Organizing Process," and I have relied upon his work in several places in this study.
18. Lyman Beecher, "The Building of Waste-Places," *Works*, (Boston, 1853), 2: 142–46.
19. For the debate over the nature and role of the new institutions of the ante-bellum period, see Stanley Elkins, *Slavery: A Problem in American Institutional Life* (New York, 1963); David Rothman, *The Discovery of the Asylum* (Boston, 1970); Rowland Berthoff, *An Unsettled People: Social Order and Disorder in American History* (New York, 1971); Oscar and Mary Handlin, *The Dimensions of Liberty* (Cambridge, Mass., 1961).
20. Richard D. Brown, "The Emergence of Urban Society in Rural Massachusetts, 1760–1820," *Journal of American History* 61 (1974): 40–41. See also Keller, *Second Great Awakening in Connecticut*; and Foster, *Errand of Mercy*.

21. See, for example, literature coming out of the American Tract Society, sermons on temperance, and the advice literature directed to youths; e.g., Joel Hawes, *Lectures Addressed to the Young Men of Hartford and New Haven* (Hartford, 1829); William Sprague, *The Dangers of Evil Company* (Boston, 1823); Lyman Beecher, *Six Sermons on the Nature, Occasions, Evils, Signs and Remedy of Intemperance* (Boston, 1828).

22. See pages 36–44 above.

23. See Hawes, *Lectures Addressed to the Young Men of Hartford*; Sprague, *Dangers of Evil Company*.

24. Walker, *The Congregationalists*, pp. 230–51.

25. This can partly be seen in the proliferation of churches in a town. See *Contributions to the Ecclesiastical History of Connecticut*. In 1828, *The Spirit of the Pilgrims* calmly avowed that "There are in the different denominations, various degrees of talent, wealth, and zeal. Some have peculiar facilities with one class of the community and some with another." ("The Rights and Duties of Different Denominations of Christians," *The Spirit of the Pilgrims* 1 [1828]: 349.) Several historians have stressed the character of churches as voluntary associations and gathered communities. See Sidney Mead, *The Lively Experiment: The Shaping of Christianity in America* (New York, 1963); and Berthoff, *An Unsettled People*, pp. 254–475.

27. I am indebted for this interpretation to conversations with Donald G. Mathews and to his forthcoming study of evangelicalism in the South.

28. See Allan S. Horlick, "Countinghouses and Clerks: The Social Control of Young Men in New York" (Ph.D. diss., University of Wisconsin, 1969). "Journal of Lucien C. Boynton," *Proceedings of the American Antiquarian Society* 43 (1911): 323–24, records Boynton's difficulties in finding a young woman of suitable evangelical character.

29. A comparison of the rhetoric on such ceremonial occasions as ordinations, fasts, and elections after about 1815 with earlier rhetoric suggests that rather than talk of structure and institutions, churchmen now spoke almost entirely of character. Moreover, these traditional occasions were becoming less and less important as vehicles of clerical expression: more important were the writings and sermons addressed to self-reformation and promulgated through the new agencies and the religious press.

30. Hawes, *Lectures Addressed to the Young Men of Hartford*, pp. 121–35.

31. Beecher, *Six Sermons*, pp. 103–5.

32. "Review of Gallaudet's Sermons and Discourses on Various Points of Christian Faith and Practice," *The Christian Spectator* 1 (1819): 27.

33. "Sketches of the Character of Miss Julia A. Strong," *The Christian Spectator* 1 (1819): 2–4.

34. Ibid., pp. 2–3.

35. This conception of the moral duties and the growth of grace through

active solicitation for the morals and salvation of others derived from Edwards' notion of true virtue and, especially, from Samuel Hopkins' development of it. By the beginning of the nineteenth century, it was a staple of almost all the theological strands within New England evangelicalism. See Oliver W. Elsbree, "Samuel Hopkins and his Doctrine of Benevolence," *New England Quarterly* 8 (1933): 534–50; Mead, *Nathaniel Taylor*; Joseph Haroutunian, *Piety versus Moralism: The Passing of New England Divinity* (Boston, 1933).

36. See, for example, Hawes, *Lectures Addressed to the Young Men of Hartford*, pp. 11–21; Lyman Beecher, *The Rights, Design and Duties of Local Churches* (Salem, 1819), p. 20.

37. Lyman Beecher, "*An Address of the Charitable Society for the Education of Indigent Pious Young Men for the Ministry of the Gospel* (New Haven, 1814), p. 20.

38. Many historians have examined evangelicalism as social doctrine. Bodo, *Protestant Clergy and Public Issues* and Cole, *Social Ideas of Northern Evangelicals* describe the ideas evangelicals held about social ills; others, like William McLoughlin, *Modern Revivalism: Charles Grandison Finney to Billy Graham* (New York, 1959), Whitney Cross, *The Burned-over District: The Social and Intellectual History of Enthusiastic Religion in Western New York, 1800–1850* (New York, 1956), and Timothy Smith, *Religion and Social Reform: American Protestantism on the Eve of the Civil War* (New York, 1957) examine revivalism and the social energies it generated; Perry Miller, "From The Covenant to the Revival," in *Nature's Nation* and *The Life of the Mind in America* (New York, 1965), considers revivalism as a basic constituent of the culture, while Donald G. Mathews, "The Second Great Awakening as an Organizing Process," examines evangelicalism as a form of social reconstruction. Rather than translate evangelical ideas into social or political categories, I have taken a more wholistic approach, asking how religious groups, institutions, and ideologies affect, express, and respond to social change, and have, consequently, construed evangelicalism as a social grammar, a basic vocabulary that shaped the evangelical's commitments, perceptions, and relationships to others.

39. Lyman Beecher, *Address of the Charitable Society*, p. 20.

Chapter 4

1. In most instances in colonial New England, the decision of an elder, usually the father, determined a young man's vocation: providing sons with their vocational base, through land, education, or apprenticeship, was considered among the most important paternal obligations. Dexter, *Biographical Sketches*, provides numerous examples of the ways in which "suitability" was determined. A useful general study of parent-

son relations is John Gillis, *Youth and History* (New York, 1974). For New England in the eighteenth century, see Greven, *Four Generations,* pp. 222–58.

2. See, for example, Dexter, *Biographical Sketches,* 1: 395, 649; 2: 273; 3: 211; Schmotter, "Provincial Professionals," is also very informative on the early eighteenth-century ministry.

3. Allmendinger, *Paupers and Scholars,* pp. 46–52; Beverly McNear, "College Founding in the American Colonies," *Mississippi Valley Historical Review* 42 (1955): 22–44.

4. Schmotter, "Ministerial Careers in Eighteenth Century New England," pp. 257–62.

5. Calhoun, *Professional Lives,* p. 150. See also Edwin Gaustad, *Historical Atlas of American Religion* (New York, 1962).

6. Allmendinger, *Paupers and Scholars,* pp. 8–23, analyzes the departure of New England youths from the hill towns of western New England. See also Lois Kimball Mathews, *The Expansion of New England* (New York, 1962); Percy Bidwell, "The Agricultural Revolution in New England," *American Historical Review* 26 (1921): 683–702; Bidwell, "Rural Economy in New England at the Beginning of the Nineteenth Century," *Transactions of the Connecticut Academy of Arts and Sciences* 20 (1916): 241–399; and Kenneth Lockridge, "Land, Population, and the Evolution of New England Society, 1630–1790," *Past and Present* 39 (1968): 62–80.

7. *Twelfth Annual Report of the American Education Society* (Andover, 1828), p. 4.

8. Allmendinger, *Paupers and Scholars,* p. 10. The figure for the percentage of college graduates heading toward the ministry is based upon the following biographical catalogues: *Amherst College Biographical Record, Centennial Issue, 1821–1921* (Amherst, 1927); *General Catalogue of Bowdoin College, 1794–1914* (Brunswick, 1912); *General Catalogue of Dartmouth College, 1769–1910* (Hanover, 1910); and Calvin Durfee, *Williams Biographical Annals* (Boston, 1971).

9. Between 1725 and 1745 this percentage dropped to between 11 and 12 percent, but until 1785 it remained between 15 and 19 percent. These figures are drawn from analysis of the biographical sketches in Dexter, *Biographical Sketches.*

10. Beecher, *An Address of the Charitable Society,* p. 14.

11. Ibid., p. 22.

12. I have drawn heavily upon Allmendinger's path-breaking study of ante-bellum New England students and colleges. In the following portion of this chapter, I have used the definition of "poor" students he gives in note 1, p. 23.

13. Allmendinger, *Paupers and Scholars,* pp. 11–12.

14. Ibid., pp. 9, 129–38.

15. Ibid., p. 11.
16. See Joseph Kett, "Growing Up in Rural New England," in Tamara Harevan, *Anonymous Americans* (New York, 1972), and "Adolescence and Youth in Nineteenth Century America," *The Journals of Interdisciplinary History* 2 (1971): 283–95. See also pp. 77–80 below.
17. Allmendinger, *Paupers and Scholars*, pp. 54–62.
18. Beecher, *Address of the Charitable Society*, p. 23.
19. Allmendinger, *Paupers and Scholars*, p. 65. For the American Education Society see Natalie Ann Naylor, "Raising a Learned Army: The American Education Society, 1815–1960" (Ph.D. diss., Columbia University, 1971); and Allmendinger, *Paupers and Scholars*, pp. 64–74. In addition, the annual reports of the society were published, and the AES published *The American Quarterly Register* as its official organ. The *Register* is an indispensable source of information about colleges, students, seminaries, and ministers. In addition, the Congregational Library in Boston, Massachusetts, possesses a number of manuscripts, especially the letterbooks of its general secretaries, Elias Corneilus and William Cogwell, which are extremely useful.
20. Allmendinger, *Paupers and Scholars*, pp. 59–60.
21. Ibid., p. 67.
22. Ibid., p. 68.
23. There is a fairly large literature on the New England tradition of a learned ministry. See especially the histories of Harvard and Yale, and Mary Gambrell, *Ministerial Training in Eighteenth Century New England* (New York, 1937). Daniel Calhoun, for example, found that of the seventy-three ministers serving in New Hampshire in 1770, only four had no higher education (Calhoun, *Professional Lives*, p. 141).
24. Carl F. Kaestle, *The Evolution of an Urban School System: New York City, 1750–1850* (Cambridge, Mass., 1973), p. 16.
25. These figures are based upon the sketches in Dexter, *Biographical Sketches*.
26. Beecher, *Address of the Charitable Society*, p. 6; See also Ebenezar Porter, *An Address on the Anniversary of the American Education Society* (Andover, 1816); and Joseph Dana, *A Sermon delivered at Ipswich before the Essex Auxiliary Society for the Education of Pious Youth for the Gospel Ministry* (Andover, 1816).
27. Allmendinger, *Paupers and Scholars*, pp. 81–86.
28. See the letters from Elias Corneilus to the AES beneficiaries at the various colleges, AES Manuscripts, *Letterbook*, 1 and 2, Congregational Library, Boston, Mass. John Todd, *John Todd, The Story of His Life, Told Mainly by Himself* (New York, 1876), gives a good sense of the purposiveness of these students. Allmendinger, *Paupers and Scholars*, gives the fullest account of them.

29. Gambrell, *Ministerial Training,* pp. 116–27; Joseph Vaill, "Theological Education in Connecticut Seventy Years Ago," *Congregational Quarterly* 14 (1864): 137–42.

30. Vaill, "Theological Education," pp. 140–42; Gambrell, *Ministerial Education,* pp. 134–42.

31. For Andover see Leonard Woods, *History of Andover Theological Seminary* (Boston, 1885); Henry K. Rowe, *History of Andover Theological Seminary* (Newton, 1933); *The Constitution and Associate Statutes of the Theological Seminary in Andover* (Boston, 1808); Timothy Dwight, *A Sermon Preached at the Opening of the Theological Seminary in Andover* (Boston, 1808); "Thoughts on the Importance of a Theological Institution," *The Panoplist* 3 (1806): 306–16.

32. See, for example, "Ministerial Sobriety," *The Spirit of the Pilgrims* 4 (1830): 11–14; William Buel Sprague, *The Causes of an Unsuccessful Ministry* (Albany, 1829); Gardiner Spring, *The Discriminating Preacher* (Hartford, 1825); and Samuel Miller, *Letters on Clerical Manners and Habits, Addressed to a Student in the Theological Seminary at Princeton, New Jersey* (New York, 1827).

33. Abel Flint, *Ordination Sermon for William Buel Sprague* (Boston, 1819), pp. 12–13.

34. Miller, *Letters on Clerical Manners,* chaps. 3–5.

35. Beecher, "Building of Waste-Places," p. 147.

36. Ibid.

37. Ibid.

38. Dexter, *Biographical Sketches,* lists the publications of ministers; from 1750 through 1770, for example, only about 12 percent published more than two sermons, and less than half published any sermons at all.

39. The religious journals and the tracts published most of their pieces anonymously, and with the rise of these forms the printed word began to take on greater importance as a devotional medium.

40. These figures are based upon systematic analysis of the *General Catalogue of the Theological Seminary, Andover, Massachusetts, 1808–1908* (Boston, 1909), which contains sketches of all Andover matriculants.

41. "Journal of Lucian Boynton," p. 352.

42. *The Panoplist* and *The Massachusetts Missionary Magazine* (*The Missionary Magazine* united with *The Panoplist* in 1806) were specifically concerned with the foreign mission movement and printed innumerable accounts of missionaries, as did *The Connecticut Evangelical Magazine,* which was more concerned with revivals. In addition, memoirs of missionaries quickly became an important form of evangelical literature. See, for example, Wayland, *Life and Labor of Adoniram Judson.* Todd, *John Todd,* pp. 124–33, contains a revealing

account of the significance attached to missions at Andover. Julian Sturtevant, *Julian M. Sturtevant: An Autobiography* (New York, 1896) contains a good account of the Yale band, as does Julian Rammelkampf, *Illinois College* (New Haven, 1928).

43. For Buel see Dexter, *Biographical Sketches,* 1: 664–69, and Lyman Beecher, *A Sermon Containing a General History of East Hampton, Long Island, from its First Settlement to the Present Time* (Sag Harbor, 1806), which contains an account of Buel's ministry. The best source for Beecher's career remains Beecher's *Autobiography*. The most complete account of Beecher's life and career is Vincent Harding, "Lyman Beecher and the Transformation of American Protestantism, 1775–1863" (Ph.D. diss., University of Chicago, 1965). See also Donald M. Scott, "Watchmen on the Walls of Zion," (Ph.D. diss., University of Wisconsin, 1968), pp. 1–55, for an analysis of Beecher's early career.

44. Beecher, *Autobiography*, 1: 105–24; Scott, "Watchmen on the Walls of Zion," pp. 22–37.

45. Beecher, *Autobiography*, 1: 147–214.

46. "Minute Adopted by the Long Island Presbytery," in Beecher, *Autobiography*, 1: 142. See Beecher, *Autobiography*, 1: 127–39 for the difficulties Beecher had at East Hampton.

47. Beecher, *Autobiography*, 2: 26–51.

48. "Careers," *International Encyclopedia of the Social Sciences*, 2: 252–53.

49. Catharine Beecher, *The Biographical Remains of Rev. George Beecher* (New York, 1844), p. 15.

50. Todd, *John Todd*, p. 124.

51. Ibid., pp. 130–31.

52. Beecher, *Biographical Remains*, p. 23.

53. Beecher, *Autobiography*, 1: 129–36.

54. Todd, *John Todd*, p. 187.

55. Calhoun suggests that Congregational consciousness emerged in the 1840s and 1850s and was finally, in the Boston Platform of 1865, codified in the 1860s; and that it emerged as the antidote to the utter collapse by 1840 of pastoral permanence. While I am in substantial agreement with Calhoun, the argument of this chapter is that a translocal group-consciousness of themselves, not as "professionals" or "Congregationalists," but as evangelical agents, emerged in the 1820s and 1830s and that this consciousness eroded the earlier sense of a minister as a permanent fixture in the church and community.

56. These figures are based on Dexter, *Biographical Sketches*; see also pp. 113–15 above.

57. These figures are drawn from the biographical entries in *General Catalogue of the Theological Seminary, Andover, Mass.*

Chapter 5

1. There is a voluminous—and still expanding—literature on abolition-
    ism. The two most useful general and comprehensive treatments of
    the whole antislavery movement are Louis Filler, *Crusade against
    Slavery, 1830–1860* (New York, 1960); and Dwight Dumond, *Anti-
    Slavery* (Ann Arbor, 1961). In addition, there is an extensive literature
    of studies of particular aspects of the movement and a number of
    very good biographies of various abolitionists. A good introduction to
    the literature is Merton Dillon, "The Abolitionists: A Decade of His-
    toriography, 1959–1969," *The Journal of Southern History* 35 (1969):
    500–522. Some excellent studies of particular abolitionists are: Benja-
    min Thomas, *Theodore Weld: Crusader for Freedom* (New Bruns-
    wick, 1950); and Aileen S. Kraditor, *Means and Ends in American
    Abolitionism: Garrison and his Critics on Strategy and Tactics, 1834–
    1850* (New York, 1967); and Bertram Wyatt-Brown, *Lewis Tappan
    and the Evangelical War against Slavery* (Cleveland, 1969). Some im-
    portant articles include David Donald's controversial application of a
    status-anxiety hypothesis to the abolitionists in his *Lincoln Recon-
    sidered: Essays on the Civil War Era* (New York, 1956); David B.
    Davis, "The Emergence of Immediatism in British and American Anti-
    Slavery Thought," *Mississippi Valley Historical Review* 49 (1962):
    209–30; Anne C. Loveland, "Evangelicalism and 'Immediate Emanci-
    pation' in American Anti-Slavery Thought," *Journal of Southern His-
    tory* 32 (1966): 172–88; and Martin Duberman, ed., *The Anti-Slavery
    Vanguard* (Princeton, 1965).
2. See, for example, Bodo, *Protestant Clergy and Public Issues*; Cole,
    Social Ideas of the Northern Evangelicals; Griffin, *Their Brothers'
    Keepers*.
3. Several dissertations contain valuable information about state and
    local societies and their personnel. See Victor Howard, "The Anti-
    Slavery Movement in the Presbyterian Church, 1835–1861" (Ph.D.
    diss., Ohio State University, 1961); Robert Senior, "New England
    Congregationalism and the Anti-Slavery Movement, 1830–1860"
    (Ph.D. diss., Yale University, 1964); and Alice Henderson, "The His-
    tory of the New York State Anti-Slavery Society" (Ph.D. diss., Uni-
    versity of Michigan, 1963). The articles by John L. Meyers are
    extremely valuable in this regard. See John L. Meyers, "The Begin-
    nings of Anti-Slavery Agencies in New York State," *New York History*
    43 (1962): 149–81; Meyers, "The Anti-Slavery Activity of Five Lane
    Seminary Boys in 1835–36," *The Historical and Philosophical Society
    of Ohio Bulletin* 21 (1963): 95–111; Meyers, "The Early Anti-Slavery
    System in Pennsylvania, 1833–1837," *Pennsylvania History* 31 (1963):
    62–86; Meyers, "The Major Effort of National Anti-Slavery Agents
    in New York, 1836–37," *New York History* 46 (1965): 162–86; and
    Meyers, "The Origins of 'the Seventy': to Arouse the North against

Slavery," *Mid-America* 48 (1966): 29–46. The notes in Gilbert H. Barnes and Dwight L. Dumond, *The Letters of Theodore Dwight Weld, Angelina Grimké Weld and Sarah Grimké, 1822–1844* (Gloucester, Mass., 1965) contain information on many abolitionists. See also Gilbert Barnes, *The Anti-Slavery Impulse* (New York, 1964), and Robert Fletcher, *A History of Oberlin College* (Oberlin, Ohio, 1943).

4. Some of the controversial literature surrounding the emergence of the more intense revivals of the late 1820s and early 1830s provides a good source for the gradualism of conversion in the early decades. See, for example, *Letters of the Rev. Dr. Beecher and Rev. Mr. Nettleton on the "New Measures" in Conducting Revivals of Religion* (New York, 1828); Tyler, *New England Revivals*; Ebenezar Porter, "Dr. Porter's Letters on Revivals of Religion," *Spirit of the Pilgrims* 5 (1832): 256–64, 318–25, 368–82, 565–72; 6 (1833): 126–34, 368–72. See also "Conversation between a Clergyman and his Parishioner," *The Christian Spectator* 1 (1819): 292–96; and Beecher, *Autobiography*, 1: 355–86.

5. For mechanisms that had been used, see "Minutes of the Conference Held at New Lebanon," *The Christian Examiner* 4 (1827): 358–70; Porter, "Dr. Porter's Letters," 6: 370–75, 380–85; "The Probationer's Class," *The Spirit of the Pilgrims*, 4 (1831): 657–58.

6. The term "rebirth" does not appear to have been used to talk of the revivals of the first two decades of the nineteenth century. It is a term more often associated with Methodist or frontier revivals and later revivals. Finney's notion of sinners bound to make themselves a "new heart" and the Beecher-Taylor notion of conversion come close to it, and the revivals of the late twenties and early thirties in New England came close to the Methodist experience.

7. See Kett, "Growing Up in New England," and "Adolescence and Youth in Nineteenth Century New England."

8. This is a constant theme of the advice literature directed toward young men, and it can also be seen in correspondence directed to young persons by their parents. See, for example, Hawes, *Lectures Addressed to the Young Men of Hartford*; Boynton, "The Journal of Lucien Boynton;" Sturtevant, *Julian M. Sturtevant*; and Mark Hopkins, *Early Letters of Mark Hopkins and Others from His Brothers and Their Mother: A Picture of Life in New England from 1770 to 1857* (New York, 1929).

9. Greven, *Four Generations*, pp. 222–58.

10. See, for example, Todd, *John Todd*; Sturtevant, *Julian M. Sturtevant*; Boynton, "Journal of Lucien Boynton"; Hopkins, *Early Letters of Mark Hopkins*.

11. Charles Beecher to Isabel Beecher, Beecher-Stowe Family Papers, Schlesinger Library, Radcliffe College.

12. Todd, *John Todd*, p. 118.

13. Ibid., p. 125. See John Cawelti, *Apostles of the Self-Made Man: Changing Concepts of Success in America* (Chicago, 1965), and Irvin G. Wyllie, *The Self-Made Man in America: The Myths of Rags to Riches* (New Brunswick, 1954), the best general treatments of the notion of self-help.

14. See, for example, Sylvester Judd, *The Life of Sylvester Judd* (Boston, 1847); Beecher, *Autobiography*, 1: 335–86, contains the letters recording Catharine Beecher's difficulty with submission. See Sklar, *Catharine Beecher*, for a superb account of her difficulties. See also "A Popular Objection to Revivals, Considered and Rejected," pp. 398–404; and "The Influence of Religion upon Health," *Quarterly Christian Spectator* 8 (1836): 51–79 for evangelical attempts to counter the notion that evangelical self-abasement led to morbidity and undermined mental stability.

15. A classic description of this kind of conversion is provided by Finney's account of his own conversion. See Finney, *A Memoir of Charles Grandison Finney, Written by Himself* (New York, 1876), pp. 32–43.

16. Tyler, *New England Revivals*, and Porter, "Dr. Porter's Letters," provide good descriptions of the relationship between individual and collective experiences in these early nineteenth-century revivals.

17. "The Probationer's Class," pp. 657–58.

18. The best indication of this can be seen in the New Lebanon controversy over the "new measures." See "Minutes of the Conference Held at New Lebanon;" and *Letters of Beecher and Nettleton*; see also the discussion in Scott, "Watchmen on the Walls of Zion," pp. 165–99.

19. For the revivals of the twenties and thirties, see Perry Miller, *The Life of the Mind in America* (New York, 1965); Cross, *The Burned over District*; McLoughlin, *Modern Revivalism*; Bernard Weisberger, *They Gathered at the River: The Story of the Great Revivalists and their Impact upon Religion in America* (New York, 1958); and Scott, "Watchmen on the Walls of Zion." Contemporary accounts can be found in Charles G. Finney, *Lectures on Revivals of Religion* (Cambridge, Mass., 1960); Charles G. Finney, *Memoir of Charles Grandison Finney*; "Report of the Suffolk South Association," *The Spirit of the Pilgrims* 6 (1833): 187–201; "Report of the Old Colony and Pilgrim Association," *The Spirit of the Pilgrims* 6 (1833): 312–16; "Report of the Hampden Association," *The Spirit of the Pilgrims* 6 (1833): 442–52; "Report of the Harmony Association," *The Spirit of the Pilgrims* 6 (1833): 304–10; "Report of the Franklin Association," *The Spirit of the Pilgrims* 6 (1833): 312–18.

20. Charles Grandison Finney, *Christian Affinity, or Can two walk together except they be agreed* (Utica, New York, 1827), pp. 6–11.

21. The best sources for the dramaturgy of these revivals are Finney, *Lectures on Revivals of Religion*; Finney, *Memoir of Charles Grandi-*

son Finney; "Report of the Suffolk South Association"; "Report of the Hampden Association"; "Report of the Franklin Association"; and "Report of the Old Colony Association."

22. See, for example, Yale, *Life of Jeremiah Hallock*; Sewell, *Memoir of Jotham Sewell*; and Cummings, *Memoir of Edward Payson*.

23. Weld's own retrospective account of his conversion is contained in Beecher, *Autobiography*, 2: 232–35. See also Thomas, *Theodore Weld*, pp. 12–16.

24. A particularly good source for the inner vocational sense is Barnes, *Weld-Grimké Letters*, and Dwight L. Dumond, *The Letters of James G. Birney* (Gloucester, Mass., 1965).

25. Lyman Beecher, *A Plea for the West* (Cincinnati, 1835), p. 10. Tuveson, *Redeemer Nation*; and David E. Smith, "Millennial Scholarship in America," *American Quarterly* 17 (1965): 535–49.

26. "The Necessity of Revivals to the Perpetuity of Our Institutions," *The Spirit of the Pilgrims* 4 (1831): 479.

27. See Barnes, *Weld-Grimké Letters*, 1: 78–99, 112–14, for examples of this spiritual style among young men converted in the revivals of the late 1820s and early 1830s.

28. A good example of transcendent spirituality is provided in Jonathan Edwards' description of the piety of his wife, Sarah Pierpont Edwards; Faust and Johnson, *Jonathan Edwards: Selections*, p. 56.

29. Beriah Green, *The Divine Significance of Work: A Valedictory Address at Oneida Institute* (Oneida, 1842), p. 27.

30. Barnes, *Weld-Grimké Letters*, 7: 112–13.

31. Barnes, *Anti-Slavery Impulse*; Fletcher, *History of Oberlin*; and John Meyers, "The Agency System of the Anti-Slavery Movement and its Antecedents in Other Benevolent and Reform Societies" (Ph.D. diss., University of Michigan, 1961), provide a wealth of information on the earlier vocational activities of those who eventually enlisted themselves as antislavery activists.

32. For Andover, see Woods, *History of Andover*. For the best treatment of Oneida, see Fletcher, *History of Oberlin*. Barnes, *Anti-Slavery Impulse*; Fletcher, *History of Oberlin*; Thomas, *Theodore Weld*; and Scott, "Watchmen on the Walls of Zion" all discuss Lane Seminary. Quotation from Beecher, *Autobiography*, 2: 189.

33. See Barnes, *Weld-Grimké Letters*, 1: 78–91, 92–94, 106–114, for the Lane seminarians' activities. See also Allmendinger, *Paupers and Scholars*, pp. 118–25.

34. M. Brainerd, *The Life of the Rev. Thomas Brainerd* (New York, 1870), p. 58.

35. See, for example, Barnes, *Weld-Grimké Letters*, 1: 78–87, 112–15. See also Meyers, "Agency System of the Anti-Slavery Movement."

36. For the life of an agent, see William Hallock, *Journal Kept While An Agent of the New England Tract Society*, MSS, Congregational Li-

brary. See also the letters from Oneida and Lane students out in the field in Barnes, *Weld-Grimké Letters*.

37.   Barnes, *Weld-Grimké Letters*, pp. 52–150, gives a very good sense of the spiritual intensity the students felt once they were back together in a seminary. See also Fletcher, *History of Oberlin*, and Scott, "Watchmen on the Walls of Zion," for discussion of Lane.

38.   Green, for example, had left the pastorate to teach at Western Reserve as had Elizur Wright, and Amos Phelps converted to antislavery views shortly after moving from his first pastorate. See Meyers, "Early Anti-Slavery System in Pennsylvania," "Major Effort of National Anti-Slavery Agents in New York," and "Origins of the 'Seventy,'" for the best information on who the antislavery agents were.

39.   See H. Shelton Smith, *Changing Conceptions of Original Sin: A Study in American Theology Since 1750* (New York, 1955).

40.   See, for example, Edward Hitchcock, "On Intemperance in Eating," *The American National Preacher* 8 (1834): 337–60, 369–80; Sylvester Graham, *A Lecture to Young Men on Chastity Intended Also for the Serious Consideration of Parents and Guardians* (Boston, 1841); Hawes, *Lectures Addressed to the Young Men of Hartford*; and Beecher, *Six Sermons*.

41.   Beriah Green, *The Divine Significance of Work*, p. 8.

42.   Samuel Crothers, *An Address to the Churches on the Subject of Slavery* (Georgetown, Ohio, 1831), p. 10.

43.   See, for example, Samuel Crothers, *Strictures on African Slavery* (Rossville, Ohio, 1833); James T. Dickinson, *Sermon Preached in the Second Congregational Church, Norwich, Connecticut* (Norwich, 1834); Beriah Green, *Four Sermons Preached in the Chapel of Western Reserve College* (Cleveland, 1833); Theodore Weld, *American Slavery As It Is: The Testimony of a Thousand Witnesses* (New York, 1839); Amos Phelps, *Lectures on Slavery and its Remedy* (Boston, 1834). Essential for slavery and conceptions of sin are David Brion Davis, *The Problem of Slavery in Western Culture* (Ithaca, 1966) and David Brion Davis, *The Problem of Slavery in the Age of Revolution, 1770–1823* (Ithaca, 1975).

44.   Green, *Four Sermons*, pp. 41–42.

45.   James A. Thome, *Speech of James A. Thome of Kentucky Delivered at the Annual Meeting of the American Anti-Slavery Society, May 6, 1834* (Boston, 1834), p. 7.

46.   Barnes, *Weld-Grimké Letters*, 1: 56.

47.   The character and importance of these bonds can be seen in the correspondence between the Oneida seminarians in the *Weld-Grimké Letters*, 1: 26–38, 52–54, 78–94, 106–9, 112–14, 178–204; and in the *Letters of James Birney*. Accounts of the conversion of Weld are in Barnes, *Anti-Slavery Impulse* and in Thomas, *Theodore Weld*. Good accounts of Weld's effectiveness as an apostle of abolitionism are con-

tained in Meyers, "Major Effort of National Anti-Slavery Agents in New York"; Meyers, "Origins of the 'Seventy.'" A superb study of female bonding in this period, which is suggestive of the bonds the abolitionists established, is in Carroll Smith-Rosenberg, "The Female World of Love and Ritual: Relations between Women in Nineteenth Century America," *Signs: Journal of Women in Culture and Society* 1 (1975): 1–31.

48. For the Lane episodes see Robert Fletcher, *History of Oberlin College*, 1: 150–65; Barnes, *Anti-Slavery Impulse*, pp. 64–73; Scott, "Watchmen on the Walls of Zion," pp. 329–89. Contemporary accounts are contained in H. B. Stanton, "Letter," *The New York Evangelist*, 10 March 1834; Huntington Lyman, "Letter," Ibid.; Augustus Wattles, "Letters," *The Emancipator*, 22 April 1834; Barnes, *Weld-Grimké Letters*, 1: 137–40.

49. *Statement of the Reasons which Induced the Students of Lane Seminary to Dissolve their Connection with that Institution* (Cincinnati, 1834), p. 4.

50. Ibid.

51. See Davis, "Emergence of Immediatism in British and American Anti-Slavery Thought"; and Loveland, "Evangelicalism and 'Immediate Emancipation' in American Anti-Slavery Thought." As a "disposition" in this sense, immediatism could go in a number of specific tactical directions. See Kraditor, *Means and Ends in American Abolitionism*.

52. Gerrit L. Smith to Lyman Beecher, *The Philanthropist* 1, 23 September 1836.

53. There is a rich literature on the relationship between evangelicalism and abolition beginning with Barnes and continuing with the work of David B. Davis, Anne Loveland, Bertram Wyatt-Brown, and Donald Mathews. My own interpretation of necessity builds upon this scholarship. However, I have approached evangelicalism less as a source of abolitionist ideas than as a style of commitment and have focused on the psyche of the process, on how conversion to both evangelicalism and immediatism operated as a psychological episode fixing identity and commitment. Similarly, the youthfulness of much of the abolition cadre had been noted by David Donald and Lois Banner. In analyzing immediatism from a generational perspective, however, I have placed the adoption of abolition in the context of generational change and the transformation of the clergy and asked what it was about them and their ministerial situation and generational situation that made them susceptible to the abolitionist imperative.

Chapter 6

1. See, for example, *The Colonizationist and Journal of Freedom* (Boston 1833–34), a journal designed to take a firm antislavery, but still

colonizationist, stand; articles from 1833 to 1836 on slavery and abolitionism in the *Quarterly Christian Spectator;* "Colonization and Emancipation," *The Spirit of the Pilgrims* 6 (1833): 392–402; Leonard Bacon, *Slavery Discussed in Occasional Essays from 1833 to 1846* (New York, 1846). See also Senior, "New England Congregationalists and Anti-Slavery," and Lorman Ratner, *Powder Keg: Northern Opposition to the Anti-Slavery Movement, 1831–1840* (New York, 1968).

2. For abolitionists' tactics see Leonard L. Richards, *Gentlemen of Property and Standing: Anti-Abolition Mobs in Jacksonian America* (New York, 1970); Kraditor, *Means and Ends in American Abolitionism;* Barnes, *Anti-Slavery Impulse;* Wyatt-Brown, *Lewis Tappen;* Meyers, "Major Effort of National Anti-Slavery Agents in New York," and "Origins of the 'Seventy.' " See also Barnes, *Weld-Grimké Letters* for the behavior and attitudes of the antislavery agents.

3. Barnes, *Weld-Grimké Letters,* 1: 242–43.

4. See Tyler, *New England Revivals;* and "Dr. Porter's Letters on Revivals."

5. "Report of the Hampden Association" 6; "Report of the Suffolk South Association" 6; *Minutes of the Hampden Association, Feb. 14, 1832,* Hampden Association Manuscripts, Congregational Library.

6. Quoted in Thomas, *Theodore Weld,* p. 86. See also James Hall, "Education and Slavery," *Western Monthly Magazine* 2 (1834): 270–74. "Fanaticism," *Quarterly Christian Spectator* 6 (1834): 118–40. See also Richards, *Gentlemen of Property and Standing,* pp. 60–61; and David Grimstead, "Rioting in its Jacksonian Setting," *American Historical Review* 77 (1972): 361–97.

7. *Report of the Executive Committee of the Board of Trustees of Lane Theological Seminary,* Lane Theological Seminary Papers, McGaw Library, McCormick Theological Seminary.

8. For the democratization of American political culture in the 1820s and 1830s, see Marvin Meyers, *The Jacksonian Persuasion* (New York, 1960), and Berthoff, *An Unsettled People.*

9. See, for example, Hall, "Education and Slavery," pp. 264–73; "Necessity of Revivals to the Perpetuity of Our Institutions"; Parsons Cooke, *Moral Machinery Simplified* (Andover, 1839); *Regulations Adopted by the Board of Trustees of Lane Theological Seminary, October 6, 1834,* Lane MSS. Constance Rourke, *Trumpets of Jubilee: Henry Ward Beecher, Harriet Beecher Stowe, Lyman Beecher, Horace Greeley, P. T. Barnum* (New York, 1963) is a suggestive study of the commotion and rhetoric of the American public life in these years.

10. Hall, "Education and Slavery," p. 270.

11. Cooke, *Moral Machinery Simplified,* p. 4.

12. Hall, "Education and Slavery," pp. 266–67.

13. *Regulations Adopted by the Board of Trustees of the Lane Theological Seminary;* Cooke, *Moral Machinery Simplified,* pp. 6–11.

14. Hall, "Education and Slavery," p. 271.
15. Roy P. Basler, ed., *The Papers of Abraham Lincoln* (New Brunswick, 1960), 1: 108–15.
16. Barnes, *Weld-Grimké Letters*, 1: 318–19.
17. See Perry Miller, "The Location of American Religious Freedom," *Nature's Nation*, pp. 150–62; William McLoughlin, "The Role of Religion in the Revolution," in Stephan M. Kurtz and James H. Hutson, eds., *Essays on the American Revolution* (New York, 1973), pp. 197–255.
18. Perhaps the best single source for religion and home as counters to the turbulance of democratic life is Catharine Beecher, *A Treatise on Domestic Economy for the Use of Young Ladies at Home and at School* (New York, 1848). See Sklar, *Catharine Beecher*, and Bernard Wishy, *The Child and the Republic: The Dawn of Modern Child Nurture* (Philadelphia, 1969).
19. See Mead, *The Lively Experiment*; and Robert N. Bellah, "Civil Religion in America," in William G. McLoughlin and Robert N. Bellah, eds., *Religion in America* (Boston, 1966), pp. 3–23. The debate on women and antislavery activity is a particularly good source for the boundaries between religion and public activity. See, for example, Catharine Beecher, *An Essay on Slavery and Abolitionism with Reference to the Duty of American Females* (Philadelphia, 1837), and Angelina Grimké, *Letters to Catharine Beecher in Reply to an Essay on Slavery and Abolitionism Addressed to Angelina E. Grimké* (Boston, 1838).
20. Thomas, *Theodore Weld*, pp. 100–132, 179–91; Filler, *The Crusade Against Slavery*, pp. 1–137; Kraditor, *Means and Ends in American Abolitionism*, pp. 3–32, 118–36.
21. Richards, *Gentlemen of Property and Standing*, pp. 20–82.
22. See, for example, Cooke, *Moral Machinery Simplified*; Beecher, *Essay on Slavery and Abolitionism*; Calvin Colton, *Abolition and Sedition, by a Northerner* (Philadelphia, 1839) and *Protestant Jesuiticism* (New York, 1837).
23. See Meyers, *Jacksonian Persuasion*, and John William Ward, *Andrew Jackson: Symbol for an Age* (New York, 1953) for discussion of this style of thought.
24. For a general discussion of the voluntaristic nature of American society in these years see Berthoff, *An Unsettled People*, pp. 244–47; see also Grimstead, "Rioting in its Jacksonian Setting," p. 370.
25. See, for example, Weld's discussion of his brushes with danger and death, Barnes, *Weld-Grimké Letters*, 1: 60–66, 309–11. See also Richards, *Gentlemen of Property and Standing*, pp. 20–46; and Sylvan Tomkins, "The Psychology of Commitment: The Constructive Role of Violence and Suffering for the Individual and His Society," in Duberman, *The Anti-Slavery Vanguard*, pp. 270–98.

26. See, for example, Bacon, *Slavery Discussed in Occasional Essays;* see also Senior, "New England Congregationalists and Anti-Slavery."

27. Cooke, *Moral Machinery Simplified,* p. 3.

28. See Bacon, *Slavery Discussed in Occasional Essays;* Beecher, *Essay on Slavery and Abolitionism;* Hall, Education and Slavery."

29. Hall, "Education and Slavery," pp. 270–71.

30. See McLoughlin, *Modern Revivalism;* Cross, *The Burned-over District;* and Finney, *Memoir of Charles Grandison Finney,* for accounts of the Rochester revivals.

31. Barnes, *Weld-Grimké Letters,* 1: 326–27.

32. "Declaration of the Faculty of Lane Seminary," *Boston Recorder* 19, 7 November 1834.

33. *Report of the Executive Committee of the Board of Trustees of Lane Theological Seminary.*

34. See, for example, James G. Birney, *Letter on Colonization, Addressed to the Rev. Thornton J. Mills, Corresponding Secretary of the Kentucky Colonization Society* (New York, 1834); and Phelps, *Lectures on Slavery and its Remedy.*

35. Cooke, *Moral Machinery Simplified,* p. 5.

36. "Necessity of Revivals of Religion to the Perpetuity of Our Institutions," p. 465.

37. Cooke, *Moral Machinery Simplified,* p. 8.

38. See, for example, Gerrit Smith to Lyman Beecher, *The Philanthropist* 23 September 1836, p. 1.

39. See the various arguments over the legitimacy of withholding Christian fellowship from slaveholders; for example, Amos A. Phelps, *Letters to Professor Stowe and Dr. Bacon on God's Real Method with Great Social Wrongs in which the Bible is Vindicated from Grossly Erroneous Interpretations* (New York, 1848); and Bacon, *Slavery Discussed in Occasional Essays,* pp. 131–247. See also Edward Beecher's twelve sermons on "Organic Sin," in the *Boston Recorder* from 25 October through 25 December 1845.

40. See Robert Merideth, "Introduction" to Edward Beecher, *Narrative of Riots at Alton, Illinois in Connection with the Death of Rev. Elijah P. Lovejoy* (New York, 1965); Robert Merideth, *The Politics of the Universe: Edward Beecher, Abolition, and Orthodoxy* (Nashville, 1968); and Kraditor, *Means and Ends in American Abolitionism,* pp. 141–78.

41. Bacon, *Slavery Discussed in Occasional Essays,* pp. 57–58.

42. See, for example, James G. Birney, *The American Churches the Bulwark of Slavery* (Boston, 1843). See also Thomas, *Theodore Weld,* pp. 86–87; Barnes, *Anti-Slavery Impulse,* pp. 95–99.

43. R. L. Hightower, "Joshua Wilson, Frontier Controversialist," *Church History* 3 (1935): 300–316.

44. See also Beecher, *Autobiography,* 2: 261–73; Lyman Beecher, *Works,* 3, which contains the proceedings of the trial.

45. John Jay Shipherd to Fayette Shipherd, 23 December 1834, quoted in Fletcher *History of Oberlin*, 1: 173. See also Gamaliel Bailey to James G. Birney, 14 October 1837, in Dumond, *Letters of James G. Birney*, 1: 427; Arthur Tappen to Lyman Beecher, 20 January 1838, Lane MSS.

46. See Bertram Wyatt-Brown, "Stanley Elkins' *Slavery*: The Anti-Slavery Interpretation Reexamined," *American Quarterly* 25 (1973): 154–76.

Chapter 7

1. E. D. Moore, *On Living Peaceably with All Men, A Farewell Sermon, Preached at Barre, Mass.* (Boston, 1842), p. 19.

2. Ibid., pp. 6–17; see also W. Barrows, *Ministerial Freedom, A Sermon to the Orthodox Congregational Church and Society in Norton, Mass.* (Boston, 1850).

3. See the letter of Henry Ward Beecher to Lyman Beecher, 12 September 1844, Beecher-Stowe Family papers, Schlesinger Library, Radcliffe College, for a discussion of the difficulties Charles Beecher, who forswore any "party" label, encountered from doctrinal factions in his Fort Wayne, Indiana, congregation.

4. See, for example, Barrows, *Ministerial Freedom*, and Milton Bramen, *Obstacles to the Gospel, A Sermon Dedicating the Meeting House at North Danvers* (Salem, 1840).

5. Bramen, *Obstacles to the Gospel*, p. 44.

6. Charles Brooks, *Statement of Facts from Each Religious Denomination in New England Respecting Ministerial Salaries* (Boston, 1854). Financial pressures on ministers were such that many appear to have been forced to supplement their clerical earnings with outside "secular callings." See *Report to the Hampden Association*, Hampden West Association Papers, Congregational Library. The Congregational Library contains a large collection of unopened and uncatalogued materials which the various ministerial associations have deposited there. Buried in these papers are reports of committees on a wide range of problems, the minutes of association meetings, and letters to and from clergymen. See also Amzi Benedict, "Ministerial Support," *American National Preacher* 29 (1855): 129–40.

7. These figures are based upon the histories of the individual churches contained in *Contributions to the Ecclesiastical History of Connecticut*, an extremely valuable source for specific information about the individual churches and their pastors.

8. Todd, *John Todd*, pp. 120–22, 289–96.

9. Ibid., pp. 307–10.

10. These figures are based upon the *General Catalogue of the Theological Seminary, Andover, Massachusetts*.

11. These figures show up most frequently among the matriculants who did not complete a full course of theological study. It was not, how-

ever, uncommon for men to leave the ministry after a full course of study.

12. *General Catalogue*, p. 137.

13. *The Congregational Quarterly* annually printed a state-by-state compilation of church and ministerial statistics, in which they record the number of ministers settled, on stated supply, and "other" or "without charge." A certain number of those recorded as "other" or "without charge" were undoubtedly retired. Although ministers still can be found serving well into their seventies, the overwhelming portion of those listed in the *General Catalogue* were putting aside regular pastoral labor in their mid-sixties. The letters in the Suffolk North Association Papers, Congregational Library, requesting dismissal from the association invariably stress the fellowship the association provided.

14. See Calhoun, *Professional Lives*, pp. 136–45.

15. Brooks, *Statement of Facts*, p. 2.

16. Ibid., p. 16.

17. Ibid., p. 10.

18. Ibid., p. 15.

19. Ibid., p. 4.

20. Ibid., p. 20.

21. See, for example, Sprague, *Causes of an Unsuccessful Ministry*; and William Gould, *Sermon Delivered in Dracut, First Parish, Oct. 19, 1817, The Sabbath after the Dissolution of his Pastoral Relation with the Church* (Haverhill, 1817).

22. See, for example, Jonathan Lee, *The Labors of a Pastor Defeated and his Hopes Disappointed* (Middlebury, 1837); Moore, *On Living Peaceably with All Men*; George Allen, *Speech on Ministers Leaving a Moral Kingdom* (Boston, 1838); Joseph Henry Allen, *The Account Rendered, A Sermon at the Resignation of his Jamaica Plain Ministry* (Boston, 1847).

23. Barrows, *Ministerial Freedom*, pp. 11–13.

24. See pages 86–88 above.

25. Todd, *John Todd*, p. 45. For analysis of Todd as an example of aspiration and mobility see Scott, "Watchmen on the Walls of Zion," pp. 283–95; and Allmendinger, *Paupers and Scholars*, pp. 38–42.

26. See, for example, "The General Assembly's Board of Education and the American Education Society," *Biblical Repertory* 1 (1829): 351–64. Moses Stuart, "Examination of the Strictures Upon the American Education Society," *American Quarterly Register* 2 (1829): 79–104. Bela Edwards, "The Necessity of Education Societies," *American Biblical Repository*, 8 (1842): 444–63; and Julian Sturtevant, "The Education of Indigent Young Men for the Ministry," *American Biblical Repository* 10 (1843): 465–68.

27. See Donald M. Scott, *Pastors and Providence: Changing Ministerial Styles in Nineteenth Century America* (Evanston, 1976) for a somewhat broader analysis of this particular style.

28. This was a period which saw an enormous expansion of the number of "intellectual careers" as journalists, reformers, and publicists of various sorts began to sustain themselves by writing and activism. As biographical registers of colleges and seminaries suggest, many young men who forged such careers had initially considered the clergy. Clerical fathers, moreover, frequently placed enormous pressures upon their intellectually inclined sons to enter the ministry, and those who did break with the ministry frequently did so only after considerable inner turmoil. The whole problem of the relationship between the ministry and the newer careers needs further exploration. See George Fredrickson, *The Inner Civil War: Northern Intellectuals and the Crisis of the Union* (New York, 1965); and Wilson Smith, *Professors and Public Ethics: Studies of Northern Moral Philosophers Before the Civil War* (Ithaca, 1956).

29. See, for example, Edward A. Park, *Writings of Professor Bela Bates Edwards, with a Memoir by Edwards A. Park* (Boston, 1853); H. Humphrey, *A Memoir of John Humphrey* (New York, 1858); and Beecher, *Autobiography*, 2: 344–52. Scott, "Watchmen on the Walls of Zion," pp. 298–315, contains an analysis of these pressures as Lyman Beecher's children faced them.

30. *Minutes of the Hampden Association*, 14 February 1832, Hampden Association MSS., Congregational Library.

31. *Contributions to the Ecclesiastical History of Connecticut*, p. 424.

32. Ibid., p. 346.

33. See Calhoun, *Professional Lives*, pp. 88–94, 133–35, for discussion of these forms.

34. Alonzo Quint, "American Congregational Statistics for 1858," *Congregational Quarterly* 1 (1859): 77–89; "Annual Statistics," *Congregational Quarterly* 4 (1863): 76–93.

35. See Heman Humphrey, *Thirty-four Letters to a Son in the Ministry* (Amherst, 1834), pp. 33–35; Pond, *The Young Pastor's Guide, or, a Lecture on Pastoral Duty* (New York, 1844), pp. 39–43; Calhoun, *Professional Lives*, p. 165.

36. See pages 5–6 above.

37. Pond, *Young Pastor's Guide*, p. 67.

38. Ibid.

39. Beecher, "The Building of Waste-Places," p. 146.

40. Moore, *On Living Peaceably with All Men*, appendix.

41. *Result of the Ecclesiastical Council Convened at Beverly, Mass., Dec. 26, 1833* (Salem, 1834), p. 4.

42. See, for example, Humphrey, *Thirty-four Letters*, p. 39; Beecher, "The Building of Waste-Places," pp. 119–20; Calhoun, *Professional Lives*.

43. See Humphrey, *Thirty-four Letters*, pp. 54–64; and Pond, *Young Pastor's Guide*, pp. 27–53.

44. Humphrey, *Thirty-four Letters*, pp. 27–29.

45. Ibid., p. 36.

46. Miller, *Letters on Clerical Manners*, pp. 37–164.
47. Pond, *Young Pastor's Guide*, p. 67.
48. A good source for the extent to which seminary training had become the essential form of ministerial training is Henry Hazen, "Ministry and Churches of New Hampshire," *Congregational Quarterly* 18 (1877): 283–313, which lists all ministers serving Congregational and Presbyterian churches in New Hampshire through 1872 and includes their educational histories. See also Calhoun, *Professional Lives*, which bases much of its statistical analysis upon Hazen.
49. A good portrait of the seminaries as bastions of one or another of the various doctrinal tendencies is provided by Mead, *Nathaniel Taylor*, which discusses Yale, Andover, and East Windsor, and Fletcher, *History of Oberlin*, which discusses the struggles over the kind of doctrinal emphasis Lane Seminary was to have.
50. Todd, *John Todd*, pp. 174–216.
51. Ibid., pp. 227–56.
52. Henry Ward Beecher, *Sermon Book*, Beecher Family Papers, Yale University Library, nos. 90–96.
53. Henry Ward Beecher, *Journal of Events, Thoughts, Feelings, Plans, etc., just as they have met me, thus giving in part a transcript of my inner and outer life. Begun June 1835 at Lane Theological Seminary* (Beecher Family Papers). Entry for 27 September 1838.
54. Moore, *On Living Peaceably with All Men*, appendix.
55. Todd, *John Todd*, pp. 299–310.
56. The Congregational Library in Boston possesses, in various locations, a number of documents concerning Oliphant's problems—petitions from both sides, letters to the two councils that were called, Oliphant's recollections in his manuscript *Autobiography*, and the printed result of the council.
57. *Report of the Committee to Propose a Plan of Union*, Hampden North Association Papers, Congregational Library.
58. See, for example, H. B. Elliott, *Church Establishment: Pastor and People Mutually Encouraged* (New York, 1854); Daniel Crosby, *Good Men Love the Sanctuary* (Boston, 1834); Arthur Swazey, *The Work of the Ministry* (Galena, 1856). See also Bacon, *The American Church* (New York, 1850); Pond, *Young Pastor's Guide*, pp. 34–40; and Humphrey, *Thirty-four Letters*, pp. 32–47.
59. Todd, *John Todd*, p. 310.
60. See, for example, Crosby, *Good Men Love the Sanctuary*; Swazey, *Work of the Ministry*; Bramen, *Obstacles to the Gospel*; Pond, *Young Pastor's Guide*; and Humphrey, *Thirty-four Letters*. See also Calhoun, *Professional Lives*, pp. 182–85.
61. See pages 12–16 below.
62. "Necessity of Revivals of Religion to the Perpetuity of Our Institutions," pp. 467–72.
63. Elliott, *Church Establishment*, p. 16.

64. Bramen, *Obstacles to the Gospel*, p. 27.
65. See, for example, Crosby, *Good Men Love the Sanctuary*; Bramen, *Obstacles to the Gospel*; Swazey, *Work of the Ministry*; Barrows, *Ministerial Freedom*; Lee, *Labors of a Pastor Defeated*.
66. Swazey, *Work of the Ministry*, p. 19.
67. Barrows, *Ministerial Freedom*, p. 8–9.
68. Much of Daniel Calhoun's analysis in *Professional Lives* is concerned with the extent to which mastery and control over a body of learning confers authority. See, especially, pp. 1–19, 178–97.
69. See Pond, *Young Pastor's Guide*, and Humphrey, *Thirty-four Letters* for the sense of professional limits and decorum required of young men, and especially for the need for survival. In fact, these manuals can be read as survival kits for young ministers. See also Barrows, *Ministerial Freedom*, pp. 7–10; Swazey, *Work of the Ministry*, pp. 7–15; Moore, *On Living Peaceably with All Men*, pp. 9–19; Allen, *Speech on Ministers Leaving a Moral Kingdom*, pp. 3–11.
70. Miller, *Letters on Clerical Manners*, pp. 27–47, 107–37; Pond, *Young Pastor's Guide*, pp. 77–93; Humphrey, *Thirty-four Letters*, pp. 98–103, 192–211.
71. See Erving Goffman, *The Presentation of Self in Everyday Life* (New York, 1968), and Erving Goffman, *Behavior in Public Places: Notes on the Social Organization of Gatherings* (New York, 1963). In both of these works, Goffman provides an interesting treatment of etiquette and guidebooks.
72. Although this interpretation of the character of the ministry in mid-nineteenth-century New England draws upon Mead's "Rise of the Evangelical Conception of the Ministry in America" and Calhoun's *Professional Lives in America*, it approaches the problem from a rather different angle of vision. Mead traces the distinctive character of the pastoral office in America to the evangelical concern with the salvational episode and the character of the church as a voluntarily gathered body of seekers, while I have focused more upon the social conditions that informed the devotional needs of parishioners and impinged upon the character of the relationship between pastor and people. In his brilliant analysis of pastoral permanence, Calhoun explores how, in response to the destruction of permanence, ministers shifted their orientation away from lifelong identity with the particular communion toward the collective clerical community. In this chapter, I have approached the adoption of the language of profession less in terms of ministerial organization than in terms of the problem of the general crisis in pastoral relations.

Chapter 8

1. Samuel Miller, *Holding Fast the Faithful Word* (Albany, 1829), p. 14.
2. See, for example, Crosby, *Good Men Love the Sanctuary*; Bramen,

Obstacles to the Gospel; David Grosvenor, *The Glory of the Sanctuary* (Boston, 1834).

3. Leonard Woods, "Remarks on Voluntary and Ecclesiastical Organizations," *Biblical Repository and Quarterly Review* 12 (1838): 261.

4. *Minutes of the Suffolk North Association,* Manuscript, Congregational Library, 13 August 1833.

5. See, for example, "Report of the Old Colony and Pilgrim Association," pp. 312–14; "Report of the Harmony Association," pp. 308–9; "Report of the Franklin Association," pp. 317–18; "Report of the Hampden Association," p. 450.

6. Hampden Association, "Report on the Granting of Licenses to Preach the Gospel," Hampden Association Manuscripts, Congregational Library.

7. Barnes, *Anti-Slavery Impulse,* pp. 84–85.

8. Grosvenor, *Glory of the Sanctuary,* p. 18.

9. See *Minutes of the General Assembly of the Presbyterian Church in the United States of America* (Philadelphia, 1837); Zebulon Crocker, *The Catastrophe of the Presbyterian Church* (New Haven, 1838). See also George M. Marsden, *The Evangelical Mind and the New School Presbyterian Experience* (New Haven, 1970).

10. *Minutes of the Hampden Association,* 11 October 1832; 12 February 1833. See also Mead, *Nathaniel Taylor.*

11. See Marsden, *Evangelical Mind,* pp. 88–127; Robert Nichols, *Presbyterianism in New York State* (Philadelphia, 1963); and C. Bruce Staiger, "Abolition and the Presbyterian Schism, 1837–38," *Mississippi Valley Historical Review* 36 (1939): 391–414.

12. In 1836, the Rock Island City, Illinois, free Congregational church was formed with the standing rule that "this church will receive no individual to its fellowship who does not adopt the principles of immediate abolition, and such as are willing to do what they can to break every yoke." "Anti-Slavery Ecclesiastics," *The Philanthropist* 1, 1 November 1836. The antislavery press is the best source for abolitionist churches. *The Philanthropist* had a regular weekly feature entitled "Anti-Slavery Ecclesiastics," which reported the formation of abolitionist churches and reprinted antislavery resolutions.

13. See Jonathan Edwards, *Thoughts on Revivals of Religion.* See also Perry Miller, *Jonathan Edwards* (New York, 1949).

14. See, for example, Finney, *Lectures on Revivals of Religion;* Porter, "Dr. Porter's Letters"; Albert Barnes, *Revivals of Religion* (Philadelphia, 1844); William Sprague, *Revivals of Religion* (New York, 1838).

15. "Report of the Suffolk South Association," p. 197; "Report of the Old Colony and Pilgrim Association," pp. 312–14; "Report of the Harmony Association," pp. 308–9; "Report of the Hampden Association," pp. 447–53; Porter, "Dr. Porter's Letters," pp. 387–88.

16. Porter, "Dr. Porter's Letters," 6: 369–88; Leonard Woods, *Letters to*

Young Ministers (Andover, 1834); Edward Hooker, *Preaching the Word* (Andover, 1830).

17. "Report of the Old Colony and Pilgrim Association," pp. 312–14; "Report of the Harmony Association," pp. 308–9; "Report of the Hampden Association," p. 447.

18. "Report of the Franklin Association," p. 317; "Report of the Old Colony and Pilgrim Association," pp. 308–9; "Report of the Hampden Association," pp. 448–50.

19. Finney, *Lectures on Revivals of Religion*, pp. 263–67; Wright, *Charles G. Finney*, pp. 26–58.

20. "The Probationer's Class," p. 657.

21. See, for example, Finney, *Christian Affinity*; and Scott, "Watchmen on the Walls of Zion," pp. 165–98.

22. Finney, *Lectures on Revivals of Religion*, pp. 263–67, 292–93.

23. Ibid., pp. 310–11.

24. Porter, "Dr. Porter's Letters," 5: 369.

25. "When I attempted moderation, I have lost the revival for want of moral power and when to avoid this, I have taxed my own and the system of others, I have found exhausted nature to be the occasion of shortening the date of special mercy. I have tried by many soundings and careful observations, to find the safe middle channel of so much excitement, and efforts as can be steadily endured, and at the same time so condensed and applied as shall rouse and command and control public sentiment and feeling, as the means in the hand of God of a perpetual revival; but as yet, I must say, I have not found it." Lyman Beecher to the editor of *The New York Evangelist*, reprinted in *The Western Luminary 10*, 10 February 1834. See also Pond, *Young Pastor's Guide*, pp. 146–50, 170–74; Humphrey, *Thirty-four Letters*, pp. 270–72.

26. Finney, *Lectures on Revivals of Religion*, pp. 284–85, 432–70.

27. See, for example, Samuel Harris, *Christ: the Theme of the Sanctuary* (Northampton, 1847); Asa Smith, "Christ—the Preacher's Model," *American Biblical Repository* 9 (1843): 149–64; Henry N. Day, "The Training of the Preacher," *American Biblical Repository* 8 (1842): 71–87. See also Henry Ward Beecher, *Journal*, for a good portrait of how one minister came to focus his ministry on Christ. See Scott, "Watchmen on the Walls of Zion," pp. 438–50.

28. For the moral government scheme see Mead, *Nathaniel Taylor*, and Haroutunian, *Piety Versus Moralism*.

29. George Beecher's report of how his Rochester, New York, congregation received his sermon of April 1838 on heaven suggests the appeal of the theme: "It was listened to with breathless attention and I have been urged to preach it again." Beecher, *Biographical Remains*, p. 63. In addition to the sources referred to in note 19 above, see the discussions of pulpit eloquence which began appearing more and more

frequently in those journals directed to the pastor in the field. ". . . the love of Christ burning on his lips, and speaking from his eye, [the minister] breaks up the lethargy of sin, convinces the unbelieving, enlightens the ignorant, melts the insensible, subdues the perverse and obstinate, comforts and cheers the troubled and desponding, and transfuses all hearts with the power and blessedness of the love of Christ." Day, "Training of the Preacher," p. 75. See also Todd, *John Todd*, pp. 440 57, and Harris, *Christ the Theme of the Sanctuary*, pp. 5–13.

30. Beecher, *Biographical Remains*, pp. 150–51.

31. One of the key discussions urging "holiness" was Edward Beecher's set of six sermons which were printed in 1835 in the *American National Preacher*, a journal designed to help local pastors work up their own sermons—Edward Beecher, "The Nature, Importance and Means of Eminent Holiness throughout the Church," *American National Preacher* 6 (1835): 542–60. Other sources for this emphasis are the increasing numbers of articles describing Christ in the religious press. "Holiness" appears also to have been a major theme of many sermons about Christ. See, for example, Harris, *Christ the Theme of the Sanctuary*; see also the constant striving after greater inner holiness and tranquility in the *Weld-Grimké Letters*. See Smith, *Revivalism and Social Reform*, pp. 103–13, 135–47; Fletcher, *History of Oberlin*, pp. 207–36.

32. Beecher, *Biographical Remains*, p. 56.

33. See Stephen Nissenbaum, "Careful Love: Sylvester Graham and Victorian Sexual Theory" (Ph.D. diss., University of Wisconsin, 1968).

34. Henry Ward Beecher, *Journal*, entry for 3 March 1836.

35. Graham, *Lecture to Young Men on Chastity*, p. 39.

36. Ibid., p. 92.

37. See, for example, William Alcott, *The Young Man's Guide* (Boston, 1834); William P. Dewees, *Treatise on the Physical and Medical Treatment of Children* (Philadelphia, 1843). See also Nissenbaum, "Careful Love."

38. See "Thoughts on Revivals of Religion"; "Popular Objection to Revivals, Considered and Rejected"; and "Religion and Health."

39. Beecher, *Journal*, entry for 14 September 1839.

40. Henry Fowler, *Journal Kept by Henry P. Fowler*, Manuscript, Congregational Library.

41. See, for example, William Alcott, *The Young Wife, or Duties of Women in the Marriage Relation* (Boston, 1838); Beecher, *Treatise on Domestic Economy*; T. S. Pinnea, *The Hemans Reader for Female Schools* (New York, 1847). See also, Sklar, *Catharine Beecher*, and William R. Taylor, *Cavalier and Yankee* (New York, 1962).

42. Henry Ward Beecher, untitled manuscript sermon, delivered May 1846, Beecher Family Papers, Yale University Library. See also Crosby,

Good Men Love the Sanctuary, and Grosvenor, *The Glory of the Sanctuary*.

43. H. Crosby Englizian, *Brimstone Corner: Park Street Church, Boston* (Chicago, 1968), p. 118. See also "Spiritual Songs for Social Worship, *Quarterly Christian Spectator* 6 (1834): 209–22. See also Sandy Sizer, "Gospel Hymns: A Cultural Analysis" (Ph.D. diss., University of Chicago, 1976).

44. This hymn from the *Plymouth Church Collection of Christian Hymns* was attached to Henry Ward Beecher, *How to Become a Christian* (New York, 1862), p. 13.

45. Englizian, *Brimstone Corner*, pp. 113–24.

46. Fowler, *Journal of Henry Fowler*. See also, Smith, *Revivalism and Social Reform*.

47. Calhoun, *Intelligence of a People*, contains a brilliant and provocative discussion of the differences between eighteenth-century sermons and those of the mid-nineteenth century.

48. This analysis of the sermon as a rhetorical event draws upon the models of rhetorical analysis contained in Calhoun, *Intelligence of a People*; Taylor, *Cavalier and Yankee*; and Clifford Geertz, "Deep Play: Notes on the Balinese Cockfight," in Geertz, *Myth, Symbol, and Culture* (Cambridge, Mass., 1972).

49. Henry Ward Beecher, *Yale Lectures on Preaching* (New York, 1872), pp. 226–27.

50. Beecher, *Journal*, entries for 15 September 1839 and 10 December 1839.

51. See, for example, Day, "Training of the Preacher"; Harris, *Christ: The Theme of the Sanctuary*; Henry N. Day, "The Ideal of a Perfect Pulpit Discourse," *American Biblical Repository and Classical Review* 5 (1849): 191–22; and Henry P. Tappen, "The Philosophy of Expression in Oratory," *Biblical Repository and Classical Review* 4 (1848): 698–711.

52. See note 29 above. See also Todd, *John Todd*, pp. 423–46. See Calhoun, *Intelligence of a People*, pp. 256–91.

53. Beecher, *Yale Lectures on Preaching*, pp. 226–27.

54. Quoted in Neil Harris, *Humbug: The Art of P. T. Barnum* (Boston, 1973), p. 136.

55. Ibid., p. 141.

56. Henry Ward Beecher, *How to Become a Christian, an Address Delivered in Burton's Old Theater* (New York, 1857), pp. 1–6.

57. Ibid., p. 2.

58. Ibid., p. 1.

59. Ibid., pp. 6–9.

60. Ibid., p. 10.

61. Ibid., p. 11.

62. Ibid.

Chapter 9

1. In recent years a number of historians have begun to view the 1850s as a time when Americans, recoiling from the individualism and apparent anarchy of the 1830s and 1840s, began to lay the foundations for a new cultural and social order. See George Fredrickson, *Inner Civil War*; Daniel Howe, ed., *Victorian Culture in America* (Philadelphia, 1976); and the last chapter of Calhoun, *Professional Lives*.

2. This notion of the cultural significance of religion, which underlies much of this book, has been informed by Clifford Geertz, "Religion as a Cultural System" in Geertz, *The Interpretation of Cultures* (New York, 1973), pp. 87–125.

3. The pastoral role in eighteenth-century New England was in some ways more formal than confessional and devotional. Eighteenth-century communicants were frequently less dependent upon their pastors for maintaining an ongoing relationship to God than their nineteenth-century counterparts were. While the relationship to God certainly was keyed to the minister's conduct of public worship, it was basically sustained privately, by family devotions, private or "closet" prayer, introspection, and the keeping of a spiritual diary.

4. See Timothy Smith, *Revivalism and Social Reform*, for the fullest account of the resurgence of clerical social thought in the 1850s.

5. Burton Bledstein, *The Culture of Professionalism: The Middle Class and the Development of Higher Education in America* (New York, 1976), pp. 46–79, has a suggestive discussion of space. This discussion of how religion was stationed within the society of the 1850s differs from the approach of such historians as William Clebsch, *From Sacred to Profane America* (New York, 1968), and Martin Marty, *Righteous Empire* (New York, 1970), who have perceived religion and culture as separate entities and tried to describe how religion influenced the culture. My concern has not been with influence nor with secularization. Instead I have analyzed its place within the culture and viewed church and clergy as part of the social order.

6. Fredrickson, *Inner Civil War* contains a suggestive analysis of how the crisis of the union and the Civil War provided an opportunity for spokesmen and ideas that had seemed to lose sway in the 1830s and 1840s to regain influence.

7. My concern has been more structural, attempting to analyze how religion was situated in the society, than Smith's, which is mainly concerned with establishing that religion was socially engaged and with connecting this engagement, not to religious liberalism, but to evangelcal pietism.

8. For discussion of the reformer and agitator as a new and self-conscious social type see Richard Hofstadter, *The American Political Tradition*

(New York, 1948) and Kraditor, *Means and Ends in American Abolitionism.*

9. See Calhoun, *Professional Lives*, pp. 172–75.
10. See Carroll Smith-Rosenberg, *Religion and the Rise of the American City* (Ithaca, 1971).
11. See Smith, *Professors and Public Ethics.*
12. Bledstein, *Culture of Professionalism*, pp. 80–129.
13. Calhoun, *Professional Lives*, p. 174.

Index